Probability and Mathematical Statistics (Contin

SEBER • Linear Regression Analysis

SEBER • Multivariate Observations

SEN • Sequential Nonparametrics: Invariance Principles and Statistical Inference

SERFLING • Approximation Theorems of Mathematical Statistics

TJUR • Probability Based on Radon Measures

WILLIAMS • Diffusions, Markov Processes, and Martingales, Volume I: Foundations

ZACKS • Theory of Statistical Inference

Applied Probability and Statistics

ABRAHAM and LEDOLTER • Statistical Methods for Forecasting

AGRESTI • Analysis of Ordinal Categorical Data

AICKIN • Linear Statistical Analysis of Discrete Data

ANDERSON, AUQUIER, HAUCK, OAKES, VANDAELE, and WEISBERG • Statistical Methods for Comparative Studies

ARTHANARI and DODGE • Mathematical Programming in Statistics

BAILEY • The Elements of Stochastic Processes with Applications to the Natural Sciences

BAILEY • Mathematics, Statistics and Systems for Health

BARNETT • Interpreting Multivariate Data

BARNETT and LEWIS • Outliers in Statistical Data

BARTHOLOMEW • Stochastic Models for Social Processes, *Third Edition*

BARTHOLOMEW and FORBES • Statistical Techniques for Manpower Planning

BECK and ARNOLD • Parameter Estimation in Engineering and Science

BELSLEY, KUH, and WELSCH • Regression Diagnostics: Identifying Influential Data and Sources of Collinearity

BHAT • Elements of Applied Stochastic Processes

BLOOMFIELD • Fourier Analysis of Time Series: An Introduction

BOX • R. A. Fisher, The Life of a Scientist

BOX and DRAPER • Evolutionary Operation: A Statistical Method for Process Improvement

BOX, HUNTER, and HUNTER • Statistics for Experimenters: An Introduction to Design, Data Analysis, and Model Building

BROWN and HOLLANDER • Statistics: A Biomedical Introduction

BROWNLEE • Statistical Theory and Methodology in Science and Engineering, *Second Edition*

CHAMBERS • Computational Methods for Data Analysis

CHATTERJEE and PRICE • Regression Analysis by Example

CHOW • Analysis and Control of Dynamic Economic Systems

CHOW • Econometric Analysis by Control Methods

COCHRAN • Sampling Techniques, *Third Edition*

COCHRAN and COX • Experimental Designs, *Second Edition*

CONOVER • Practical Nonparametric Statistics, *Second Edition*

CONOVER and IMAN • Introduction to Modern Business Statistics

CORNELL • Experiments with Mixtures: Designs, Models and The Analysis of Mixture Data

COX • Planning of Experiments

DANIEL • Biostatistics: A Foundation for Analysis in the Health Sciences, *Third Edition*

DANIEL • Applications of Statistics to Industrial Experimentation

DANIEL and WOOD • Fitting Equations to Data: Computer Analysis of Multifactor Data, *Second Edition*

DAVID • Order Statistics, *Second Edition*

DAVISON • Multidimensional Scaling

DEMING • Sample Design in Business Research

DILLON and GOLDSTEIN • Multivariate Analysis: Methods and Applications

DODGE and ROMIG • Sampling Inspection Tables, *Second Edition*

DOWDY and WEARDEN • Statistics for Research

DRAPER and SMITH • Applied Regression Analysis, *Second Edition*

continued on back

LOSS
DISTRIBUTIONS

LOSS DISTRIBUTIONS

ROBERT V. HOGG

STUART A. KLUGMAN

Department of Statistics and Actuarial Science
The University of Iowa

WITH THE ASSISTANCE OF

Charles C. Hewitt   **and**   **Gary Patrik**

Metropolitan Reinsurance Company   *North American Reinsurance Corporation*

JOHN WILEY & SONS

New York • Chichester • Brisbane • Toronto • Singapore

Library of Congress Cataloging in Publication Data:

Hogg, Robert V.
  Loss distributions.

Includes bibliographical references and index.

    1. Insurance—Statistical methods. 2. Insurance—
Mathematical models. I. Klugman, Stuart A., 1949–
II. Title.
HG8781.H63   1984   368'.015   83-19663
ISBN 0-471-87929-0

Printed in the United States of America

10 9 8 7 6

Preface

This book is devoted to the problem of fitting probability distribution models to data. While most of the data sets used here are related to losses in the insurance industry and thus are heavy-tailed and skewed to the right, the statistical methods applied are also appropriate for other kinds of distributions. A reasonable prerequisite for the understanding of this work is a substantial undergraduate course in mathematical statistics. Also, some readers may find it helpful to review in advance the materials on loss distributions contained in the Proceedings of the Casualty Actuarial Society.

Initially the title of the text was to be *Size-of-Loss Distributions*, but this was shortened to *Loss Distributions*, which we preferred for its brevity and its consistency with the well-known actuarial topic "life contingencies." In any case, it should be understood that this work deals with the distribution of single losses that are, in some sense, related to claims made against various types of insurance policies. That is, we do not consider the probabilities of the occurrence of various numbers of claims or the combination of the same to determine the aggregate losses of a contract, line of business, or company. This latter type of situation is dealt with in many treatises on "mathematical risk theory." We look at only the distribution of the size of the loss, once it is given that such a loss has occurred.

A variety of statistical methods are studied, and each is accompanied by algorithms for computations and numerous examples. After an introductory chapter, Chapters 2 and 3 include a review of the statistical foundations and also derivations of a number of heavy-tailed, skewed distributions. The fitting techniques are discussed in Chapter 4, along with examples of models that are appropriate for the insurance industry. The material in Chapter 5 illustrates the numerous ways in which the fitted models can be used in actuarial analysis. Specific examples include deductibles, increased limits factors, leveraging, and the value of a layer of insurance.

While the reader is taken from the statistical foundations through the use of models in actuarial practice, the text is written with the practitioner in mind. Thus the numerous illustrations and great detail make it possible to apply the methods to real insurance problems. The addition of exercises also makes the book suitable for instructional purposes and inclusion on the syllabus of examinations of an actuarial society.

The text promotes a philosophy that fitted models are more appropriate than the empirical distributions. In most cases, standard actuarial calculations are much easier to make and update with the fitted parametric distributions than with the actual data. In particular, emphasis is placed on the work of fitted models when the data have been collected in a grouped format.

We are indebted to a number of people. Through lengthy discussions with C.K. Khury, FCAS, Vice President and Actuary, Prudential Property and Casualty Insurance Company, one of us (Hogg) was introduced to this topic and, without Mr. Khury's generous help and encouragement, never would have been involved in this project. In addition, Daniel J. McNamara, President, and Sheldon Rosenberg, Actuary and Manager, of the Insurance Services Office were extremely helpful in acquiring good data sets for our illustrations. Of course, without the financial support of the Actuarial Education and Research Fund and the administrative help of its research director, Cecil J. Nesbitt, FSA, we would not have gotten very far. Dr. Nesbitt not only acted as a guide to our efforts but also supplied substantial feedback. Two members of the AERF Steering Committee, Charles C. Hewitt, Jr., FCAS, President and Chief Executive Officer, Metropolitan Reinsurance Company, and Gary S. Patrik, FCAS, at time of writing of the book Director, Prudential Reinsurance Company, now Vice President, North American Reinsurance Company, were most helpful. Messrs. Hewitt and Patrik were especially effective in guiding the "practical" side of the text and helped to keep our presentation consistent with current actuarial practice and terminology. Not only that, but they actually picked up the pen on many occasions and did some writing. This type of involvement is most unusual and accounts for the acknowledgment of their assistance on the title page of this book. There were a number of people associated with our department, who on their extra time helped out; so we owe thanks to Irene Pearson, Ada Burns, Deborah Tomlinson, Laurie Estrem, Karen Horner, and Paul Novotny, as well as the University of Iowa for the computer support. And finally, but not least, we thank our wives, Carolyn and Marie, for their patience and understanding during the preparation of this manuscript. We feel blessed for all this genuine support because without it we could not have completed this work.

ROBERT V. HOGG
STUART A. KLUGMAN

Iowa City, Iowa
January 1984

The preparation of this book was funded by contributions to the Actuarial Education and Research Fund by the following organizations:

American Academy of Actuaries

Canadian Reinsurance Company

Casualty Actuarial Society

Employers Reinsurance Corporation

Firemen's Fund Insurance Company

General Reinsurance Corporation

International Actuarial Association (ASTIN Section)

Metropolitan Life Foundation

Munich American Reinsurance Company

North American Reinsurance Corporation

Contents

LOSS
DISTRIBUTIONS

CHAPTER 1

Introduction

1.1. BASIC TERMINOLOGY

Losses caused by occurrences of unexpected events are problems both for individuals and for society as a whole. Insurance is a mechanism for spreading these losses. Examples of **insured events** and their consequences are property damage due to fire, theft, flood, hail, or car accident (replacement cost); disability or death (loss of future income and support); illness (cost of medical treatment); and personal injury resulting from accidents or medical malpractice (cost of treatment and personal suffering). These are just a few of the many insured events, and we will assume that most readers understand the basic ones, which are used as illustrations throughout this book. The more complicated insurances will be described at the time of their use.

Clearly, the actuary wants to know something about the probability of an insured event occurring. In particular, it is important to know the expected number of occurrences for a specific measure of exposure to the risk. For a simple example, we might observe the number of claims occurring during the next year for a certain group of insured cars. Upon dividing by the number of cars, we obtain an estimate of the expected number of claims for one car in one policy year. This ratio is the **mean frequency** and is defined as

$$\frac{\text{number of occurrences}}{\text{exposure (to risk) basis}}.$$

However, from usage in business, this ratio is usually called, more simply, **frequency**, and we adopt this terminology here.

Unlike its connotation in statistics, frequency, as used here, is not a count nor is it necessarily a probability estimate, as would be a "relative frequency" in statistical usage. To illustrate this latter statement, in the foregoing example, the exposure might have been measured in units of 100 car-years; again, in case of air travel insurance, exposure might be in terms of 1000 passenger-hours. One notes, however, that frequency is an estimate of the expected number of insured events per exposure unit. Sometimes, when the meaning is clear, the word frequency is used for that expected value itself.

Although frequency is not the principal topic of this text, it is obviously an extremely important measure in placing a value on an insurance contract. It should also be noted that the terms of the insurance contract itself have a determining effect on frequency. For example, if Automobile Collision Insurance excludes payment for the first $250 of any loss, then there will be no payment at all for losses under $250 and hence the number of occurrences of insured events is reduced. Alternatively, if Accident and Sickness Insurance excludes disability for periods of seven days or less, then there will be no payment for periods of disability fewer than eight days and hence the number of reported cases is smaller.

Most important, for the purpose of this text, is the question "If the insured event occurs, what will be the cost to the insurer?" This cost (or loss) is, of course, a random variable. One characteristic of several such costs, arising from the occurrence of similar insured events, is the mean value, sometimes referred to as a **mean severity**, or, to conform with business usage, simply **severity**. That is, severity is the ratio

$$\frac{\text{total losses from all occurrences}}{\text{number of occurrences}}.$$

One notes that severity estimates the expected value of the individual loss random variable, and sometimes severity refers to that expected value when there is no chance for confusion.

Since the amount of an insured loss normally is expressed in dollars (or other currency), the severity normally is expressed as an average dollar amount per loss. A notable exception appears in some forms of Disability Insurance in which the average length of the period of disability can express the severity.

Severity and losses that enter into the computation of severity are the principal topics of this book; severity, like frequency, is an extremely important measure in placing a value on an insurance contract. Almost without exception the terms of the insurance contract have a determining effect on severity. For example, if Automobile Liability Insurance limits payment for personal injury to one claimant to $10,000, then there will be no payments for losses to one claimant in excess of $10,000. Hence the total payments for these losses could be reduced with a consequent effect on the average payment (severity). Alternatively, if the face amount of a Life Insurance policy is $50,000, then the amount paid upon the death of the insured is $50,000—no more, no less.

The **pure premium** is the average amount of loss per exposure to risk. Thus pure premium is the ratio

$$\frac{\text{total amount from all occurrences}}{\text{exposure (to risk) basis}},$$

which clearly equals the product

$$(\text{frequency})(\text{severity}).$$

Pure premium is an indirect topic of this book. Only as the pure premium is affected by the specific terms of an insurance contract with consequent effect upon the severity, and possibly upon the frequency, is the pure premium of concern. For example, if a Theft Insurance policy excludes payment for the first $100 of value of a loss and also limits the amount to be paid for the loss of any one article to $1000, then

1. There will be no payment for thefts under $100 and frequency is affected.
2. The first $100 of a loss larger than $100 will be excluded and severity is affected.
3. Theft losses per article of over $1100 will not be reimbursed and severity is affected.

Clearly, pure premium is affected in any one of several ways by this insurance contract.

Certainly the reader is already familiar with the term **premium** as it relates to the purchase price of an insurance contract. There is a relationship between the premium and the pure premium which may be expressed as follows:

$$\text{premium} = \left(\begin{array}{c}\text{pure}\\\text{premium}\end{array} \times \text{exposure}\right) + \begin{array}{c}\text{expenses of}\\\text{doing business}\end{array} + \begin{array}{c}\text{risk}\\\text{charge}\end{array}$$

Expenses of doing business may include commissions to agents or brokers, salaries to employees, rental of building space or equipment, supplies, taxes, and so on. Expenses, typically, can be measured as a percentage of the premium, or as a flat (dollar) amount per unit of exposure to risk or even per contract. The **risk charge** is payment to which the insurer is entitled for exposing its surplus and hence its shareholders or other policyholders to risk fluctuations. Risk fluctuations may result either from failure to estimate the pure premium or expenses correctly or from fluctuations of the pure premium or expenses about the expected value. The risk charge is typically a greater proportion of the premium for those lines of insurance where there is greater likelihood of risk fluctuations, such as Medical Malpractice Insurance, and less for those lines of insurance where there is less likelihood of risk fluctuations, such as Automobile Collision Insurance.

Neither expense nor risk charge is a principal topic of this book, although both may be affected to some degree by contractual terms as these terms bear upon severity and frequency.

Actuaries may concern themselves with the evaluation of the distribution of single losses, as such distribution bears on the costing of limitations of coverage within the insurance contract. Or they may concern themselves with the evaluation of multiple losses whose collective distribution bears upon the costing limitations of a single contract, or upon the aggregation of losses of a whole portfolio of contracts. Since this book deals solely with the distributions of single losses, aggregations of individual losses are not treated. The reader, who quite legitimately may be concerned with collections of losses, is referred to any one of the many treatises on mathematical risk theory.

At this juncture, it is necessary to make clear to the reader the sense in which the text considers a single loss and, by contrast, the sense in which reference may occasionally be made to collective losses. Generally speaking, *a **single loss** is one that counts as one occurrence in the determination of the frequency as heretofore defined. A **collective loss** is an aggregation of losses, where each loss in the aggregation counts as one occurrence when determining frequency.*

Example 1. Automobile Bodily Injury Liability Insurance often specifies two different limits within a single insurance contract—a limit per injured person and a limit per accident. Thus a certain contract may have limits of $100,000/$300,000, generally written 100/300—meaning that no injured person will receive more than $100,000 for injuries incurred in one accident and that, if more than one person is injured in the same accident, the insurer will not pay more than $300,000 as a result of that one accident. If frequency is being measured on a *per person* or per claimant basis, then the payments to each of the injured persons severally are single losses. By the same token, if frequency is measured on a per person basis and there is more than one claimant per accident, total payments on that accident are collective losses. On the other hand, if frequency is being measured on a *per accident* basis, the total payments on that accident constitute a single loss.

Example 2. Homeowners Insurance provides coverage for a number of different perils, for example, fire, windstorm, liability, theft. It is conceivable that a single occurrence may result in payment under more than one of the perils insured against. If frequency is being measured for each peril separately, then the payment under each insured peril is a single loss and, if there is more than one insured peril involved, total payments on that occurrence are collective losses. On the other hand, if frequency is being measured on a per occurrence basis, the payments on that occurrence constitute a single loss.

From this point, loss means single loss unless otherwise stated. In some forms of insurance the amount of the loss is specified given the occurrence of the insured event. The best known example is, of course, Life Insurance in which the amount payable upon the death of the insured is fixed in the contract. However, in most forms of property and liability insurance the amount of the loss may be less than the limit insured; thus the actuary must deal with indeterminate and partial loss amounts.

The need to deal with indeterminate losses gives rise to the need to know the distribution of losses by size. The study of loss distributions thus becomes a principal effort of the casualty actuary and even of the life actuary if one recognizes that the duration of a life annuity creates, in effect, an indeterminate loss. Both life and casualty actuaries may become involved in evaluating contracts of Accident and Sickness in which the duration of disability or of a hospital stay is a form of indeterminate loss. If all forms of insurance reimbursed the claimant or policyholder without any restriction, then a study of partial losses would involve only a study of the distribution of losses, and, in particular, the average value of losses, that is, severity. However, virtually every contract of insurance modifies or limits the benefit or amount of recovery thereunder, as seen in the following section.

Exercises

1. Describe an insured event that could be interpreted as either a single loss or a collective loss depending on the company's method of recording claims. Explain your answer.

2. What would be a logical exposure basis in
    (a) Group Life Insurance,
    (b) Workers' Compensation Insurance, and
    (c) Homeowners Insurance?

3. Company A has the following experience for Workers' Compensation:

	Year 1	Year 2
Exposure (payroll)	$2,400,000	$3,600,000
Losses—number	20	40
Losses—amount	$30,000	$54,000

If the exposure unit is $100 of payroll, then for each year separately and for the two years combined determine (a) frequency, (b) severity, and (c) pure premium.

4. The probability that a particular house will have a fire in the next 12 months is 0.001. If a fire does occur, the respective conditional probabilities of partial or total loss are:

% of Insured Value	Conditional Probability
25	0.5
50	0.2
75	0.1
100	0.2

If the pure premium for one year is $60, what is the insured value of the house?

1.2. COVERAGE LIMITATIONS

A contract of insurance without some limitation as to maximum amount or maximum duration of benefits is virtually unknown. As a matter of fact, in many jurisdictions a contract without some limitation would be illegal. Even if an insurer could and would provide unlimited insurance, the cost of such coverage might exceed the ability or willingness of the proposed insured to pay. Therefore, by agreement between the insurer and the insured most contracts of insurance carry some form of limitation of coverage. Examples include limiting the payment on a theft coverage to the value of the article and limiting the payment on a liability coverage to a specified dollar amount.

At the opposite end of the amount-of-loss spectrum, many insureds and insurers choose to exclude coverage for small losses. This election reduces the cost of the coverage purchased and eliminates the need for the insurer to become involved in the processing of small claims, which is often a relatively expensive and time-consuming process. The most common form of loss exclusion on smaller losses is the **deductible**. In the deductible, the insured agrees to absorb the full cost of losses which fall below an amount specified in the contract and, furthermore, to absorb this agreed-upon amount on all losses which exceed this deductible limit. In Disability Insurance a waiting period before commencement of benefits is a form of deductible. Other forms of the deductible are the disappearing deductible and franchise deductible.

In the **disappearing deductible**, the insured absorbs the full cost of losses that fall below the amount of the deductible; however, if the loss amount exceeds the deductible, the insured pays only a percentage of the deductible with the percentage decreasing as the amount by which the actual loss exceeds the deductible increases until at some amount of loss the amount of the deductible is waived entirely. Hence the name disappearing deductible.

In the **franchise deductible**, the entire deductible is waived as soon as the amount of loss exceeds the deductible amount. A form of this is found in Workers' Compensation: If the period of temporary disability extends beyond a specified waiting period, then the insured is reimbursed for the loss of time during the waiting period.

As the size of the deductible increases, at some point there is a change in terminology and it becomes known as the **retention**. Thus the insurer and the insured may speak of a *$500 deductible*, but a *$10,000 retention*. However, the principle is the same: The insured absorbs the amount of the retention and, furthermore, pays the amount of the retention on all losses that exceed the amount of the retention. The larger the value of the insured item, the larger the retention the insured is willing to assume. Retentions are common in contracts between an insurer and its reinsurer.

Another method of coverage limitation is for the insured to assume some percentage of all losses. This participation by the insured is generally referred to as **pro rata** or **quota share** insurance or reinsurance. A good reason for this type of risk sharing is found when the insured or reinsured has a great deal to say in the settlement of the loss or in the utilization of services that affect the amount of the loss. Typically, forms of Medical Insurance or Hospitalization Insurance may require the insured to pay a percentage, say 20%, of the loss. This encourages the insured to hold down medical treatment or shorten the duration of a hospital stay. Workers' Compensation and Disability Insurance customarily pay on disability claims a percentage of the average wage, possibly between 65 and 80%, in order to discourage malingering on the part of the injured, thus reducing the amount of the loss.

We have seen that the basic limitations on coverage for a single loss are (*a*) deductible or retention, (*b*) maximum or limit, and (*c*) pro rata share. Combinations of these basic limitations are common.

Example 1. Disability payments under Workers' Compensation Insurance may provide for a waiting period (deductible), followed by periodic payments equal to a fixed percentage of wages (pro rata), and terminating after a specified number of periodic payments (maximum).

Exercises

1. A Workers' Compensation Law in a certain state calls for the following benefits for temporary disability:

   (a) $66\frac{2}{3}\%$ of weekly wages up to a maximum weekly benefit of $200.

   (b) No payment for the first seven days of disability unless disability extends *beyond* 28 days; if disability is 29 days or more, payment is made retroactively for the first seven days.

   (c) Maximum number of weeks = 104.

Given	Worker 1	Worker 2	Worker 3
Weekly wage	$150	$240	$360
Length of disability in weeks	125	5	3

   Calculate the weekly benefit and total benefits for each worker.

2. A disappearing deductible of $500 per claim is applied. If the claimant receives $1.50 for every $1 by which the loss exceeds $500 until the deductible is fully recovered, what is the recovery for losses of $250, $500, $600, $1000, $1500, and $2000? What is the effective deductible for losses of $500, $600, and $1000?

3. A reinsurer agrees to pay 90% of each catastrophe loss in excess of $1,000,000 except that no loss on any one insured risk may contribute more than $50,000 to the total catastrophe loss. A hurricane produces the following: 5 losses of $100,000 each (risk), 10 losses of $75,000 each (risk), and other losses totaling $2,500,000, no one of which is over $50,000. Determine: (a) gross loss, i.e., before any recovery, (b) amount of recovery from reinsurer, and (c) net loss to the primary insurer.

1.3. EVALUATION OF COVERAGE LIMITATIONS

In this discussion, the term "pricing" is strictly avoided; "evaluation" or "valuing" refers to either the *severity* or the *pure premium*. Pricing deals with the determination of the premium, which includes expenses and a risk charge as explained earlier.

In evaluation of a particular coverage limitation, it is helpful to know the proportion of losses (by amount) that would be eliminated by such coverage limitation, called the **loss elimination ratio** (LER), given by

$$\text{LER} = \frac{\text{amount of losses eliminated}}{\text{total amount of losses}}$$

or, equivalently,

$$\text{LER} = \frac{\text{severity of losses eliminated}}{\text{total severity}}.$$

The computation and use of an LER is illustrated in the next three examples; the first concerns a retention (deductible), the second a limit (maximum), and the third the value of a "layer". In Chapter 5 we learn how to handle these situations more formally and with fitted distributions, using notation from mathematical statistics, but for the present we use the simple data set involving the following 10 losses (in $10,000 units) by 10 insureds of a certain insurer:

$$7, 9, 21, 29, 47, 62, 87, 113, 140, \text{ and } 306 .$$

Example 1. A retention of 10 units ($100,000) was accepted by each insured. That is, each insured pays the first $100,000 of each loss. Since the first two losses are under the value of the retention, they are paid in full by the insureds, but the others cost the insureds only 10 units each. Thus the LER, from the point of view of the insurer, is

$$\text{LER} = \frac{7+9+10+10+10+10+10+10+10+10}{7+9+21+29+47+62+87+113+140+306} = \frac{96}{821},$$

that is, here the LER $= 0.117$.

Example 2. If the coverage is limited to 100 units ($1,000,000) per loss, then the insureds receive the first seven amounts in full, but only 100 units for each of the last three. Thus the respective loss eliminations of $113 - 100 = 13$, $140 - 100 = 40$, and $306 - 100 = 206$ occur in those three cases and accordingly

$$\text{LER} = \frac{13+40+206}{821} = \frac{259}{821} = 0.315.$$

Example 3. An insurer agreed to a retention of $100,000 by each of the insureds and purchased reinsurance coverage on losses of more than $900,000 over this $100,000 retention. That is, for a loss of x dollars, this insurer is obligated to pay

$$0 \text{ when } x \leq 100,000,$$
$$x - 100,000 \text{ when } 100,000 < x \leq 1,000,000,$$
$$900,000 \text{ when } 1,000,000 < x.$$

The **relative value** of this layer is

$$\frac{11+19+37+52+77+90+90+90}{821} = \frac{466}{821} = 0.568,$$

which equals the coverage value remaining after subtracting from 1 the sum of the previous two LERs found in Examples 1 and 2:

$$1 - 0.117 - 0.315 = 0.568.$$

We discuss these relationships involving the LER more fully in Chapter 5. Moreover, in doing so, we find useful the notions of truncated and censored distributions, which are introduced in Chapter 2.

Exercises

1. Let the following amounts represent the respective costs to repair 12 cars, each of which had been damaged in an accident and was covered by a $250 deductible:

    $579, $110, $842, $213, $98, $445, $1332, $162, $131, $276, $312, $482 .

    From the point of the insurer, compute the LER.

2. Eight accidents involving automobiles, each having liability insurance with a limit of $100,000, resulted in the following losses:

    $86,000, $123,000, $423,000, $43,000, $213,000, $28,000, $52,000, $178,000 .

    From the point of view of the insurer, determine the LER.

3. An insurance company had agreed to cover each of a number of insureds with a layer of medical insurance as follows: A $50,000 retention with a limit of $500,000. If six settlements were for the amounts $153,000, $1,652,000, $78,000, $35,000, $178,000, and $827,000, respectively, compute the relative value of this layer for these six cases and show that it is equal to one minus the sum of two LERs, one for the retention and one for the limit.

1.4. DATA COLLECTION AND MODELING

Before presuming knowledge with respect to either the form of a loss distribution or its parameters one normally has collected actual information with respect to the subject insured event or events. There are matters pertaining to the collection of loss data that should be considered.

The settlement process with respect to indeterminate and partial losses tends to produce a **clustering** of values about particular numbers. For example, claims adjusters have authority to settle losses up to and including $1000; above that amount they must refer the matter to a supervisor. This situation often results in a clustering of loss values at or just below the maximum authorization point—in this case $1000. The reverse side of this is the relative absence of loss amounts just above the point of maximum authorization. Also, human nature tends to think in terms of round numbers. An insured is much more likely to settle a loss for $500 than $494.67—and so is the individual claims adjuster!

Policies with deductibles or limits tend to be susceptible to this type of distortion. In automobile collision claims it is not uncommon for the repair bill to be escalated as the amount approaches the deductible amount from below. However, there are contraphenomena. Insureds may be reluctant to report or press claims when the amount recoverable after application of a deductible is small. Attorneys often are reluctant to press legal actions when the amount recoverable is negligible. At the other end of the size-of-loss spectrum adjusters frequently are willing to settle at or just below policy limits when it is clear that a claim if pressed to adjudication might substantially exceed those limits.

This phenomenon makes it difficult to obtain good fits of mathematical models to "raw" data when, in fact, the mathematical model may more accurately describe the random process that determines true loss amounts. The actuary therefore is urged not to fall victim to the deadly trap that "raw" data are most expressive of the true loss process.

To help simplify the fitting of size-of-loss data it is often useful to choose intervals so that "cluster points" occur near the middle of the interval and not at the boundaries.

Actual claims data are obtained by reporting events that have occurred in the past. The longer the lag time between the happening of an event and the date for which the data are to be used for analysis and forecasting, the greater the likelihood that some intervening event has occurred to impair the relevance of available data. For example, if the definition of coverage afforded has changed or benefit levels have changed, as in Workers' Compensation, the data may require adjustment before being used to fit a model.

Inflation, which is now common to most economies, affects loss amounts and hence contaminates loss distributions over time. Normally, some adjustment is necessary, assuming an inflation rate, in order to place various loss amounts on a more homogeneous time basis to prevent such contamination. One technique that is independent of the particular model or parameters selected is to leave the frequency counts alone and simply adjust the boundaries of the intervals used in the size-of-loss distributions. For example, if it is assumed that there is a 100% inflation factor between the time of the events for which data have been gathered and the time for which the evaluation is being made, then the frequency of the interval (a, b) for the inflated variable equals the frequency of the interval $(a/2, b/2)$ for the original observed variable.

There are many other ways of **trending**. For example, if a model has been determined, we can find the distribution of the transformed variable.

However, not all size-of-loss distribution models are susceptible to this approach, as seen in subsequent chapters.

An important reason for studying loss distributions is to understand that certain changes in these distributions often have different effects on differing layers of coverage. If the severity doubles over a period of time, the value of a particular layer may be more than double—or it may be less than double. This phenomenon, particularly with respect to the evaluation of increased limits or of reinsurance excess or of catastrophe coverage, is known as **leverage** and is considered in detail in Chapter 5.

In fitting size-of-loss distributions, attention should be paid to the purpose for which the data are to be used. If the data set is to be used for valuing deductibles or retentions, then the selected model and parameters should stress the goodness-of-fit at the lower loss amounts, at least within reason. If, on the other hand, the problem is to value increased limits, then the model and parameters selected should emphasize the fit at the upper values of loss.

A separate problem is the establishment of interval means for the purpose of assigning loss amounts to grouped data. If the loss interval is from $1000 to $2000, does $1500 represent the mean value for the losses in that interval? In most situations in property and liability insurance, as well as in accident and sickness insurance, the answer is "No." As will be seen when data are analyzed in Chapters 4 and 5, most loss distributions in these lines of insurance are heavy-tailed. One of the advantages of assuming a model is that it will enable the analyst to assign a more realistic value to the interval mean and, if the loss distribution is open-ended on the right, to assign a mean value to the uppermost interval, if such mean exists.

The next two chapters review the basic concepts of mathematical statistics: random variables and their distributions, including the Gamma, Lognormal, Weibull, Burr, Pareto, and generalizations that are particularly useful to actuaries; various methods of estimation; tests of hypotheses, including goodness-of-fit tests; and algorithms and techniques needed to use these statistical procedures. The emphasis throughout the remainder of this book is placed upon model building. Obviously, it is impossible to determine the exact distributions of certain losses. Thus, in practice, the objective is to find reasonable and usable approximations to those distributions. These will range from very simple nonparametric descriptions, such as histograms, to fairly complex mathematical models depending on one or more parameters. As a matter of fact, the reader is encouraged to try different models for one situation, checking on the degree of agreement among the various solutions. With good agreement, we can feel comfortable with the recommendations arising therefrom. However, with substantial disagreement, the reader should take another hard look at the data before accepting some fitted distribution as a reasonable approximation.

Once a fitted model has been selected, it will be taken as a mathematical description of a situation which has some meaningful relationship with the real system. That is, reality should suggest the appropriate model, but there should be a continuous process of checking and changing any usable model with each set of newly observed data. This "give and take" in model building is important in any scientific investigation and is at the heart of the scientific method.

Once determined, appropriate mathematical models are not only extremely good descriptions of size-of-loss distributions, but they are much more convenient than the raw or empirical distributions when changes are necessary, for example, to predict future situations. That is, empirical distributions, such as histograms, could be satisfactory descriptions of historical data; however, in most instances, a forecast of the real system at some future time is desired, and this can frequently be done by changing a parameter of a fitted distribution. Of course, this introduces more subjectiveness into the solution, like personal guesses about the inflationary trends. While this text does not go into details of this type of forecasting, it does suggest how Bayesian methods can be used to introduce subjective ideas about the model. That is, actuaries are encouraged to introduce any sound *a priori* beliefs into the inference, whether Bayesian or not.

After adequate treatments of various models in Chapter 2 and the corresponding statistical inferences in Chapter 3, these results are applied to distributions of losses described in and treated in detail in Chapters 4 and 5.

Exercises

1. Consider the 50 losses from automobile accidents that are summarized in the following grouped data set:

Interval	Counts	Interval Average
1–100	8	79
101–300	14	212
301–500	16	430
501–800	6	689
801–1500	4	992
1501–2500	2	1714
	50	

Due to the method of settlement, some clustering is expected about $500.

(a) Determine another grouped data summary by combining the intervals 301–500 and 501–800, computing the average of this new interval.

(b) Draw the histogram for each of the old and new grouped data summaries. Since the intervals are of unequal lengths, take care to adjust the heights in the histograms. For example, if 8 is the height of 1–100, then $14/2 = 7$ is the height of 101–300 since the second interval is twice as long as the first.

2. Suppose a very simple distribution of losses due to automobile accidents is given by

Loss	Probability
0	0.9
50	0.05
100	0.03
200	0.01
500	0.01

With a $100 deductible, the insurance company expects to pay

$$(200 - 100)\,(0.01) + (500 - 100)\,(0.01) = 5$$

Suppose, over a certain period of time, inflation has caused prices to double. Now, what does the company expect to pay on a $100 deductible? Is this double the previous expectation? If not, this is a simple example of leveraging.

CHAPTER 2

Models for
Random Variables

2.1. MODELS

In the applications of mathematics to the real world, the selection of a suitable model is extremely important. For the actuary, models for distributions of random variables are of great concern, for example, the length of life of an individual or the damage due to a fire. Assuming the reader has a reasonably good background in mathematical statistics, we review, primarily with examples, some of the topics of that subject, placing enough emphasis on the importance of the model. [For those needing a little more review than given in Chapters 2 and 3, we refer you to *Introduction to Mathematical Statistics* by Hogg and Craig (1978). Frequently we refer to a particular section of that book by HC, 3.1, meaning Section 3.1.] In this presentation we stress the underlying assumptions of the models and some of the consequences if part of the assumptions do not hold.

Recall (HC, 3.1) the situation in which we have n independent trials of a random experiment, the outcome of which could be classified in one of two mutually exclusive and exhaustive ways (say, success or failure). If the respective probabilities p and $1 - p$ of success and failure are the same on each trial, then the number X of successes in n trials has a *binomial distribution* with p.d.f.

$$f(x) = \frac{n!}{x!(n-x)!} p^x (1-p)^{n-x}, \qquad x = 0, 1, 2, \ldots, n.$$

(As a convenience, the names probability density function, density func-

18   MODELS FOR RANDOM VARIABLES

tion, probability function, and frequency function are denoted by p.d.f. and we give the formula only on the region of positive density or *support*, as in this case: $x = 0, 1, 2, \ldots, n$.) To compute probabilities involving X, we sum the p.d.f. over the proper region; that is, the probability that X is in the set A is given by

$$\Pr(X \in A) = \sum_{x \in A} f(x).$$

There are two major difficulties that could create problems in the use of the binomial probability formula: lack of independence and p varying from trial to trial. Possibly the breakdown of the independence assumption is the most serious. As an extreme case, say that the outcomes of the second and subsequent trials would be exactly the same as the outcome on the first trial; thus each trial would have probability p of success but they would be totally dependent (as might be in the case of flight insurance on n executives in one company when they always fly to meetings together). Here the p.d.f. of X is

$$f(x) = \begin{cases} 1 - p, & x = 0 \\ p, & x = n \end{cases},$$

which is very different from the usual binomial p.d.f. The change in the distribution of X if p varies from trial to trial is considered in Sections 2.5 and 2.7.

With the simple binomial distribution, let us review two important characteristics of a distribution: The *mean* is

$$\mu = E(X) = \sum_{x=0}^{n} x \frac{n!}{x!(n-x)!} p^x (1-p)^{n-x}$$

and the *variance* is

$$\sigma^2 = E[(X - \mu)^2] = E(X^2) - \mu^2 = \sum_{x=0}^{n} x^2 \frac{n!}{x!(n-x)!} p^x (1-p)^{n-x} - \mu^2.$$

In Exercise 1, the reader is asked to evaluate these two summations and to show that $\mu = np$ and $\sigma^2 = \text{var}(X) = np(1-p)$.

In most courses in mathematical statistics, we often find that it is more convenient, as in this case, to use the *moment-generating function* (m.g.f.) to find these characteristics. Here the m.g.f. is

$$M(t) = E(e^{tX})$$

$$= \sum_{x=0}^{n} e^{tx} \frac{n!}{x!(n-x)!} p^x (1-p)^{n-x}$$

$$= \sum_{x=0}^{n} \frac{n!}{x!(n-x)!} (pe^t)^x (1-p)^{n-x}$$

$$= (1 - p + pe^t)^n$$

because the binomial expansion is

$$(a + b)^n = \sum_{x=0}^{n} \frac{n!}{x!(n-x)!} b^x a^{n-x}.$$

It can be shown that, for a general $M(t)$, $E(X^r) = M^{(r)}(0)$. Here the first two derivatives of this $M(t)$ are

$$M'(t) = n(1 - p + pe^t)^{n-1}(pe^t)$$

and

$$M''(t) = n(n-1)(1 - p + pe^t)^{n-2}(pe^t)^2 + n(1 - p + pe^t)^{n-1}(pe^t).$$

Thus

$$\mu = M'(0) = np \quad \text{and} \quad E(X^2) = M''(0) = n(n-1)p^2 + np.$$

Hence

$$\sigma^2 = M''(0) - [M'(0)]^2 = n(n-1)p^2 + np - (np)^2 = np(1-p).$$

Possibly more important than an aid in computing moments is the uniqueness property of the m.g.f. That is, an m.g.f. uniquely determines a distribution of probability; so, theoretically, the person with the m.g.f. is just as well off as the person with the p.d.f.

Example 1. Let $M(t) = E(e^{tX}) = (\frac{3}{4} + \frac{1}{4}e^t)^3$. From the uniqueness property of the m.g.f., we know X has a binomial distribution with $n = 3$ and $p = \frac{1}{4}$. Thus the probability that X equals zero or one is given by

$$\text{Pr}(X = 0, 1) = \sum_{x=0}^{1} \frac{3!}{x!(3-x)!} \left(\frac{1}{4}\right)^x \left(\frac{3}{4}\right)^{3-x} = \left(\frac{3}{4}\right)^3 + 3\left(\frac{1}{4}\right)\left(\frac{3}{4}\right)^2 = \frac{27}{32}.$$

Example 2. Consider a sequence of independent trials, each with probability of success $p = \frac{1}{3}$. The probability of obtaining the second success on the fifth trial is the product of the probability of having one success in four trials and the probability of a success on the fifth trial:

$$\left[\frac{4!}{1!\,3!}\left(\frac{1}{3}\right)\left(\frac{2}{3}\right)^3\right]\left(\frac{1}{3}\right) = \frac{32}{243}.$$

This example is generalized to the *negative binomial distribution* along with a special case, the *geometric distribution*, in Exercise 3.

Exercises

1. (a) For the binomial distribution, evaluate μ by writing $E(X)$ as

$$\sum_{x=1}^{n} x \frac{n!}{x!(n-x)!} p^x (1-p)^{n-x}$$
$$= np \sum_{x=1}^{n} \frac{(n-1)!}{(x-1)!(n-x)!} p^{x-1}(1-p)^{n-x}.$$

   Note the lower limit of summation is $x = 1$. Why can this be written this way?

   (b) Evaluate σ^2 by first noting that $E(X^2) = E[X(X-1)] + E(X)$. The first term in the right-hand member of this equation can be evaluated in a manner similar to part (a), except now the lower limit of the summation is $x = 2$. Why?

2. Let $E(e^{tX}) = (0.9 + 0.1e^t)^n$. Determine the smallest value of n so that $\Pr(1 \le X) \ge 0.6$. *Hint*: $\Pr(1 \le X) = 1 - \Pr(X = 0)$.

3. (a) Consider a sequence of independent repetitions of a random experiment with constant probability p of success. Let X be the number of trials needed to obtain exactly r successes. Argue that the p.d.f. of X is that of the *negative binomial distribution*, namely

$$f(x) = \frac{(x-1)!}{(r-1)!(x-r)!} p^r (1-p)^{x-r}, \qquad x = r, r+1, \ldots.$$

   Hint: This probability can be thought of as the product of the probability of obtaining exactly $r-1$ successes in $x-1$ trials and the probability of success on the xth trial.

   (b) Let $r = 1$ and obtain the p.d.f. of the *geometric distribution*, namely $f(x) = p(1-p)^{x-1}$, $x = 1, 2, 3, \ldots$.

4. Cast a fair die a number of independent times. Compare the probability of obtaining two "sixes" in five such trials to the probability of getting the second "six" on the fifth trial.

5. Show that the moment-generating function of the negative binomial distribution, as given in Exercise 3, is

$$M(t) = (pe^t)^r [1 - (1 - p)e^t]^{-r}.$$

Find the mean and the variance of this distribution. *Hint*: In the summation representing $M(t)$, make use of the MacLaurin's series for $(1 - w)^{-r}$.

2.2. THE POISSON PROCESS AND RELATED MODELS

The Poisson process is considered in many books; for example, see HC, 3.2. Let $g(x, w)$ be the probability of x changes (accidents, claims, etc.) in a fixed interval (of time, space, etc.) of length w. The Poisson postulates are essentially the following:

1. For a small length $w = h$, the probability $g(1, h)$ of one change is about proportional to that length, say λh, where λ represents a positive proportionality factor (later seen to be the failure rate or, in actuarial terms, the force of mortality or morbidity, or the accident rate).

2. For a small length $w = h$, the probability $\sum_{x=2}^{\infty} g(x, h)$ of two or more changes is essentially zero; in particular,

$$\lim_{h \to 0} \sum_{x=2}^{\infty} g(x, h) = 0.$$

3. The numbers of changes in nonoverlapping intervals are independent.

Initially taking λ to be a positive constant function of time, these postulates lead to a set of differential equations (HC, 3.2) for $g(x, w)$, $x = 0, 1, 2, \ldots$, the solution of which is

$$g(x, w) = \frac{(\lambda w)^x e^{-\lambda w}}{x!}, \qquad x = 0, 1, 2, \ldots.$$

We recognize this to be the p.d.f. of a *Poisson distribution* with mean $\mu = \lambda w$. That is, the number X of changes in an interval w has the p.d.f.

$$f(x) = \frac{\mu^x e^{-\mu}}{x!}, \qquad x = 0, 1, 2, \ldots,$$

where μ equals the product of the constant λ and the length w. It is a basic exercise (Exercise 1) to show that

$$M(t) = E(e^{tX}) = e^{\mu(e^t - 1)}$$

and that both the mean and the variance are equal to μ.

Example 1. If $E(e^{tX}) = e^{2(e^t - 1)}$, then X has a Poisson distribution with $\mu = 2$ and the probability that X equals 0, 1, 2, or 3 is

$$\Pr(X = 0, 1, 2, 3) = \sum_{x=0}^{3} \frac{2^x e^{-2}}{x!} = e^{-2}\left(1 + \frac{2}{1!} + \frac{2^2}{2!} + \frac{2^3}{3!}\right) = 0.857.$$

It is interesting to turn this around a little and consider the distribution of a random length W until the first change is obtained. In particular, the distribution function of W is given by, for $0 < w$,

$$G(w) = \Pr(W \le w) = 1 - \Pr(W > w).$$

However, the event $W > w$ is equivalent to the event in which there are no changes in an interval of length w, the probability of which is $g(0, w)$. Thus

$$G(w) = 1 - g(0, w) = 1 - e^{-\lambda w}, \qquad 0 < w,$$

and the p.d.f. of this random variable W of the continuous type is

$$g(w) = G'(w) = \lambda e^{-\lambda w}, \qquad 0 < w.$$

Thus W has the well-known *exponential distribution*. The *failure rate* is

$$\frac{-(d/dw)[1 - G(w)]}{1 - G(w)} = \frac{g(w)}{1 - G(w)} = \frac{\lambda e^{-\lambda w}}{1 - (1 - e^{-\lambda w})} = \lambda.$$

In this case, we assume λ to be a constant function of time. Thus viewing

λ as a force of mortality, the probability of death is constant regardless of age. With λ as an accident rate, the chances of being involved in an accident are the same no matter how much time, w, has elapsed since the last accident.

Example 2. Let the length T of life of a certain part have a constant failure rate of $\lambda = 0.005$. To find probabilities associated with a random variable of a continuous type, we integrate to determine an area under the p.d.f.; for instance,

$$\Pr\,(100 < T < 200) = \int_{100}^{200} (0.005)e^{-0.005t}\,dt$$

$$= e^{-1} - e^{-2} = 0.233\,.$$

Of course, engineers and actuaries recognize that failure rates of various equipment and human beings are not usually constant functions of time. Hence we let λ vary with w, say $\lambda(w)$. We can either return to those original differential equations associated with the Poisson process or simply set

$$\frac{g(w)}{1 - G(w)} = \lambda(w)\,, \qquad \text{where } g(w) = G'(w)\,.$$

The solution of this simple differential equation, with boundary condition $G(0) = 0$, is

$$\ln\,[1 - G(w)] = -\int_0^w \lambda(t)\,dt\,.$$

We solve this for $G(w)$ and find that

$$G(w) = 1 - \exp\left[-\int_0^w \lambda(t)\,dt\right], \qquad 0 < w\,.$$

Thus, with a nonconstant failure rate, the p.d.f. of W, the time (or length) until the first change, is

$$g(w) = G'(w) = \lambda(w)\exp\left[-\int_0^w \lambda(t)\,dt\right].$$

Example 3. Let $\lambda(w) = c\tau w^{\tau-1}$ for $0 < w$, where $\tau > 0$. The failure rate is an increasing function of w when $\tau > 1$ and a decreasing function of w

when $0 < \tau < 1$. The corresponding p.d.f. is $f(w) = c\tau w^{\tau-1} \exp(-cw^{\tau})$, $0 < w$, and the random variable W is said to have a *Weibull distribution*. We find that this distribution provides a good model for size of claims in casualty insurance (malpractice, windstorms, etc.), particularly when $0 < \tau < 1$. See the appendix for a summary of the characteristics and graphs of the Weibull p.d.f.

Example 4. The exponential failure rate $\lambda(w) = Bc^w$, $a > 0$, $b > 0$, means

$$g(w) = Bc^w \exp\left[\frac{B}{\ln c}(1 - c^w)\right], \qquad 0 < w,$$

is the p.d.f. associated with *Gompertz's law*. If this is modified slightly so that

$$\lambda(w) = A + Bc^w,$$

then

$$g(w) = (A + Bc^w) \exp\left[\frac{B}{\ln c}(1 - c^w) - Aw\right], \qquad 0 < w,$$

is the p.d.f. associated with *Makeham's law*.

Using one of the four models—exponential, Weibull, Gompertz, and Makeham—for the distribution of W, we can think of one "change" being enough to "terminate life." That is, W is the random length of life until one change that could cause the "death" of the item under consideration. Many times, however, we are interested in the random variable W, which is the time needed to produce exactly k changes. If we again assume that λ is a constant, the distribution function of W is

$$G(w) = \Pr(W \le w) = 1 - \Pr(W > w), \qquad 0 < w.$$

However, here $W > w$ is equivalent to at most $k - 1$ changes in the interval $(0, w)$. Hence we have

$$\Pr(W > w) = \sum_{x=0}^{k-1} \frac{(\lambda w)^x e^{-\lambda w}}{x!}$$

and thus

$$G(w) = 1 - \sum_{x=1}^{k-1} \frac{(\lambda w)^x e^{-\lambda w}}{x!} - e^{-\lambda w}.$$

The p.d.f. of W is $G'(w) = g(w)$, which is equal to

$$g(w) = -\sum_{x=1}^{k-1} \left[\frac{(-\lambda)(\lambda w)^x e^{-\lambda w}}{x!} + \frac{\lambda(\lambda w)^{x-1} e^{-\lambda w}}{(x-1)!} \right] + \lambda e^{-\lambda w}$$

$$= \frac{\lambda^k w^{k-1} e^{-\lambda w}}{(k-1)!}, \qquad 0 < w.$$

If we let $k = \alpha$ and recall that $\Gamma(k) = (k-1)!$, we see that W has a *gamma distribution* with p.d.f.

$$g(w) = \frac{\lambda^\alpha}{\Gamma(\alpha)} w^{\alpha-1} e^{-\lambda w}, \qquad 0 < w.$$

It is an easy exercise (Exercise 2) to show that

$$M(t) = E(e^{tW}) = \left(\frac{\lambda}{\lambda - t} \right)^\alpha, \qquad t < \lambda,$$

and

$$\mu = \frac{\alpha}{\lambda} \qquad \text{and} \qquad \sigma^2 = \frac{\alpha}{\lambda^2}.$$

See the appendix for graphs of the p.d.f. for various values of the parameters.

The mean waiting time until exactly $k = \alpha$ changes is k/λ; this makes sense since the mean waiting time for one change is $1/\lambda$, the reciprocal of the failure rate. Recall that here λ is a constant; the resulting p.d.f. is much more complicated if λ varies with w. Incidentally, the gamma distribution is a good model for many situations involving the size of loss in casualty insurance. This is demonstrated later.

One final remark: while Poisson postulates (1) and (2) are reasonably accurate in these kinds of situations, assumption (3) concerning the independence of the numbers of changes in nonoverlapping intervals often is questionable. For example, a car might be so badly damaged at a given time that it has no chance of being damaged again in the near future because it is being repaired. Or, if the Poisson process involves the number of accidents on a given highway, an accident at a given time may very well influence what happens in the next few minutes because there might be a chain of automobile accidents (a contagion). Clearly, a violation of this independence postulate greatly influences the distributions given here. So again the reader is cautioned about difficulties created by lack of independence.

Exercises

1. (a) Show that the m.g.f. of a Poisson distribution is $M(t) = e^{\mu(e^t - 1)}$.
         Hint:

$$\sum_{x=0}^{\infty} e^{tx}\frac{\mu^x e^{-\mu}}{x!} = e^{-\mu}\sum_{x=0}^{\infty}\frac{(\mu e^t)^x}{x!}$$

         and recall that $e^z = \sum_{x=0}^{\infty} z^x/x!$, for all real z.

    (b) Show that $M'(0) = \mu$ and $M''(0) - [M'(0)]^2 = \mu$; thus both the mean and the variance are equal to μ.

2. (a) Show that the m.g.f. of a gamma distribution is $\lambda^\alpha(\lambda - t)^{-\alpha}$, $t < \lambda$.
         Hint:

$$\int_0^\infty \frac{e^{tw}\lambda^\alpha w^{\alpha-1}e^{-\lambda w}}{\Gamma(\alpha)}\,dw = \int_0^\infty \frac{\lambda^\alpha w^{\alpha-1}e^{-(\lambda-t)w}}{\Gamma(\alpha)}\,dw\,;$$

         simply write down the value of the latter integral after letting $\lambda - t$ equal a new λ.

    (b) Show that $M'(0) = \alpha/\lambda$ and $M''(0) - [M'(0)]^2 = \alpha/\lambda^2$.

3. Let w, the time to remarriage of the spouse in a fatal worker's compensation accident, have a Weibull distribution with $\lambda(w) = cw$. Find c so that $\Pr(W > 5) = e^{-1/4} = 0.7788$.

4. Suppose the length W of a human life has a Gompertz distribution with force of mortality $\lambda(w) = B(1.1)^w$. Determine the constant B so that $\Pr(W > 65) = 0.5$.

5. Let W have the Weibull distribution of Example 3. Show that $E(W^k) = \Gamma[(k + \tau)/\tau]/c^{k/\tau}$. *Hint*: In the integral representing $E(W^k)$, change the variable by letting $y = cw^\tau$.

6. Show that the p.d.f.s having the respective failure rates $\lambda_1(w) = \alpha/(\lambda + w)$, $\alpha > 0$, $\lambda > 0$, and $\lambda_2(w) = \alpha\tau w^{\tau-1}/(\lambda + w^\tau)$, $\alpha > 0$, $\lambda > 0$, $\tau > 0$, are

$$f_1(w) = \frac{\alpha \lambda^\alpha}{(\lambda + w)^{\alpha+1}}, \qquad 0 < w < \infty,$$

and

$$f_2(w) = \frac{\alpha \tau \lambda^\alpha w^{\tau-1}}{(\lambda + w^\tau)^{\alpha+1}}, \qquad 0 < w < \infty.$$

The corresponding distributions are called the *Pareto* and the *Burr*, respectively.

2.3. MODELS FOR JOINT RANDOM VARIABLES

Distributions of two or more random variables play an important role in actuarial science. For example, it is absolutely necessary to understand the *joint distribution* of the lengths of the lives of a husband and wife in the consideration of a joint annuity. In this section, we use one extremely simple, but somewhat realistic, distribution just to illustrate the concepts. This distribution is of the continuous type, so integration is used to compute probabilities and various characteristics, but in discrete cases, summations replace the integrations (HC, 2.2 and 2.3).

Let X be the loss amount due to damage of an automobile and Y be the allocated loss adjustment expense associated with this accident. Say X and Y have the *joint p.d.f.*

$$f(x, y) = \frac{5}{10^6} e^{-x/1000}, \qquad 0 < 5y < x < \infty.$$

To indicate the use of a joint p.d.f., let us compute the following probability.

$$
\begin{aligned}
\Pr(X < 1000, Y < 100) &= \Pr(5Y < X < 1000, 0 < Y < 100) \\
&= \int_0^{100} \left(\int_{5y}^{1000} \frac{5}{10^6} e^{-x/1000} dx \right) dy \\
&= \int_0^{100} \frac{5}{1000} (e^{-5y/1000} - e^{-1}) \, dy \\
&= 1 - e^{-1/2} - \frac{e^{-1}}{2} = 0.21 \ .
\end{aligned}
$$

Suppose that we want probabilities associated only with X, like

$$\Pr(X < 1000) = \int_0^{1000} \left(\int_0^{x/5} \frac{5}{10^6} e^{-x/1000} dy \right) dx$$

$$= \int_0^{1000} \left(\frac{x}{(1000)^2} e^{-x/1000} \right) dx \, .$$

While this integral can be completed easily using integration by parts, we note that the integrand is a gamma p.d.f. with $\alpha = 2$ and $\lambda = 1/1000$. Thus X has this *marginal distribution*. That is, in general, the marginal p.d.f.s are

$$f_1(x) = \int_y f(x, y) \, dy \, ,$$

$$f_2(y) = \int_x f(x, y) \, dx \, .$$

In this case, the marginal p.d.f. of Y is

$$f_2(y) = \int_{5y}^{\infty} \frac{5}{10^6} e^{-x/1000} dx$$

$$= \frac{5}{1000} e^{-5y/1000} = \frac{1}{200} e^{-y/200} \, , \qquad 0 < y \, ,$$

which is exponential (or gamma with $\alpha = 1$ and $\lambda = 1/200$).

From the marginal distributions, it is easy to compute the means and the variances of X and Y. They are:

$$\mu_X = 2(1000) = 2000, \qquad\qquad\qquad \mu_Y = 200 \, ,$$

$$\sigma_X^2 = 2(1000)^2 = 2{,}000{,}000, \quad \text{and} \quad \sigma_Y^2 = (200)^2 = 40{,}000 \, .$$

There is a characteristic, however, that requires the joint p.d.f. in its computation, the *covariance* of X and Y,

$$\text{cov}(X, Y) = E[(X - \mu_X)(Y - \mu_Y)] = E(XY) - \mu_X \mu_Y \, .$$

In our example,

$$E(XY) = \int_0^\infty \left(\int_0^{x/5} xy \, \frac{5}{10^6} \, e^{-x/1000} dy \right) dx$$

$$= \int_0^\infty \frac{x}{2} \left(\frac{x^2}{25} \right) \left(\frac{5}{10^6} \right) e^{-x/1000} dx$$

$$= \frac{1}{10^7} \int_0^\infty x^3 e^{-x/1000} dx \ .$$

Comparing the integrand to the gamma p.d.f. with $\alpha = 4$ and $\lambda = 1/1000$, we see that

$$E(XY) = \left(\frac{1}{10^7} \right) (1000)^4 \Gamma(4) = (6)(10^5) \ .$$

Thus

$$\text{cov } (X, Y) = (6)(10^5) - (2000)(200) = (2)(10^5) \ .$$

We can then compute the *correlation coefficient*

$$\rho = \frac{\text{cov } (X, Y)}{\sigma_X \sigma_Y} = \frac{(2)(10^5)}{\sqrt{(2)(10^6)(4)(10^4)}} = \frac{1}{\sqrt{2}} = 0.707 \ .$$

Frequently *conditional distributions* are useful. The conditional p.d.f.s are

$$f(y|x) = \frac{f(x, y)}{f_1(x)} = \frac{\left(\frac{5}{10^6} \right) e^{-x/1000}}{\frac{x}{(1000)^2} e^{-x/1000}} = \frac{5}{x}, \qquad 0 < y < \frac{x}{5},$$

and

$$f(x|y) = \frac{f(x, y)}{f_2(y)} = \frac{\left(\frac{5}{10^6} \right) e^{-x/1000}}{\left(\frac{5}{1000} \right) e^{-5y/1000}} = \left(\frac{1}{1000} \right) e^{-(x-5y)/1000},$$

where $5y < x < \infty$. Also note the important relationship

$$f(x, y) = f_1(x)f(y|x) = f_2(y)f(x|y) \ .$$

Of course, with conditional distributions we can also determine conditional means and variances. For illustration, with our example, we have the conditional means

$$\mu_{Y|x} = E(Y|x) = \int_0^{x/5} y\left(\frac{5}{x}\right)dy = \left(\frac{5}{2x}\right)\left(\frac{x}{5}\right)^2 = \frac{x}{10}$$

and

$$\mu_{X|y} = E(X|y) = \int_{5y}^{\infty} x\left(\frac{1}{1000}\right)e^{-(x-5y)/1000}\,dx$$

$$= 5y + 1000 .$$

Each of these conditional means is linear. In the case of a linear conditional mean, there exists (HC, 2.3) the interesting formula

$$\mu_{Y|x} = \mu_Y + \rho\frac{\sigma_Y}{\sigma_X}(x - \mu_X) .$$

Substituting the computed characteristics into this formula, we obtain

$$\mu_{Y|x} = 200 + \left(\frac{1}{\sqrt{2}}\right)\sqrt{\frac{4(10)^4}{2(10)^6}}(x - 2000) = \frac{x}{10} ,$$

the same as before. Similarly,

$$\mu_{X|y} = \mu_X + \rho\frac{\sigma_X}{\sigma_Y}(y - \mu_Y)$$

$$= 2000 + \left(\frac{1}{\sqrt{2}}\right)\sqrt{\frac{2(10)^6}{4(10)^4}}(y - 200)$$

$$= 5y + 1000 .$$

Frequently it is true that

$$f(x, y) \equiv f_1(x)f_2(y) ;$$

that is, $f_1(x) = f(x|y)$ and $f_2(y) = f(y|x)$. In such cases, we say that X and Y are *independent random variables*. In our example, $f(x, y) \neq f_1(x)f_2(y)$ since

$$\left(\frac{5}{10^6}\right)e^{-x/1000} \neq \left[\left(\frac{x}{10^6}\right)e^{-x/1000}\right]\left[\left(\frac{1}{200}\right)e^{-y/200}\right],$$

so X and Y are *dependent random variables*. Of course, we can also observe this dependence from the support $0 < 5y < x < \infty$, where clearly y depends on the value of x.

If X and Y are independent random variables, then

$$E[u(X)v(Y)] = \int_{-\infty}^{\infty}\int_{-\infty}^{\infty} u(x)v(y)f_1(x)f_2(y) \, dx \, dy$$

$$= \left(\int_{-\infty}^{\infty} u(x)f_1(x) \, dx\right)\left(\int_{-\infty}^{\infty} v(y)f_2(y) \, dy\right)$$

$$= E[u(X)]E[v(Y)] ;$$

that is, in this case, the *expected value* of a product is the product of the expected values. In particular, the covariance of X and Y is

$$\text{cov}(X, Y) = E[(X - \mu_X)(Y - \mu_Y)]$$

$$= E(X - \mu_X)E(Y - \mu_Y)$$

$$= [E(X) - \mu_X][E(Y) - \mu_Y] = 0 .$$

Thus if X and Y are independent, then the correlation coefficient is

$$\rho = \frac{\text{cov}(X, Y)}{\sigma_X\sigma_Y} = \frac{0}{\sigma_X\sigma_Y} = 0 .$$

However, the converse of this is not true; zero correlation does not imply independence (Exercise 1).

If we have more than two random variables, say $X_1, X_2, \ldots, X_n$, most of the preceding concepts generalize rather naturally. In particular, if $f(x_1, x_2, \ldots, x_n)$ is the joint p.d.f., let the marginal p.d.f. of X_i be given by

$$f_i(x_i) = \int_{-\infty}^{\infty}\int_{-\infty}^{\infty} \cdots \int_{-\infty}^{\infty} f(x_1, x_2, \ldots, x_n)dx_1 \ldots dx_{i-1}dx_{i+1} \ldots dx_n ,$$

where the $(n - 1)$-fold integral is over the support of $x_1, \ldots, x_{i-1}, x_{i+1}, \ldots, x_n$, given x_i. Then $X_1, X_2, \ldots, X_n$ are *mutually independent* if and only if

$$f(x_1, x_2, \ldots, x_n) \equiv f_1(x_1)f_2(x_2) \ldots f_n(x_n) .$$

Exercises

1. Let X and Y have the joint p.d.f.

$$f(x, y) = \frac{1}{\pi}, \quad x^2 + y^2 < 1 .$$

   (a) Show that the marginal p.d.f. of X is $f_1(x) = (2/\pi)\sqrt{1 - x^2}$, $-1 < x < 1$. From symmetry, what is that of Y?
   (b) Show that X and Y are dependent.
   (c) Show that $\mu_X = \mu_Y = 0$.
   (d) Show that cov $(X, Y) = E(XY) = 0$, demonstrating that $\rho = 0$ does not imply the independence of X and Y.

2. Let X and Y have the joint p.d.f.

$$f(x, y) = x + y, \quad 0 < x < 1, 0 < y < 1 .$$

   (a) Show that $f_1(x) = x + \frac{1}{2}, 0 < x < 1$, and $f_2(y) = y + \frac{1}{2}, 0 < y < 1$, are the marginal p.d.f.s; thus X and Y are dependent.
   (b) Show that $\mu_X = \mu_Y = \frac{7}{12}$ and $\sigma_X^2 = \sigma_Y^2 = \frac{11}{144}$.
   (c) Show that cov $(X, Y) = -\frac{1}{144}$ and $\rho = -\frac{1}{11}$.
   (d) Show that $\mu_{Y|x} = (3x + 2)/(6x + 3), 0 < x < 1$.

3. Let X and Y have the joint discrete p.d.f. described as follows:

(x, y)	$(0, 0)$	$(1, 0)$	$(0, 1)$	$(1, 1)$
$f(x, y)$	1/10	3/10	4/10	2/10

   Find the correlation coefficient ρ.

4. Let X and Y be independent random variables with Weibull distributions with respective failure rates $\lambda(x) = 2x$ and $\lambda(y) = 3y^2$. Compute Pr $[\min (X, Y) > \frac{1}{2}]$. *Hint:* Pr $[\min (X, Y) > \frac{1}{2}] = $ Pr $(X > \frac{1}{2}, Y > \frac{1}{2})$.

2.4. NORMAL MODELS

In 1733 De Moivre proved that the binomial distribution could be approximated by a normal distribution provided n is large. He did this by examining the probabilities associated with X, the binomial random variable with parameters n and p. In most modern courses, the limit, as $n \to \infty$, of the m.g.f. of

$$Y = \frac{X - np}{\sqrt{np(1-p)}}$$

is found in order to prove this fact. The m.g.f. of Y is

$$M_Y(t) = E\left\{\exp\left[t\,\frac{X - np}{\sqrt{np(1-p)}}\right]\right\} = \exp\left[-\frac{tnp}{\sqrt{np(1-p)}}\right]E\left[\exp\frac{tX}{\sqrt{np(1-p)}}\right]$$

$$= \exp\left[-\frac{tnp}{\sqrt{np(1-p)}}\right]\left[1 - p + p\exp\left(\frac{t}{\sqrt{np(1-p)}}\right)\right]^n.$$

It is left as an exercise (Exercise 1) to show that, for fixed p,

$$\lim_{n\to\infty} M_Y(t) = \exp\left(\frac{t^2}{2}\right).$$

This, of course, is the m.g.f. of the *standard normal distribution* with p.d.f.

$$\frac{1}{\sqrt{2\pi}}\exp\left(\frac{-y^2}{2}\right), \qquad -\infty < y < \infty.$$

This result suggests that the discrete probabilities of X (or Y) can in some way be approximated by the probabilities associated with the continuous-type normal random variable. To do this, think of the probability of $\Pr(X = k)$, where k is one of the nonnegative integers 0, 1, 2, ..., n, as being approximated by the area between $x = k - \frac{1}{2}$ and $x = k + \frac{1}{2}$, above the x-axis, and under a normal curve that more or less passes through the points $(x, \Pr[X = x])$, $x = 0, 1, 2, \ldots, n$. Thus we can write

$$\Pr(X = k) = \Pr\left(k - \tfrac{1}{2} < X < k + \tfrac{1}{2}\right)$$

$$= \Pr\left[\frac{k - \frac{1}{2} - np}{\sqrt{np(1-p)}} < \frac{X - np}{\sqrt{np(1-p)}} < \frac{k + \frac{1}{2} - np}{\sqrt{np(1-p)}}\right]$$

$$\approx \Phi\left[\frac{k + \frac{1}{2} - np}{\sqrt{np(1-p)}}\right] - \Phi\left[\frac{k - \frac{1}{2} - np}{\sqrt{np(1-p)}}\right],$$

where $\Phi(\cdot)$ is the distribution function of a standard normal random variable,

$$\Phi(z) = \int_{-\infty}^{z} \frac{1}{\sqrt{2\pi}} \exp\left(-\frac{y^2}{2}\right) dy .$$

The latter expression is usually tabled in books on statistics.

Example 1. Let X have a binomial distribution with $n = 100$ and $p = \frac{1}{2}$ so that $np = 50$ and $np(1-p) = 25$. Then

$$\Pr(X = 45, 46, \ldots, 55) = \Pr(44.5 < X < 55.5)$$

$$= \Pr\left(\frac{44.5 - 50}{5} < \frac{X - 50}{5} < \frac{55.5 - 50}{5}\right)$$

$$\approx \Phi(1.1) - \Phi(-1.1) = 0.7286 .$$

If Y has a standard normal distribution, then its mean and variance equal zero and one, respectively (HC, 3.4). Thus $Y = (X - \mu)/\sigma$ means that $X = \sigma Y + \mu$, where $\sigma > 0$, has mean

$$E(X) = \sigma E(Y) + \mu = \mu$$

and variance

$$E[(X - \mu)^2] = E[(\sigma Y + \mu - \mu)^2] = \sigma^2 E(Y^2) = \sigma^2 .$$

Moreover, the distribution function of X is

$$F(x) = \Pr(X \le x) = \Pr(\sigma Y + \mu \le x)$$

$$= \Pr\left(Y \le \frac{x - \mu}{\sigma}\right)$$

$$= \int_{-\infty}^{(x-\mu)/\sigma} \frac{1}{\sqrt{2\pi}} \exp\left(-\frac{y^2}{2}\right) dy .$$

Accordingly, the p.d.f. $f(x) = F'(x)$ of X is

$$f(x) = \frac{1}{\sqrt{2\pi}\sigma} \exp\left[\frac{-(x - \mu)^2}{2\sigma^2}\right], \qquad -\infty < x < \infty,$$

by one form of the fundamental theorem of calculus. This latter p.d.f. can be depicted by Figure 2.1. The points of inflection occur at $x = \mu - \sigma$ and $x = \mu + \sigma$. A random variable X that has a p.d.f. of the form $f(x)$ is said

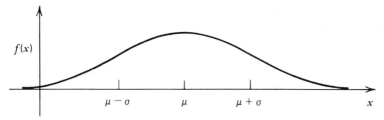

Figure 2.1. The normal p.d.f.

to have a *normal distribution* with mean μ and variance σ^2. It occurs so frequently in statistics, we denote this distribution by $N(\mu, \sigma^2)$. Thus $N(0, 1)$ refers to the standard normal distribution.

It is left as an exercise (Exercise 2) to show that the m.g.f. of $N(\mu, \sigma^2)$ is

$$M(t) = E(e^{tX}) = \exp\left(\mu t + \frac{\sigma^2 t^2}{2}\right).$$

Example 2. Let $E(e^{tX}) = \exp(-6t + 25t^2/2)$. Then X is $N(-6, 25)$ and, for illustration,

$$\Pr(-11 < X < 4) = \Pr\left(\frac{-11+6}{5} < \frac{X+6}{5} < \frac{4+6}{5}\right)$$

$$= \Phi(2) - \Phi(-1)$$

$$= 0.9772 - (1 - 0.8413) = 0.8185.$$

For the purpose of modeling distributions of claims, the normal distribution is not very valuable, although actuaries sometimes find that the logarithm of the claim has an approximate normal distribution. Moreover, the normal distribution is extremely useful in providing some approximate error structure for many random variables (statistics). For example, if X is binomial, the function X/n is an estimator p; and we have seen that it has an approximate normal distribution with mean p and variance $p(1-p)/n$. Later, we find that two or more statistics (estimators of two or more parameters) frequently have joint normal distributions. Hence we take this opportunity to describe briefly the basic features of a bivariate normal distribution. Let X and Y have a bivariate normal distribution with means μ_X and μ_Y, variances σ_X^2 and σ_Y^2, and correlation coefficient ρ. It can be shown (HC, 3.5) that:

1. The marginal distributions of X and Y are $N(\mu_X, \sigma_X^2)$ and $N(\mu_Y, \sigma_Y^2)$, respectively.

2. The conditional distribution of Y, given $X = x$, is

$$N\left[\mu_Y + \rho\frac{\sigma_Y}{\sigma_X}(x - \mu_X), \sigma_Y^2(1 - \rho^2)\right]$$

and that of X, given $Y = y$, is

$$N\left[\mu_X + \rho\frac{\sigma_X}{\sigma_Y}(y - \mu_Y), \sigma_X^2(1 - \rho^2)\right].$$

It is interesting to note that each conditional mean is linear and that each conditional variance does not depend on the given value of the other variable. Of course, from facts (1) and (2), we can find the joint p.d.f. $f(x, y)$ of X and Y by multiplying the marginal p.d.f. of X and the conditional p.d.f. of Y, given $X = x$. It can then be shown, by considering the identity $f(x, y) \equiv f_1(x)f_2(y)$, that $\rho = 0$ is a necessary and sufficient condition for the independence of X and Y when they have a joint normal distribution. However, as we have seen, $\rho = 0$ is not, in general, a sufficient condition for the independence of two random variables.

Exercises

1. Write $M_Y(t)$ as

$$\left\{(1-p)\exp\left[-\frac{tp}{\sqrt{np(1-p)}}\right] + p\exp\left[\frac{t(1-p)}{\sqrt{np(1-p)}}\right]\right\}^n,$$

expand each exponential factor in a series using

$$e^w = 1 + \frac{w}{1!} + \frac{w^2}{2!} + \frac{w^3}{3!} + \cdots,$$

simplify the resulting expression, and take the limit as $n \to \infty$ to obtain $\exp(t^2/2)$.

2. Evaluate

$$\int_{-\infty}^{\infty}\left(\frac{1}{\sqrt{2\pi}\sigma}\right)\exp\left[tx - \frac{(x - \mu)^2}{2\sigma^2}\right]dx$$

by noting (through completing the square) that the exponent

$$tx - \frac{(x-\mu)^2}{2\sigma^2} = -\frac{\mu^2 - (\mu + \sigma^2 t)^2 + (x - \mu - \sigma^2 t)^2}{2\sigma^2}$$

and by recalling that

$$\int_{-\infty}^{\infty} \frac{1}{\sqrt{2\pi}b} \exp\left[-\frac{(x-a)^2}{2b^2} \right] dx = 1$$

for every real a and every real $b > 0$.

3. Let X be binomial with parameters n and p, such that $np = c$, a constant.

   (a) Show that

$$\lim_{n \to \infty} E(e^{tX}) = \lim_{n \to \infty} \left[1 + \frac{c(e^t - 1)}{n} \right]^n = e^{c(e^t - 1)},$$

   the Poisson m.g.f. with $\mu = c$.

   (b) Let $n = 200$ and $p = 0.01$ and use the result in (a) to approximate $\Pr(X < 5) = \Pr(X = 0, 1, 2, 3, 4)$ by referring to appropriate Poisson tables.

4. Let $p = 0.98$ be the probability that a person belonging to a certain class of drivers drives for 3 years without a claim.

   (a) If we are to observe 50 such persons and if we assume independence, find the probability that at least 48 of them drive 3 years without a claim.

   (b) Find an approximation to the result of part (a) by using a Poisson approximation. *Hint*: Let $p' = 1 - p = 0.02$ and redefine success.

5. Let X and Y have a bivariate normal distribution with parameters $\mu_X = -3$, $\mu_Y = 10$, $\sigma_X^2 = 25$, $\sigma_Y^2 = 9$, and $\rho = 3/5$. Compute (a) $\Pr(-5 < X < 5)$, (b) $\Pr(-5 < X < 5 | Y = 13)$, (c) $\Pr(7 < Y < 16)$, and (d) $\Pr(7 < Y < 16 | X = 2)$.

2.5. LINEAR FUNCTIONS OF RANDOM VARIABLES

Functions of random variables are most important in probability and statistics, and we begin our study of these functions by considering linear functions. For illustration, an insurance company is very much concerned about the sum of the claims from the policies it writes on fire insurance.

Let $X_1, X_2, \ldots, X_n$ be the random variables under consideration. Say X_i has mean μ_i and variance σ_i^2, $i = 1, 2, \ldots, n$. We want to consider some of the characteristics of the distribution of the linear function

$$Y = k_1 X_1 + k_2 X_2 + \cdots + k_n X_n = \sum_{i=1}^{n} k_i X_i,$$

where $k_1, k_2, \ldots, k_n$ are real constants (HC, 4.9). Because the expectation E is a linear operator, the mean of Y is

$$\mu_Y = E\left[\sum_{i=1}^{n} k_i X_i\right] = \sum_{i=1}^{n} k_i E(X_i) = \sum_{i=1}^{n} k_i \mu_i,$$

which is not a surprising result. The variance of Y is

$$\sigma_Y^2 = E\left[\left(\sum_{i=1}^{n} k_i X_i - \sum_{i=1}^{n} k_i \mu_i\right)^2\right] = E\left[\left\{\sum_{i=1}^{n} k_i(X_i - \mu_i)\right\}^2\right],$$

and, by squaring the multinomial in the right-hand member, we get

$$\sigma_Y^2 = E\left[\sum_{i=1}^{n} k_i^2(X_i - \mu_i)^2 + 2\sum\sum_{i<j} k_i k_j(X_i - \mu_i)(X_j - \mu_j)\right]$$

$$= \sum_{i=1}^{n} k_i^2 E[(X_i - \mu_i)^2] + 2\sum\sum_{i<j} k_i k_j E[(X_i - \mu_i)(X_j - \mu_j)]$$

$$= \sum_{i=1}^{n} k_i^2 \sigma_i^2 + 2\sum\sum_{i<j} k_i k_j \, \text{cov}(X_i, X_j).$$

If we denote the correlation coefficient of X_i and X_j by $\rho_{ij} = \text{cov}(X_i, X_j)/\sigma_i \sigma_j$, this last result can be written

$$\sigma_Y^2 = \sum_{i=1}^{n} k_i^2 \sigma_i^2 + 2\sum\sum_{i<j} k_i k_j \rho_{ij} \sigma_i \sigma_j.$$

Moreover, if $X_1, X_2, \ldots, X_n$ are mutually independent so that $\text{cov}(X_i, X_j) = 0$, $i \neq j$, then we have

$$\mu_Y = \sum_{i=1}^{n} k_i \mu_i \quad \text{and} \quad \sigma_Y^2 = \sum_{i=1}^{n} k_i^2 \sigma_i^2.$$

Example 1. If X and Y have respective parameters $\mu_X = 6$, $\sigma_X^2 = 16$, $\mu_Y = 1$, $\sigma_Y^2 = 9$, and $\rho_{XY} = \frac{1}{2}$, then $Z = X - Y$ has mean $\mu_Z = 6 - 1 = 5$ and variance

$$\sigma_Z^2 = 16 + (-1)^2 9 + 2(1)(-1)(\tfrac{1}{2})(4)(3) = 13 .$$

If, instead of $\rho = 1/2$, X and Y are independent so that $\rho = 0$, then $\mu_Z = 6 - 1 = 5$ and $\sigma_Z^2 = 16 + 9 = 25$. That is, the positive correlation reduced the variance of the difference $X - Y$.

Example 2.   In this example, we address a problem proposed in Section 2.1: What about the distribution of the number of successes if the probability of success changes from trial to trial? Let Y_i have p.d.f.

$$p_i^{y_i}(1 - p_i)^{1 - y_i} , \qquad y_i = 0, 1, i = 1, 2, \ldots , n ,$$

so that $\mu_i = p_i$ and $\mathrm{var}(Y_i) = p_i(1 - p_i)$, $i = 1, 2, \ldots , n$; and let Y_1, $Y_2, \ldots , Y_n$ be mutually independent. If $X = Y_1 + Y_2 + \cdots + Y_n$, then

$$\mu_X = p_1 + p_2 + \cdots + p_n = n\bar{p}, \qquad \bar{p} = \sum_{i=1}^{n} \frac{p_i}{n}$$

and

$$\sigma_X^2 = \sum_{i=1}^{n} p_i(1 - p_i) = \sum_{i=1}^{n} (\bar{p} + d_i)(1 - \bar{p} - d_i) ,$$

where $d_i = p_i - \bar{p}$ so that $\Sigma d_i = 0$. Thus

$$\sigma_X^2 = n\bar{p}(1 - \bar{p}) - \bar{p}\sum_{i=1}^{n} d_i + (1 - \bar{p})\sum_{i=1}^{n} d_i - \sum_{i=1}^{n} d_i^2 = n\bar{p}(1 - \bar{p}) - \sum_{i=1}^{n} d_i^2 .$$

Hence we note that if all the p values are the same $(\bar{p})$, the mean of X does not change, but the variance increases to $n\bar{p}(1 - \bar{p})$ because $d_i = 0$, $i = 1, 2, \ldots , n$. That is, the variance of the number of successes is actually less than $n\bar{p}(1 - \bar{p})$ when the p values change from trial to trial, a result that is surprising to a number of persons.

So we see that it is relatively easy to compute the mean and the variance of a linear function of random variables. These are important characteristics of a distribution, but what about the distribution itself? With linear functions, the *moment-generating function technique* is a particularly attractive method of finding the distribution, especially if the random variables are mutually independent. That is,

$$M_Y(t) = E\left[\exp\left(t \sum k_i X_i \right) \right] = E[\exp(k_1 t X_1) \exp(k_2 t X_2) \ldots \exp(k_n t X_n)] .$$

If we assume mutual independence so that the expected value of the product is the product of the expected values, we obtain

$$M_Y(t) = E[\exp(k_1 t X_1)]E[\exp(k_2 t X_2)] \dots E[\exp(k_n t X_n)]$$
$$= M_1(k_1 t)M_2(k_2 t) \dots M_n(k_n t),$$

where $M_i(t) = E[\exp(tX_i)]$ is the m.g.f. of X_i, $i = 1, 2, \dots, n$. If we can recognize that $M_Y(t)$ is the m.g.f. of a certain distribution, then Y has that particular distribution; this follows from the uniqueness property of the m.g.f.

Example 3.   Let X and Y be independent random variables with normal distributions $N(3, 7)$ and $N(5, 8)$, respectively. The m.g.f. of $Z = 2X + Y$ is

$$M_Z(t) = E\{\exp[t(2X + Y)]\} = E[\exp(2tX)]E[\exp(tY)]$$

$$= \exp\left[3(2t) + \frac{7(2t)^2}{2}\right]\exp\left(5t + \frac{8t^2}{2}\right)$$

$$= \exp\left(11t + \frac{36t^2}{2}\right).$$

Thus Z is normal with mean 11 and variance 36; that is, Z is $N(11, 36)$.

Before demonstrating another application of the m.g.f. technique, we mention a very special distribution in statistics. Let r be a positive integer. A *chi-square distribution* with r *degrees of freedom* is a special gamma distribution in which $\alpha = r/2$ and $\lambda = 1/2$; it occurs so frequently in statistics we denote it by $\chi^2(r)$. So if X is $\chi^2(r)$, its p.d.f. is

$$f(x) = \frac{1}{\Gamma(r/2)2^{r/2}} x^{r/2-1} e^{-x/2}, \qquad 0 < x < \infty,$$

its m.g.f. is

$$M(t) = (1 - 2t)^{-r/2}, \qquad t < 1/2,$$

and its mean and variance are

$$\mu = \left(\frac{r}{2}\right)2 = r \qquad \text{and} \qquad \sigma^2 = \left(\frac{r}{2}\right)2^2 = 2r.$$

There are four important results (HC, 4.7), the proofs of which are extremely easy and thus left as exercises:

1. The sum of k mutually independent chi-square random variables with respective degrees of freedom $r_1, r_2, \ldots, r_k$ is chi-square with $r_1 + r_2 + \cdots + r_k$ degrees of freedom (Exercise 1).

2. The sum of k mutually independent Poisson random variables with respective means $\mu_1, \mu_2, \ldots, \mu_k$ is Poisson with mean $\mu_1 + \mu_2 + \cdots + \mu_k$ (Exercise 2).

3. The sum of k mutually independent binomial random variables with respective parameters $n_1, n_2, \ldots, n_k$ and a common p is binomial with parameters $n_1 + n_2 + \cdots + n_k$ and p (Exercise 3).

4. If $X_1, X_2, \ldots, X_n$ are n mutually independent normal variables with means $\mu_1, \mu_2, \ldots, \mu_n$ and variances $\sigma_1^2, \sigma_2^2, \ldots, \sigma_n^2$, respectively, then

$$Y = \sum_{i=1}^{n} k_i X_i \quad \text{is} \quad N\left(\sum_{i=1}^{n} k_i \mu_i, \sum_{i=1}^{n} k_i^2 \sigma_i^2\right).$$

See Exercise 4.

It is interesting to note that if X is $N(\mu, \sigma^2)$, then $Y = [(X - \mu)/\sigma]^2$ has the m.g.f.

$$M_Y(t) = \int_{-\infty}^{\infty} \exp\left[t\left(\frac{x-\mu}{\sigma}\right)^2\right] \frac{1}{\sqrt{2\pi}\sigma} \exp\left[-\frac{(x-\mu)^2}{2\sigma^2}\right] dx$$

$$= \int_{-\infty}^{\infty} \frac{1}{\sqrt{2\pi}\sigma} \exp\left[-\frac{(x-\mu)^2}{2}\left(\frac{1-2t}{\sigma^2}\right)\right] dx$$

$$= \frac{1}{\sqrt{1-2t}} \int_{-\infty}^{\infty} \frac{1}{\sqrt{2\pi}\sqrt{\sigma^2/(1-2t)}} \exp\left\{-\frac{(x-\mu)^2}{2\sigma^2/(1-2t)}\right\} dx$$

$$= (1-2t)^{-1/2},$$

provided $1 - 2t > 0$, that is, $t < \frac{1}{2}$. Hence the square of a standard normal variable, $Y = [(X - \mu)/\sigma]^2$, is $\chi^2(1)$. This means that if $X_1, X_2, \ldots, X_n$ are normally distributed as hypothesized in result (4), then $[(X_i - \mu_i)/\sigma_i]^2$ is $\chi^2(1)$, $i = 1, 2, \ldots, n$; and by result (1),

$$\sum_{i=1}^{n} \left(\frac{X_i - \mu_i}{\sigma_i}\right)^2 \quad \text{is} \quad \chi^2(n),$$

an important fact in statistics.

The final point that we wish to develop in this section is the well-known *convolution formula*. Let X_1 and X_2 be independent random variables with respective p.d.f.s $f_1(x_1)$ and $f_2(x_2)$ so that the joint p.d.f. is $f_1(x_1)f_2(x_2)$. Let $Y_1 = X_1 + X_2$ and $Y_2 = X_2$; that is, the *inverse transformation* (HC, 4.3) is defined by $x_1 = y_1 - y_2$, $x_2 = y_2$ and its *Jacobian* is

$$J = \begin{vmatrix} \dfrac{\partial x_1}{\partial y_1} & \dfrac{\partial x_1}{\partial y_2} \\[2mm] \dfrac{\partial x_2}{\partial y_1} & \dfrac{\partial x_2}{\partial y_2} \end{vmatrix} = \begin{vmatrix} 1 & -1 \\ 0 & 1 \end{vmatrix} = 1 \, .$$

Thus the joint p.d.f. of Y_1 and Y_2 is

$$g(y_1, y_2) = f_1(y_1 - y_2)f_2(y_2) \cdot |J| = f_1(y_1 - y_2)f_2(y_2) \, .$$

The marginal p.d.f. of Y_1 is

$$g_1(y_1) = \int_{-\infty}^{\infty} f_1(y_1 - y_2)f_2(y_2) \, dy_2 \, ;$$

while we indicate that this integral is over all reals ($-\infty$ to ∞), frequently $f_1(y_1 - y_2)$ or $f_2(y_2)$ is equal to zero for some of those y_2 values and we can disregard those parts of the integral. It is equally clear that the roles of X_1 and X_2 could be reversed. In any case, we obtain the well-known *convolution formula* for the p.d.f. of the sum of two independent random variables, say $Y = X_1 + X_2$, namely

$$\int_{-\infty}^{\infty} f_1(y - z)f_2(z)dz = \int_{-\infty}^{\infty} f_1(z)f_2(y - z) \, dz \, .$$

If we have the sum of three or more mutually independent random variables, say $Z = X_1 + X_2 + X_3$, we could first find the p.d.f. of $Y = X_1 + X_2$ by the convolution formula and then that of $Z = Y + X_3$ by the convolution formula. As the following example indicates, it is frequently easier to use the m.g.f. technique, if at all possible, rather than the convolution formula.

Example 4. Let the independent random variables X_1 and X_2 have the same exponential p.d.f. $f(x) = e^{-x}$, $0 < x < \infty$. Thus the p.d.f. of $Y = X_1 + X_2$ is, for $0 < y < \infty$,

$$g(y) = \int_0^y e^{-z}e^{-(y-z)}dz,$$

where the limits are from 0 to y since $f(z)$ is zero when $z < 0$ and $f(y - z)$ is zero when $z > y$. If we evaluate this integral, we obtain

$$g(y) = \int_0^y e^{-y}dz = ye^{-y}, \qquad 0 < y < \infty.$$

If a third independent random variable X_3 is introduced, then the sum $Z = Y + X_3$ has the p.d.f.

$$h(z) = \int_0^z we^{-w}e^{-(z-w)}dw = \frac{z^2 e^{-z}}{2}, \qquad 0 < z < \infty.$$

Of course, this can be continued for the sum of n independent such random variables, say $W = X_1 + X_2 + \cdots + X_n$, but it seems much easier to us to find the m.g.f.

$$M_W(t) = E\{\exp[t(X_1 + X_2 + \cdots + X_n)]\}$$
$$= (1 - t)^{-1}(1 - t)^{-1}\ldots(1 - t)^{-1} = (1 - t)^{-n}, \qquad t < 1.$$

That is, W has a gamma distribution with parameters $\alpha = n$, $\lambda = 1$; in particular, Y is gamma ($\alpha = 2$, $\lambda = 1$) and Z is gamma ($\alpha = 3$, $\lambda = 1$).

Exercises

1. Let $X_1, X_2, \ldots, X_k$ be mutually independent where X_i is $\chi^2(r_i)$, $i = 1, 2, \ldots, n$. Show that

$$E[e^{t(X_1+X_2+\cdots+X_n)}] = (1 - 2t)^{-(r_1+r_1+\cdots+r_n)/2}.$$

2. Let $X_1, X_2, \ldots, X_k$ be mutually independent Poisson random variables with respective means $\mu_1, \mu_2, \ldots, \mu_k$. Show that

$$E[e^{t(X_1+X_2+\cdots+X_k)}] = e^{(\mu_1+\mu_2+\cdots+\mu_k)(e^t-1)}.$$

3. Let $X_1, X_2, \ldots, X_k$ be mutually independent binomial random variables with respective parameters $n_1, n_2, \ldots, n_k$ and common p. Show that

$$E[e^{t(X_1+X_2+\cdots+X_k)}] = (1 - p + pe^t)^{n_1+n_2+\cdots+n_k}.$$

4. Show that a linear combination of n mutually independent normal random variables is normal; that is, show that

$$E\left[\exp\left(t\sum k_i X_i\right)\right] = \exp\left[\left(\sum k_i \mu_i\right)t + \left(\sum k_i^2 \sigma_i^2\right)t^2/2\right].$$

5. Let X_1 and X_2 be independent random variables, each being $N(\mu, \sigma^2)$. Find the distribution of $Y = X_1 + X_2$ (a) by the convolution formula and (b) by the m.g.f. technique.

6. Let X_1, X_2, X_3 be three random variables with common variance σ^2. Find the variance of $Y = X_1 + X_2 + X_3$ (a) if $\rho_{12} = \rho_{13} = \rho_{23} = 0$ and (b) if $\rho_{12} = \rho_{13} = \rho_{23} = 1/4$. Does it agree with your intuition that the variance of the sum increases with positive correlation among the random variables?

7. Let X_1, X_2, and X_3 be three independent random variables so that the variances are $\sigma_1^2 = 4$, $\sigma_2^2 = 3$, and $\sigma_3^2 = k$. Given that the variance of $X_1 + 2X_2 - 3X_3$ is 28, find k.

8. Let X_1, X_2, and X_3 be three random variables with $\mu_1 = 4$, $\mu_2 = 6$, $\mu_3 = 3$, $\sigma_1^2 = 5$, $\sigma_2^2 = 8$, $\sigma_3^2 = 7$, $\rho_{12} = \frac{1}{2}$, $\rho_{13} = \frac{1}{3}$, and $\rho_{23} = \frac{1}{4}$. Find the mean and the variance of $Y_1 = 2X_1 - X_2 + X_3$. If $Y_2 = X_1 + 3X_2 - 2X_3$, find the correlation coefficient of Y_1 and Y_2. *Hint*: In computing the variances and the covariances of Y_1 and Y_2 the means of X_1, X_2, and X_3 are unimportant; so let $\mu_1 = \mu_2 = \mu_3 = 0$ and determine cov (Y_1, Y_2) by computing

$$E(Y_1 Y_2) = E[(2X_1 - X_2 + X_3)(X_1 + 3X_2 - 2X_3)].$$

2.6. FUNCTIONS OF RANDOM VARIABLES

In Section 2.5, we treated the important case of linear functions of random variables. In this section, we consider other functions; the reader who wants more material on this is referred to HC, 4.2–4.5. And through these functions (transformations) we can create more distributions, some of which are skewed with heavier tails than those of the normal distribution. That is, in this section and the next, we develop some distributions that, along with the binomial, Poisson, normal, exponential, Weibull, Gompertz, Makeham, and gamma, are extremely useful to actuaries.

The first is the *lognormal distribution*. Let X be $N(\mu, \sigma^2)$ and consider the transformation $X = \ln Y$ or, equivalently, $Y = e^X > 0$; that is, here we are assuming that the logarithm of a random variable has a normal distribution. Thus we see that Y is a positive random variable with the lognormal p.d.f.

$$g(y) = \frac{1}{\sqrt{2\pi}\sigma} \exp\left[-\frac{(\ln y - \mu)^2}{2\sigma^2}\right]\left(\frac{1}{y}\right), \qquad 0 < y < \infty,$$

where $1/y$ is the Jacobian of the transformation $x = \ln y$. To find the moments of Y, it is extremely easy to compute $E(Y) = E(e^X)$ and $E(Y^2) = E(e^{2X})$ by recognizing that these are the values of the m.g.f. of X evaluated at $t = 1$ and $t = 2$, respectively. That is, since $M_X(t) = \exp(\mu t + \sigma^2 t^2/2)$, we have

$$\mu_Y = E(Y) = M_X(1) = \exp\left(\mu + \frac{\sigma^2}{2}\right),$$

$$E(Y^2) = M_X(2) = \exp(2\mu + 2\sigma^2),$$

and

$$\sigma_Y^2 = \exp(2\mu + 2\sigma^2) - \exp(2\mu + \sigma^2) = \exp(2\mu + \sigma)^2[\exp(\sigma^2) - 1].$$

While all of the moments exist, the m.g.f. of Y does not exist. See the appendix for a graph of a lognormal p.d.f.

The *loggamma p.d.f.* can be found in a similar manner. If X has a gamma distribution with parameters α and λ, then $Y = e^X$ has p.d.f.

$$g(y) = \frac{\lambda^\alpha}{\Gamma(\alpha)} (\ln y)^{\alpha - 1} e^{-\lambda(\ln y)}\left(\frac{1}{y}\right), \qquad 1 < y < \infty.$$

That is,

$$g(y) = \frac{\lambda^\alpha (\ln y)^{\alpha - 1}}{\Gamma(\alpha) y^{1 + \lambda}}, \qquad 1 < y < \infty.$$

Since $M_X(t) = \lambda^\alpha(\lambda - t)^{-\alpha}$, when $t < \lambda$, then $E(Y^k) = E(e^{kX})$ exists only provided $k < \lambda$. In particular, the mean exists if $\lambda > 1$ and the variance exists if $\lambda > 2$; they are

$$\mu_Y = E(Y) = M_X(1) = \lambda^\alpha(\lambda - 1)^{-\alpha},$$

$$E(Y^2) = M_X(2) = \lambda^\alpha(\lambda - 2)^{-\alpha},$$

and

$$\sigma_Y^2 = \frac{\lambda^\alpha}{(\lambda - 2)^\alpha} - \frac{\lambda^{2\alpha}}{(\lambda - 1)^{2\alpha}} \cdot$$

The m.g.f. of Y again does not exist.

Another important distribution in statistics and actuarial science is derived as follows. This derivation should help the reader review the *change of variable* technique for determining the distribution of a function of two or more random variables. Let X_1 and X_2 be two independent gamma random variables with joint p.d.f.

$$\frac{\lambda^\alpha}{\Gamma(k)\Gamma(\alpha)} x_1^{k-1} x_2^{\alpha-1} e^{-x_1 - \lambda x_2}, \qquad 0 < x_1 < \infty, 0 < x_2 < \infty.$$

We are interested in the distribution of the ratio $Y_1 = X_1/X_2$. Let $Y_2 = X_2$ be an auxiliary variable. The corresponding transformation and its inverse, $x_1 = y_1 y_2$ and $x_2 = y_2$, map $\{(x_1, x_2); 0 < x_1 < \infty, 0 < x_2 < \infty\}$ onto $\{(y_1, y_2); 0 < y_1 < \infty, 0 < y_2 < \infty\}$, and the inverse transformation has the Jacobian

$$J = \begin{vmatrix} y_2 & y_1 \\ 0 & 1 \end{vmatrix} = y_2.$$

Thus the joint p.d.f. of Y_1 and Y_2 is

$$g(y_1, y_2) = \frac{\lambda^\alpha |y_2|}{\Gamma(k)\Gamma(\alpha)} (y_1 y_2)^{k-1} y_2^{\alpha-1} e^{-y_1 y_2 - \lambda y_2},$$

$$0 < y_1 < \infty, 0 < y_2 < \infty.$$

The marginal p.d.f. of Y_1 equals

$$g_1(y_1) = \int_0^\infty \frac{\lambda^\alpha y_1^{k-1}}{\Gamma(k)\Gamma(\alpha)} y_2^{k+\alpha-1} \exp\left[-(\lambda + y_1)y_2\right] dy_2.$$

By comparing the integrand of this integral to the p.d.f. of a gamma distribution with parameters $k + \alpha$ and $(\lambda + y_1)$, we see that

$$g_1(y_1) = \frac{\Gamma(k + \alpha)\lambda^\alpha y_1^{k-1}}{\Gamma(k)\Gamma(\alpha)(\lambda + y_1)^{k+\alpha}}, \qquad 0 < y_1 < \infty.$$

There are a few interesting observations that can be made about this p.d.f. of Y_1 and the corresponding distribution.

1. If $k = r_1/2$, $\alpha = r_2/2$, and $\lambda = r_2/r_1$, where r_1 and r_2 are positive integers, then Y_1 had the well-known *Fisher's F*-distribution with r_1 and r_2 degrees of freedom.

2. If $k = 1$, so that X_1 has an exponential distribution, then Y_1 has the p.d.f.

$$g_1(y_1) = \frac{\alpha \lambda^\alpha}{(\lambda + y_1)^{\alpha+1}}, \qquad 0 < y_1 < \infty,$$

which is that of a *Pareto distribution*, a very useful model for the distributions of losses in casualty insurance.

3. The right tail of the skewed distribution described by $g_1(y_1)$ is much thicker than the tails of either of the original gamma random variables. Frequently, in statistics, thicker tailed distributions are created by forming the ratio of two independent random variables; that is, measuring one thing per another, where the latter is also a random variable.

Since the Pareto distribution is a special case of the distribution of $Y_1 = X_1/X_2$, we call the more general $g_1(y_1)$ the p.d.f. of the *generalized Pareto distribution* and it is used as a model for some loss distributions.

There are two other very important p.d.f.s in statistics that can be developed by this change-of-variables technique (HC, 4.4). The first is Student's *t*-distribution. Let W be $N(0, 1)$, let V be $\chi^2(r)$, and let W and V be independent. Then

$$T = \frac{W}{\sqrt{V/r}}$$

is said to have a *Student's t-distribution* with r degrees of freedom. If, as an exercise (Exercise 3) in the change-of-variables technique, we also let $U = V$ and find the joint p.d.f. of T and U, finally integrating out u to obtain Student's p.d.f.,

$$g(t) = \frac{\Gamma[(r+1)/2]}{\sqrt{\pi r}\,\Gamma(r/2)(1 + t^2/r)^{(r+1)/2}}, \qquad -\infty < t < \infty.$$

The special case when $r = 1$ is called a *Cauchy p.d.f.*

The other important random variable is that which has a *beta dis-*

48 MODELS FOR RANDOM VARIABLES

tribution. Let X_1 and X_2 be independent gamma random variables with joint p.d.f.

$$\frac{\lambda^{\alpha+\beta}}{\Gamma(\alpha)\Gamma(\beta)} x_1^{\alpha-1} x_2^{\beta-1} e^{-\lambda(x_1+x_2)}, \qquad 0<x_1<\infty, 0<x_2<\infty.$$

Consider the distribution of $Y_1 = X_1/(X_1+X_2)$. If $Y_2 = X_1 + X_2$ is the auxiliary variable, it is an easy exercise so show that:

1. Y_2 is a gamma random variable with parameters $\alpha + \beta$ and λ.
2. Y_2 is independent of Y_1.
3. Y_1 has p.d.f.

$$g_1(y_1) = \frac{\Gamma(\alpha+\beta)}{\Gamma(\alpha)\Gamma(\beta)} y_1^{\alpha-1}(1-y_1)^{\beta-1}, \qquad 0<y_1<1,$$

   which is the p.d.f. of a beta distribution.
4. The mean and the variance of Y_1 are

$$\mu = \frac{\alpha}{\alpha+\beta}, \qquad \sigma^2 = \frac{\alpha\beta}{(\alpha+\beta+1)(\alpha+\beta)^2}.$$

The beta distribution (with $\alpha<1$ and $\beta<1$) is seemingly a good model for certain loss distributions, like the ratio of the loss to the total policy limit for fire losses concerning unprotected frame buildings.

Exercises

1. Carry out the calculations necessary to find the beta p.d.f. *Hint*: The new support is $0<y_1<1$, $0<y_2<\infty$ and the absolute value of the Jacobian equals y_2. In the process, show that Y_1 and Y_2 are independent and the latter has a gamma distribution.

2. Show that the mean and the variance of a beta distribution are as given in the text. *Hint*: In

$$\mu = \int_0^1 y \frac{\Gamma(\alpha+\beta)}{\Gamma(\alpha)\Gamma(\beta)} y^{\alpha-1}(1-y)^{\beta-1} dy$$

$$= \frac{\Gamma(\alpha+\beta)}{\Gamma(\alpha)\Gamma(\beta)} \int_0^1 y^{\alpha+1-1}(1-y)^{\beta-1} dy,$$

evaluate the last integral by comparing its integrand to a beta p.d.f. with parameters $\alpha + 1$ and β.

3. Carry out the calculations necessary to find the Student's t p.d.f. *Hint*: The new support is given by $-\infty < t < \infty$, $0 < u < \infty$ and the absolute value of the Jacobian equals $\sqrt{u}/\sqrt{r}$.

4. Let X have the p.d.f.

$$f(x) = \frac{1}{\pi}, \qquad \frac{-\pi}{2} < x < \frac{\pi}{2}.$$

Show that $Y = \tan X$ has a Cauchy distribution.

5. Let X have the Weibull p.d.f. $f(x) = 3x^2 e^{-x^3}$, $0 < x < \infty$. Find the increasing function of X, say $Y = u(X)$, that has the exponential p.d.f. $g(y) = e^{-y}$, $0 < y < \infty$. *Hint*: Let the inverse transformation be $x = w(y)$, that is, $u^{-1} = w$; thus the Jacobian is $w'(y)$. Solve the simple differential equation

$$[w'(y)](3)[w(y)]^2 e^{-[w(y)]^3} = e^{-y} \quad \text{for} \quad w(y)$$

and then determine $u(x)$.

6. Let X_1 and X_2 have the joint p.d.f. $f(x_1, x_2) = 8x_1 x_2$, $0 < x_1 < x_2 < 1$. Find the joint p.d.f. of $Y_1 = X_1/X_2$ and $Y_2 = X_2$ and then the marginal p.d.f. of Y_1.

2.7. THE MIXTURE OF MODELS

One way in which long-tailed and/or skewed distributions arise naturally is through a *mixture of models*. For illustration, say that we are observing independent standard normal random variables but occasionally, due to some defect in the process, we observe a random variable that is $N(0, 9)$. From what type of total distribution do these observations come? To answer this, suppose "occasionally" means about one tenth of the time. Thus the underlying distribution for the observations is the mixture

$$\frac{9}{10} N(0, 1) + \frac{1}{10} N(0, 9),$$

which has p.d.f.

$$\frac{9}{10\sqrt{2\pi}}\exp\left(\frac{-x^2}{2}\right)+\frac{1}{30\sqrt{2\pi}}\exp\left(\frac{-x^2}{18}\right).$$

By recalling that the usual measures of *skewness* and *kurtosis* are the standardized third and fourth moments of a distribution, it is an easy exercise (Exercise 1) to show that this mixture distribution has the characteristics

$$\mu=0,\qquad\sigma^2=1.8,\qquad E\left[\left(\frac{X-\mu}{\sigma}\right)^3\right]=0,\qquad E\left[\left(\frac{X-\mu}{\sigma}\right)^4\right]=8.34.$$

Since the kurtosis of the normal distribution is 3, we observe that this mixture, with a kurtosis of 8.34, has much thicker tails than does a normal distribution.

The mixing idea can be extended to a mixture of more than two distributions. Suppose that we have k distributions with respective p.d.f.s $f_1(x), f_2(x), \ldots, f_k(x)$, means $\mu_1, \mu_2, \ldots, \mu_k$, and variances $\sigma_1^2, \sigma_2^2, \ldots, \sigma_k^2$, with positive mixing probabilities $p_1, p_2, \ldots, p_k$, where $p_1 + \cdots + p_k = 1$. The p.d.f. of the mixture distribution is

$$p_1 f_1(x) + p_2 f_2(x) + \cdots + p_k f_k(x) = \sum_{i=1}^{k} p_i f_i(x).$$

The mean of this distribution is

$$E(X) = \sum_{i=1}^{k} p_i \int_{-\infty}^{\infty} x f_i(x)\,dx = \sum_{i=1}^{k} p_i \mu_i = \bar{\mu},$$

a weighted average of $\mu_1, \mu_2, \ldots, \mu_k$, and the variance equals

$$\mathrm{var}\,(X) = \sum_{i=1}^{k} p_i \int_{-\infty}^{\infty} (x - \bar{\mu})^2 f_i(x)\,dx$$

$$= \sum_{i=1}^{k} p_i \int_{-\infty}^{\infty} [(x - \mu_i) + (\mu_i - \bar{\mu})]^2 f_i(x)\,dx$$

$$= \sum_{i=1}^{k} p_i \int_{-\infty}^{\infty} (x - \mu_i)^2 f_i(x)\,dx + \sum_{i=1}^{k} p_i (\mu_i - \bar{\mu})^2 \int_{-\infty}^{\infty} f_i(x)\,dx$$

as the cross-product terms integrate to zero. That is,

$$\mathrm{var}\,(X) = \sum_{i=1}^{k} p_i \sigma_i^2 + \sum_{i=1}^{k} p_i (\mu_i - \bar{\mu})^2.$$

Remark. It is extremely important to note these characteristics are associated with a mixture of k distributions and have nothing to do with a linear combination, say $\Sigma\, p_i X_i$, of k random variables.

Example 1. Actuaries have found (Hewitt and Lefkowitz, 1979) that a mixture of the loggamma and gamma distributions is an important model for claim distributions. Here, with mixing probabilities p and $(1-p)$, the corresponding p.d.f. is

$$f(x) = \begin{cases} \dfrac{(1-p)\lambda_2^{\alpha_2} x^{\alpha_2-1}\exp(-\lambda_2 x)}{\Gamma(\alpha_2)}, & 0 < x \le 1, \\[3mm] \dfrac{\lambda_1^{\alpha_1}(p)(\ln x)^{\alpha_1-1}}{\Gamma(\alpha_1)x^{1+\lambda_1}} + \dfrac{(1-p)\lambda_2^{\alpha_2}x^{\alpha_2-1}\exp(-\lambda_2 x)}{\Gamma(\alpha_2)}, & 1 < x, \end{cases}$$

and zero elsewhere. The mean and the variance of the mixture distributions are, when $\lambda_1 > 2$, $\mu = \lambda_1^{\alpha_1}(p)(\lambda_1-1)^{-\alpha_1} + (1-p)\alpha_2/\lambda_2$ and

$$\sigma^2 = p\sigma_1^2 + (1-p)\alpha_2/\lambda_2^2 + p(1-p)[\lambda_1^{\alpha_1}(\lambda_1-1)^{-\alpha_1} - \alpha_2/\lambda_2]^2,$$

where

$$\sigma_1^2 = \left(\frac{\lambda_1}{\lambda_1-2}\right)^{\alpha_1} - \left(\frac{\lambda_1}{\lambda_1-1}\right)^{2\alpha_1}.$$

It is important to note that the variance is not simply the weighted average of the two variances but also includes a positive term involving the weighted variance of the means.

The mixture of distributions, which is extremely important, is sometimes called *compounding*. Moreover, it does not need to be restricted to a finite number of distributions. A continuous weighting function, which is of course a p.d.f., can replace $p_1, p_2, \ldots, p_k$; thus integration replaces summation.

Example 2. Let X be Poisson with parameter θ. We want to mix an infinite number of Poisson distributions, each with a different value of θ. We let the weighting function be a p.d.f. of θ, namely, a gamma with parameters α and λ. Hence the compound distribution is

$$\int_0^\infty \left[\frac{\lambda^\alpha}{\Gamma(\alpha)}\theta^{\alpha-1}e^{-\lambda\theta}\right]\left[\frac{\theta^x e^{-\theta}}{x!}\right]d\theta = \frac{\lambda^\alpha}{\Gamma(\alpha)x!}\int_0^\infty \theta^{\alpha+x-1}e^{-\theta(1+\lambda)}d\theta.$$

Comparing this integrand to the gamma p.d.f. with parameters $\alpha + x$ and $1 + \lambda$, we see that p.d.f. is equal to

$$\frac{\Gamma(\alpha + x)\lambda^\alpha}{\Gamma(\alpha)x!(1 + \lambda)^{\alpha + x}}, \qquad x = 0, 1, 2, \ldots .$$

If $\alpha = r$, a positive integer, and $\lambda = p/(1 - p)$, $0 < p < 1$, then this becomes

$$\frac{(r + x - 1)!}{(r - 1)!x!} p^r(1 - p)^x, \qquad x = 0, 1, 2, \ldots .$$

That is, X has a distribution that is the same as that of the number of excess trials needed to obtain r successes in a sequence of independent trials, each with probability p of success; this is one form of the *negative binomial distribution*. The negative binomial distribution has been used successfully as a model for number of accidents for motorists (see Weber, 1971).

In compounding, we can think of the original distribution of X as being a conditional one, given θ, whose p.d.f. is denoted by $f(x|\theta)$. Then the weighting function is treated as a p.d.f. for θ, say $g(\theta)$. Accordingly, the joint p.d.f. is $g(\theta)f(x|\theta)$, and the compound p.d.f. can be thought of as the marginal (unconditional) p.d.f. of X,

$$h(x) = \int_\theta g(\theta)f(x|\theta)\, d\theta,$$

where a summation replaces integration in case θ has a discrete distribution. For illustration, suppose we know that the mean of the normal distribution is zero but the variance σ^2 equals $1/\theta > 0$, where θ has been selected from some random model. For convenience, say this latter is a gamma distribution with parameters α and λ. Thus, given θ, X is conditionally $N(0, 1/\theta)$ so that the joint distribution of X and θ is

$$\frac{\sqrt{\theta}}{\sqrt{2\pi}} \exp\left(\frac{-\theta x^2}{2}\right) \frac{\lambda^\alpha}{\Gamma(\alpha)} \theta^{\alpha - 1} \exp(-\lambda\theta), \qquad \begin{matrix} -\infty < x < \infty, \\ 0 < \theta < \infty. \end{matrix}$$

Therefore, the marginal (unconditional) p.d.f. $h(x)$ of X is found by integrating out θ; that is,

$$h(x) = \int_0^\infty \frac{\lambda^\alpha \theta^{\alpha + 1/2 - 1}}{\sqrt{2\pi}\Gamma(\alpha)} \exp\left[-\theta\left(\frac{x^2}{2} + \lambda\right)\right] d\theta.$$

By comparing this integrand with a gamma p.d.f. with parameters $\alpha + \frac{1}{2}$ and $\lambda + x^2/2$, we see the integral equals

$$h(x) = \frac{\lambda^\alpha \Gamma(\alpha + \frac{1}{2})}{\sqrt{2\pi} \Gamma(\alpha)} \left(\frac{2}{2\lambda + x^2} \right)^{\alpha + 1/2}, \qquad -\infty < x < \infty.$$

It is interesting to note that if $\alpha = \lambda = r/2$, where r is a positive integer, then X has an unconditional distribution which is Student's t with r degrees of freedom. That is, we have developed a generalization of Student's distribution through this type of mixing or compounding. We note that the resulting distribution (a generalization of Student's t) has much thicker tails than those of the conditional normal with which we started.

We are now in a position to consider a question related to one raised in Section 1.1. Suppose that we are not certain about the probability p of success on a given trial, but p has been selected first by some random process, say one having a beta p.d.f. with parameters α and β. Thus X, the number of successes on n independent trials, has a conditional binomial distribution so that the joint p.d.f. of X and p is

$$\frac{n!}{x!(n-x)!} p^x (1-p)^{n-x} \frac{\Gamma(\alpha + \beta)}{\Gamma(\alpha)\Gamma(\beta)} p^{\alpha - 1} (1-p)^{\beta - 1}, \qquad \begin{array}{l} x = 0, 1, \ldots, n, \\ 0 < p < 1. \end{array}$$

Therefore, the unconditional p.d.f. of X is given by the integral

$$\int_0^1 \frac{n! \Gamma(\alpha + \beta)}{x!(n-x)! \Gamma(\alpha)\Gamma(\beta)} p^{x + \alpha - 1} (1-p)^{n - x + \beta - 1} dp$$

$$= \frac{n! \Gamma(\alpha + \beta) \Gamma(x + \alpha) \Gamma(n - x + \beta)}{x!(n-x)! \Gamma(\alpha)\Gamma(\beta)\Gamma(n + \alpha + \beta)}, \qquad x = 0, 1, 2, \ldots, n.$$

Let α and β be positive integers; since $\Gamma(k) = (k-1)!$, this unconditional (marginal or compound) p.d.f. can be written

$$\frac{n!(\alpha + \beta - 1)!(x + \alpha - 1)!(n - x + \beta - 1)!}{x!(n-x)!(\alpha - 1)!(\beta - 1)!(n + \alpha + \beta - 1)!}, \qquad x = 0, 1, 2, \ldots, n.$$

Because the conditional mean $E(X|p) = np$, the unconditional mean is $n\alpha/(\alpha + \beta)$ since $E(p)$ equals the mean $\alpha/(\alpha + \beta)$ of the beta distribution.

We now develop, by compounding, a heavy-tailed skewed distribution, a special case of which is extremely important to actuaries interested in size of loss distributions. Say X has a conditional gamma p.d.f. with parameters k and θ. The weighting function for θ is a gamma p.d.f. with parameters α and λ. Thus the unconditional (marginal or compounded) p.d.f. of X is

$$h(x) = \int_0^\infty \left[\frac{\lambda^\alpha \theta^{\alpha-1} e^{-\lambda\theta}}{\Gamma(\alpha)} \right] \left[\frac{\theta^k x^{k-1} e^{-\theta x}}{\Gamma(k)} \right] d\theta$$

$$= \int_0^\infty \frac{\lambda^\alpha x^{k-1} \theta^{\alpha+k-1} e^{-(\lambda+x)\theta}}{\Gamma(\alpha)\Gamma(k)} \, d\theta.$$

Comparing this integrand to the gamma p.d.f. with parameters $\alpha + k$ and $\lambda + x$, we see that

$$h(x) = \frac{\Gamma(\alpha+k)\lambda^\alpha x^{k-1}}{\Gamma(\alpha)\Gamma(k)(\lambda+x)^{\alpha+k}}, \qquad 0 < x < \infty,$$

which is the p.d.f. of the *generalized Pareto distribution*. Of course, when $k = 1$ (so that X has a conditional exponential distribution), the p.d.f. is

$$h(x) = \frac{\alpha\lambda^\alpha}{(\lambda+x)^{\alpha+1}}, \qquad 0 < x < \infty,$$

which is the *Pareto p.d.f.* Both of these compound p.d.f.s have thicker tails than the original (conditional) gamma distribution.

The mean and the variance of the generalized Pareto distribution can be found easily by comparing the integrals representing $E(X)$ and $E(X^2)$ with the p.d.f. of that distribution when k is $k+1$ (with α changed to $\alpha - 1$) and $k + 2$ (with α changed to $\alpha - 2$), respectively. They are

$$\mu = E(X) = \frac{\Gamma(\alpha+k)\lambda^\alpha}{\Gamma(\alpha)\Gamma(k)} \frac{\Gamma(\alpha-1)\Gamma(k+1)}{\Gamma(\alpha-1+k+1)\lambda^{\alpha-1}} = \frac{k\lambda}{\alpha-1},$$

provided $\alpha > 1$, and

$$E(X^2) = \frac{\Gamma(\alpha+k)\lambda^\alpha}{\Gamma(\alpha)\Gamma(k)} \frac{\Gamma(\alpha-2)\Gamma(k+2)}{\Gamma(\alpha-2+k+2)\lambda^{\alpha-2}} = \frac{(k+1)k\lambda^2}{(\alpha-1)(\alpha-2)},$$

provided $\alpha > 2$. Thus when $\alpha > 2$, the variance is

$$\sigma^2 = \frac{(k+1)k\lambda^2}{(\alpha-1)(\alpha-2)} - \frac{k^2\lambda^2}{(\alpha-1)^2} = \frac{k(\alpha+k-1)\lambda^2}{(\alpha-1)^2(\alpha-2)}.$$

In the special Pareto case, $k = 1$, these two characteristics are

$$\mu = \frac{\lambda}{\alpha - 1} \quad \text{and} \quad \sigma^2 = \frac{\alpha \lambda^2}{(\alpha - 1)^2(\alpha - 2)}.$$

While the distribution function of the generalized Pareto distribution cannot be expressed in a simple closed form, that of the Pareto distribution is

$$H(x) = \int_0^x \frac{\alpha \lambda^\alpha}{(\lambda + t)^{\alpha+1}} \, dt = 1 - \frac{\lambda^\alpha}{(\lambda + x)^\alpha}, \qquad 0 \le x < \infty.$$

From this, we can create another useful long-tailed distribution by letting $X = Y^\tau$, $0 < \tau$. Thus Y has the distribution function

$$G(y) = \Pr(Y \le y) = \Pr[X^{1/\tau} \le y]$$
$$= \Pr[X \le y^\tau].$$

This probability is equal to

$$G(y) = 1 - \frac{\lambda^\alpha}{[\lambda + y^\tau]^\alpha}, \qquad 0 \le y < \infty,$$

with corresponding p.d.f.

$$G'(y) = g(y) = \frac{\alpha \tau \lambda^\alpha y^{\tau-1}}{(\lambda + y^\tau)^{\alpha+1}}, \qquad 0 < y < \infty.$$

We call the associated distribution the *transformed Pareto distribution or Burr distribution* (Burr, 1942) and it has proved to be a useful one in modeling certain thicker tailed distributions. See the appendix for a summary and graphs of the Pareto, Burr, and generalized Pareto p.d.f.s.

There is another important type of compound distribution that must be mentioned. Say X is the sum of n independent claims and that its p.d.f. $f_n(x)$ can be found from the convolution formula or the m.g.f. technique. However, let us say that n, the number of claims, is the value of a random variable that has either a Poisson distribution with mean μ or a negative binomial distribution with parameters r and p. Thus the marginal (unconditional) p.d.f. $g(x)$ of X is

$$g(x) = \sum_{n=0}^{\infty} f_n(x) \frac{\mu^n e^{-\mu}}{n!} \quad \text{or} \quad \sum_{n=0}^{\infty} f_n(x) \frac{(r+n-1)!}{(r-1)!n!} p^r (1-p)^n.$$

Clearly, we must have an explicit expression for $f_n(x)$ to evaluate this summation. However, such evaluation is usually extremely difficult and numerical methods frequently are required. Over the years, several approximations (for examples, see Bohman and Esscher, 1963, 1964) have been suggested; a recent and very promising one, based on the gamma distribution, is given by Seal (1977a).

If the m.g.f. $M_n(t)$ corresponding to $f_n(x)$ is known, then, in the Poisson case,

$$E(e^{tX}) = \int_x e^{tx}g(x)dx = \sum_{n=0}^{\infty} \left(\int_x e^{tx}f_n(x)dx \right) \frac{\mu^n e^{-\mu}}{n!}$$

$$= \sum_{n=0}^{\infty} M_n(t) \frac{\mu^n e^{-\mu}}{n!}$$

often proves to be useful. For illustration, if X is the sum of n independent and identically distributed random variables, each with m.g.f. $M(t)$, then $M_n(t) = [M(t)]^n$. Hence

$$E(e^{tX}) = \sum_{n=0}^{\infty} [M(t)]^n \frac{\mu^n e^{-\mu}}{n!} = e^{\mu[M(t)-1]}.$$

Thus, for example, if the underlying distribution is exponential, with $M(t) = \lambda(\lambda - t)^{-1}$, so that X is conditionally gamma with $M_n(t) = \lambda^n(\lambda - t)^{-n}$, we have

$$E(e^{tX}) = e^{\mu t/(\lambda - t)}$$

If, instead of the m.g.f. $E(e^{tX})$, we considered the *characteristic function*

$$E(e^{itX}) = e^{i\mu t/(\lambda - it)},$$

this could be inverted using the inverse Fourier transform to obtain a numerical solution for the unconditional distribution of X; see, for example, an article by Seal (1977b).

Exercises

1. Show that the kurtosis of the mixture distribution, $(9/10)N(0, 1) + (1/10)N(0, 9)$, is 8.34.

2. Let X have the conditional geometric p.d.f. $\theta(1 - \theta)^{x-1}$, $x = 1, 2, \ldots$, where θ is a value of a random variable having a beta p.d.f. with

parameters α and β. Show that the marginal (unconditional) p.d.f. of X is

$$\frac{\Gamma(\alpha + \beta)\Gamma(\alpha + 1)\Gamma(\beta + x - 1)}{\Gamma(\alpha)\Gamma(\beta)\Gamma(\alpha + \beta + x)}, \qquad x = 1, 2, \dots .$$

If $\alpha = 1$, we obtain

$$\frac{\beta}{(\beta + x)(\beta + x - 1)}, \qquad x = 1, 2, \dots ,$$

which is one form of *Zipf's law*.

3. Repeat Exercise 2, letting X have a conditional negative binomial distribution instead of the geometric one.

4. Let X have a generalized Pareto distribution with parameters k, α, and λ. Show, by change of variables, that $Y = X/(\lambda + X)$ has a beta distribution.

5. Show that the failure rate of the Pareto distribution is

$$\frac{h(x)}{1 - H(x)} = \frac{\alpha}{\lambda + x}.$$

Find the failure rate of the Burr distribution with d.f.

$$G(y) = 1 - \left(\frac{\lambda}{\lambda + y^{\tau}}\right)^{\alpha}, \qquad 0 \le y < \infty .$$

In each of these two failure rates, note what happens as the value of the variable increases.

6. Let X be the loss amount for a liability claim against a doctor covered for professional liability. Suppose the primary insurance company purchases a reinsurance treaty with a retention of δ per claim, the reinsurer covering all loss excess of δ. Further, suppose X has a Pareto distribution with parameters α and λ. Find the (conditional) *truncated p.d.f.* of X, given $X \ge \delta$, namely $h(x)/\Pr(X \ge \delta)$, $\delta \le x < \infty$. Show that the excess claim amount, $Y = X - \delta$, given $X \ge \delta$, has a Pareto distribution with parameters α and $\lambda + \delta$; that is, the p.d.f. is

$$\frac{\alpha(\lambda + \delta)^{\alpha}}{[(\lambda + \delta) + (y)]^{\alpha+1}}, \qquad 0 < y < \infty .$$

7. For the Burr distribution, show that

$$E(X^k) = \lambda^{k/\tau}\Gamma\left(\alpha - \frac{k}{\tau}\right)\Gamma\left(\frac{k}{\tau} + 1\right)\bigg/\Gamma(\alpha),$$

provided $k < \alpha\tau$.

8. The *mean residual life* at age $\delta > 0$ is the conditional mean of $X - \delta$, given $X \geq \delta$, namely,

$$e(\delta) = E(X - \delta|X \geq \delta) = \int_\delta^\infty (x - \delta)\frac{f(x)}{\Pr(X \geq \delta)}\,dx.$$

This is related to the *excess ratio for retention*, $R(\delta)$, given by

$$R(\delta) = \frac{\int_\delta^\infty (x - \delta)f(x)dx}{E(X)} = \frac{E(X - \delta|X \geq \delta)}{E(X)/\Pr(X \geq \delta)} = \frac{e(\delta)}{E(X)/\Pr(X \geq \delta)}.$$

Show that if X has a Pareto distribution with parameters α and λ, then

$$E(X - \delta|X \geq \delta) = \frac{\lambda + \delta}{\alpha - 1},$$

a linear function of δ, and

$$R(\delta) = \left(\frac{\lambda}{\lambda + \delta}\right)^{\alpha - 1}.$$

9. Let the number X of accidents have a Poisson distribution with mean $\lambda\theta$. Suppose λ, the liability to have an accident, has, given θ, a gamma p.d.f. with parameters $\alpha = h$ and $\lambda = h$; and θ, an accident proneness factor, has a generalized Pareto p.d.f. with parameters α, $\lambda = h$, and k. Show that the unconditional p.d.f. of X is

$$\frac{\Gamma(\alpha + k)\Gamma(\alpha + h)\Gamma(h + x)\Gamma(k + x)}{\Gamma(\alpha)\Gamma(h)\Gamma(k)\Gamma(\alpha + h + k + x)x!}, \qquad x = 0, 1, 2, \ldots,$$

sometimes called the *generalized Waring* p.d.f.

10. Let X have a conditional Burr distribution with fixed parameters λ and τ, given parameter α.

(a) If α has the geometric p.d.f. $p(1-p)^\alpha$, $\alpha = 0, 1, 2, \ldots$, show that the unconditional distribution of X is a Burr distribution.

(b) If α has the exponential p.d.f. $\lambda e^{-\lambda\alpha}$, $\alpha > 0$, find the unconditional p.d.f. of X.

11. Recall that the distribution function of the largest item, Y_n, of the sample from a distribution with d.f. $F(x)$ is $[F(y_n)]^n$. If the underlying distribution is Pareto with parameters a and λ, show that

$$\lim_{n\to\infty} \Pr\left[\frac{n^{-1/a}}{\lambda} Y_n \le z\right] = \exp\left[-z^{-a}\right]$$

Hint:

$$\Pr[Y_n \le zn^{1/a}\lambda] = \left[1 - \left(\frac{1}{1 + zn^{1/a}}\right)^a\right]^n$$

$$= \left[1 - \left(\frac{z^{-a}}{n}\right)(1 + z^{-1}n^{-1/a})\right]^n .$$

This result could provide an approximate distribution for $Y_n/(n^{1/a}\lambda)$, where Y_n is the largest item of a sample from a Pareto distribution.

12. Let X have the conditional Weibull p.d.f.

$$f(x|\theta) = \theta\tau x^{\tau-1}e^{-\theta x^\tau}, \qquad 0 < x < \infty,$$

and let the p.d.f. (weighting function) $g(\theta)$ be gamma with parameters α and λ. Show that the compound (marginal) p.d.f. of X is that of Burr.

13. If X has a Pareto distribution with parameters α and λ and if c is a positive constant, show that $Y = cX$ has a Pareto distribution with parameters α and $c\lambda$.

14. Let X have a d.f. $F(x)$ and a p.d.f. $f(x)$ whose support is $0 < x < \infty$. The **limited expected value function** $E(X; d)$ of X is defined by

$$E(X; d) = \int_0^d xf(x)\,dx + d[1 - F(d)].$$

If the mean residual life function $e(d)$ exists, show that $E(X; d)$ and $e(d)$ are related through the equality

$$E(X) = E(X; d) + e(d)[1 - F(d)].$$

CHAPTER 3

Statistical Inference

3.1. MODEL-FREE ESTIMATION OF DISTRIBUTIONS

To elicit some information about an unknown distribution, the statistician takes a random sample from that distribution (or population). We want the sample to be selected in such a way that we can assume the n sample observations (items) $X_1, X_2, \ldots, X_n$ to be independent and identically distributed; that is, if $f(x)$ is the p.d.f. of the unknown distribution, then the joint p.d.f. of the sample observations is

$$f(x_1)f(x_2)\ldots f(x_n).$$

If we assume nothing more about the underlying distribution, we would estimate the probability of an event A by counting the number of items that fall in A. This number, in statistics, is called the *frequency* of A, and the *relative frequency* f/n is an estimate of $\Pr(X \in A)$. (It should be noted that in this chapter, *frequency* and *relative frequency* have their usual statistical meaning and are not to be confused with the actuarial usage; see Chapter 1.) A more formal way of thinking about this procedure is to construct an *empirical* distribution by assigning the "probability" of $1/n$ to each of the n values $X_1, X_2, \ldots, X_n$. The corresponding (cumulative) empirical distribution function is frequently denoted by $F_n(x)$; it is a nondecreasing step function with a jump of $1/n$ at each X_i. That is, $F_n(x) = $ (number of $X_i \le x)/n$, $-\infty < x < \infty$. An example, with $n = 4$, is given in Figure 3.1. The corresponding p.d.f., say $f_n(x)$, is a discrete one with a weight of $1/n$ on each X_i. The estimate of $p = \Pr(x \in A)$ is

$$\hat{p} = \sum_{x \in A} f_n(x).$$

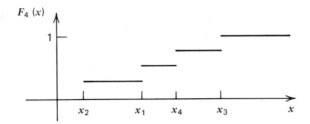

Figure 3.1. Empirical distribution function.

Not only can we compute empirical probabilities associated with this distribution determined by the sample, but also moments: the mean and the variance are, respectively,

$$\sum_x x f_n(x) = \sum_{i=1}^{n} (X_i)\left(\frac{1}{n}\right) = \frac{1}{n} \sum_{i=1}^{n} X_i = \bar{X}$$

and

$$\sum_x (x - \bar{X})^2 f_n(x) = \sum_{i=1}^{n} (X_i - \bar{X})^2 \left(\frac{1}{n}\right) = \frac{1}{n} \sum_{i=1}^{n} (X_i - \bar{X})^2 .$$

Often these characteristics of the sample are denoted by $\bar{X}$ and S^2, respectively, and these *statistics* are called the *sample mean* and the *sample variance* because they are determined by the sample items. That is,

$$\bar{X} = \frac{1}{n} \sum_{i=1}^{n} X_i \quad \text{and} \quad S^2 = \frac{1}{n} \sum_{i=1}^{n} (X_i - \bar{X})^2 ;$$

the latter is sometimes calculated using a parallel of $E(X^2) - \mu^2$:

$$S^2 = \frac{1}{n} \sum_{i=1}^{n} X_i^2 - \bar{X}^2 .$$

The positive square root, S, of S^2 is called the *sample standard deviation*.

Remark. Some statisticians define the sample variance by

$$\frac{1}{n-1} \sum_{i=1}^{n} (X_i - \bar{X})^2 ,$$

because they want an unbiased estimator of the population σ^2. Clearly, in our notation, $nS^2/(n-1)$ is that same unbiased estimator. More is said about unbiased estimation later.

There is not universal agreement on the definition of a sample percentile because the empirical distribution is a discrete one. However, all statisticians do agree that the $(100p)$th percentile, $0 < p < 1$, has about np items less than it and about $n(1-p)$ items greater than it. One way of achieving this is to select among $X_1, X_2, \ldots, X_n$, the $[(n+1)p]$th item in magnitude, provided p is such that $1 \le (n+1)p \le n$; otherwise the $(100p)$th percentile is not defined. That is, if the items $X_1, X_2, \ldots, X_n$ are ordered, say $Y_1 \le Y_2 \le \cdots \le Y_n$, and if $(n+1)p$ is an integer, then $Y_{(n+1)p}$ is the $(100p)$th sample percentile. If $(n+1)p$ is not an integer, then a weighted average of the two appropriate items is taken. For illustration, if $n = 100$ and $p = 1/4$, then $(101)/4 = 25.25$; thus we want an "observation" that is 25% of the way from Y_{25} to Y_{26}, namely

$$\frac{3}{4} Y_{25} + \frac{1}{4} Y_{26}.$$

This statistic is called the 25th sample percentile and has about 25% of the items less than it and about 75% of the items greater than it. Any slight modification of this rule is acceptable to most statisticians.

Even though $F_n(x)$, in some sense, gets close to the true d.f. $F(x)$, the discrete distribution associated with $F_n(x)$ and $f_n(x)$ is not a good way of depicting the distribution of the sample if it arises from a distribution of the continuous type. It is better to smooth $F_n(x)$ in some manner. One way to do this is simply to draw connecting line segments through $F_n(x)$; the first line segment begins at some point, say $x = c_0$, which is less than or equal to the smallest X_i, and ends at $x = c_k$, which is greater than or equal to the largest X_i. Suppose the intermediate points are $c_1 < c_2 < \cdots < c_{k-1}$, which are usually taken so as not to equal any given X_i. These points $c_0, c_1, c_2, \ldots, c_{k-1}, c_k$ do *not* need to be selected so that they are equally spaced, but they should be selected so that the line segments joining the points

$$[c_0, F_n(c_0) = 0], [c_1, F_n(c_1)], \ldots, [c_{k-1}, F_n(c_{k-1})], [c_k, F_n(c_k) = 1]$$

fit $F_n(x)$ well. Obviously, the more points the better the fit, but the principle of parsimony dictates that we should use as few line segments as possible without losing too much fit. Clearly, this method of fitting is subjective, but the spirit of this is better than given in most texts that require equally spaced values $c_0, c_1, \ldots, c_k$.

We denote the continuous function resulting from joining these line segments as $H(x)$ and call it an *ogive*. Thus $H(x)$ is an estimate of the underlying continuous d.f. $F(x)$, and its derivative $H'(x) = h(x)$ is an estimate of the underlying p.d.f. $F'(x) = f(x)$. Of course, since $H(x)$ consists of line segments, its derivative $h(x)$ is composed of slopes of those line segments, namely

$$h(x) = \frac{F_n(c_i) - F_n(c_{i-1})}{c_i - c_{i-1}}, \qquad c_{i-1} < x \le c_i.$$

If $F_n(c_i) - F_n(c_{i-1}) = f_i/n$, where f_i is the frequency of the observations in $c_{i-1} < x \le c_i$, then

$$h(x) = \frac{f_i}{n(c_i - c_{i-1})}, \qquad c_{i-1} < x \le c_i.$$

Moreover, if the lengths of the subintervals are equal, we have the usual histogram $f(x) = kf_i$, $c_{i-1} < x \le c_i$, where k is an appropriate constant. These subintervals $(c_{i-1}, c_i]$ are usually called *classes* or *cells* or *groups*. However, since it is not always desirable to use equally spaced points to describe long-tailed and skewed distributions, we encourage the reader to use the more general $h(x)$ as an estimator of the underlying $f(x)$. Please note in this general case that the height associated with the class $(c_{i-1}, c_i]$ is not only proportional to f_i, but also has the factor $1/(c_i - c_{i-1})$.

The following example indicates the importance of these concepts.

Example 1. In 1977 the following 40 losses, due to wind-related catastrophes, were recorded to the nearest $1,000,000. These data include only those losses of $2,000,000 or more; and, for convenience, they have been ordered and recorded in millions.

$$
\begin{array}{cccccccccc}
2, & 2, & 2, & 2, & 2, & 2, & 2, & 2, & 2, & 2 \\
2, & 2, & 3, & 3, & 3, & 3, & 4, & 4, & 4, & 5 \\
5, & 5, & 5, & 6, & 6, & 6, & 6, & 8, & 8, & 9 \\
15, & 17, & 22, & 23, & 24, & 24, & 25, & 27, & 32, & 43
\end{array}
$$

The mean and the standard deviation are $\bar{x} = 9.225$ and $s = 10.108$, respectively.

The empirical distribution function $F_{40}(x)$ can be depicted by the step function in Figure 3.2. It seems as if the ogive $H(x)$, which is also drawn

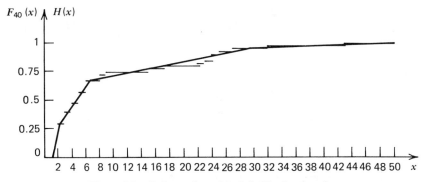

Figure 3.2. Ogive and empirical distribution function.

in Figure 3.2, given by a combination of four line segments joining the five points

$$(1.5, 0), (2.5, 0.3), (6.5, 0.675), (29.5, 0.95), (49.5, 1),$$

provides a reasonable fit to $F_n(x)$. The worst part of this fit is around $x = 22$. To fit here any better would require the ogive to be steeper around $x = 24$ and flatter around $x = 20$; this would result in a histogram that differs from our intuition. Hence we believe the given ogive smooths $F_n(x)$ reasonably well and in a manner consistent with our prior notions. Clearly there is a great subjective element in this fit and other persons would have different ones. It did, however, seem natural to choose the left-hand endpoint of 1.5 (because only values over 1,000,000 were recorded), but the right-hand endpoint of 49.5 was selected somewhat arbitrarily, although it seemed to provide a reasonable fit.

In this *grouped data*, the four frequencies for the four intervals are $f_1 = 12$, $f_2 = 15$, $f_3 = 11$, $f_4 = 2$ and the four class lengths are 1, 4, 23, 20, respectively. Thus the p.d.f. (relative frequency histogram) corresponding to $H(x)$ is given by

$$h(x) = \begin{cases} \dfrac{12}{40} = 0.3000, & 1.5 < x \le 2.5, \\[2mm] \dfrac{15}{(40)(4)} = 0.0938, & 2.5 < x \le 6.5, \\[2mm] \dfrac{11}{(40)(23)} = 0.0120, & 6.5 < x \le 29.5, \\[2mm] \dfrac{2}{(40)(20)} = 0.0025, & 29.5 < x \le 49.5; \end{cases}$$

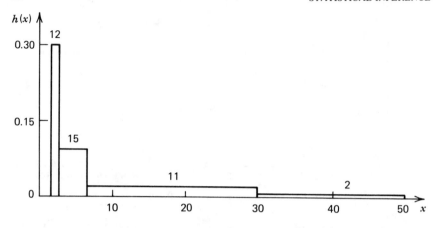

Figure 3.3. Relative frequency histogram.

and it is displayed in Figure 3.3. The numbers above the various "bars" are the respective frequencies. We will also fit this collection of data by other methods in Sections 3.4 and 3.7.

Since the sample mean $\bar{X}$ often is used as an estimator of the mean μ of the unknown underlying distribution with variance σ^2, another distributional property of $\bar{X}$ that helps to provide an error structure for this estimator should be noted. Since $\bar{X}$ is the linear function $\Sigma k_i X_i$ of X_1, $X_2, \ldots, X_n$ in which $k_1 = k_2 = \cdots = k_n = 1/n$, we have (Section 2.5)

$$\mu_{\bar{X}} = \sum_{i=1}^{n} \left(\frac{1}{n}\right)\mu = \mu \quad \text{and} \quad \sigma_{\bar{X}}^2 = \sum_{i=1}^{n} \left(\frac{1}{n}\right)^2 \sigma^2 = \frac{\sigma^2}{n}.$$

This implies that

$$Z = \frac{\bar{X} - \mu}{\sigma/\sqrt{n}}$$

has mean zero and variance one. But what is more important is that the limit of the moment-generating function of Z is

$$\lim_{n \to \infty} E(e^{tZ}) = e^{t^2/2}.$$

(For the proof, see HC, 5.4.) This result means that Z has a limiting normal distribution with mean zero and variance one, which is the well-known *Central Limit Theorem*. In applications, this means, with n large, that $\bar{X}$ has an approximate normal distribution with mean μ and variance σ^2/n and, in particular, that

$$\Pr\left(\mu - 2\frac{\sigma}{\sqrt{n}} < \bar{X} < \mu + 2\frac{\sigma}{\sqrt{n}}\right) \approx 0.95 .$$

This latter probability can be written

$$\Pr\left(\bar{X} - 2\frac{\sigma}{\sqrt{n}} < \mu < \bar{X} + 2\frac{\sigma}{\sqrt{n}}\right) \approx 0.95 .$$

Thus the observed interval $\bar{x} \pm 2\sigma/\sqrt{n}$ provides an approximate 95% *confidence interval* for the unknown μ. Of course, if σ is unknown and if n is large enough, $\sigma/\sqrt{n}$ often is approximated by $s/\sqrt{n-1}$, which is referred to as the standard error of $\bar{X}$. But, in any case, $\sigma/\sqrt{n}$ or $s/\sqrt{n-1}$ provides some information about the error structure of the estimator $\bar{X}$; that is, we have about 95% confidence that the true, but unknown, μ is within two standard errors of $\bar{X}$.

Before we leave this section, it is noted that the idea of sampling and an empirical distribution can be extended to joint distributions of two or more random variables. For illustration, if $(X_1, Y_1), (X_2, Y_2), \ldots, (X_n, Y_n)$ is a random sample from a bivariate distribution, the empirical distribution places "probability" $1/n$ on each point. Computing the characteristics of this discrete bivariate distribution, we have the respective means, variances, and correlation coefficient:

$$\bar{X} = \frac{1}{n}\sum_{i=1}^{n} X_i , \qquad S_X^2 = \frac{1}{n}\sum_{i=1}^{n} (X_i - \bar{X})^2 ,$$

$$\bar{Y} = \frac{1}{n}\sum_{i=1}^{n} Y_i , \qquad S_Y^2 = \frac{1}{n}\sum_{i=1}^{n} (Y_i - \bar{Y})^2 ,$$

and

$$R = \frac{\dfrac{1}{n}\sum_{i=1}^{n} (X_i - \bar{X})(Y_i - \bar{Y})}{S_X S_Y} .$$

If we refer to conditional means that are linear and substitute these sample characteristics for the parameters, we obtain the fitted lines (y on x)

$$\tilde{y} = \bar{Y} + R\left(\frac{S_Y}{S_X}\right)(x - \bar{X})$$

and (x on y)

$$\tilde{x} = \bar{X} + R\left(\frac{S_X}{S_Y}\right)(y - \bar{Y}).$$

Exercises

1. For each of the empirical distributions given in Tables 4.9, 4.13, and 4.17, graph reasonable ogives, $H(x)$, and their corresponding histograms, $h(x)$. In constructing the ogives it may be appropriate to use only a few of the given class boundaries.

2. Using the wind loss data of Example 1, determine the 25th, 50th, and 75th percentiles of that sample of size $n = 40$.

3. In 1971, the estimated loss payments for $n = 31$ wind catastrophes (each over $1,000,000) were (in millions) 1.6, 1.5, 1.5, 12.7, 2.4, 2.0, 1.4, 12.0, 7.0, 1.3, 13.0, 2.0, 3.5, 2.5, 7.0, 2.0, 2.7, 1.5, 1.5, 1.5, 1.5, 1.8, 1.4, 13.5, 1.5, 2.0, 1.4, 4.7, 2.0, 6.2, 9.0.

   (a) Construct the empirical distribution function.
   (b) Draw a reasonable ogive.
   (c) Find the corresponding histogram.
   (d) Compute the mean $\bar{x}$ and the standard deviation s.
   (e) Determine the 25th, 50th, and 75th percentiles of these data.

4. Consider the n data points $(X_1, Y_1), (X_2, Y_2), \ldots, (X_n, Y_n)$. Fit a straight line $y = b_1 x + b_2$ to these points by determining b_1 and b_2 that minimize

$$K(b_1, b_2) = \sum_{i=1}^{n} (Y_i - b_1 X_i - b_2)^2.$$

This method is called that of *least squares* and produces the line

$$\tilde{y} = \bar{Y} + (R)(S_Y/S_x)(x - \bar{X}).$$

3.2. ESTIMATING DISTRIBUTIONS BY SIMULATION

Sometimes it is theoretically impossible to find the p.d.f. of a function of random variables in closed form as discussed in Sections 2.5 to 2.7. First, the mathematics might be too difficult and hence some numerical methods are required. Second, it might be that the distributions of the individual variables in the function are not given in closed form or are only known approximately.

One way of attacking this important problem is through simulation. Two general references for simulation methods are *Statistical Computing* (Kennedy and Gentle, 1980, Chapter 6) and *Computational Methods for Data Analysis* (Chambers, 1977, Chapter 7). Basic elements of simulation with a view toward actuarial applications are given by Herzog (1984).

We begin by considering how to simulate the outcomes from a known distribution. Let the distribution be discrete, say

$$f(x) = \frac{x}{10}, \qquad x = 1, 2, 3, 4 .$$

Then, in a sequence of simulated observations, we desire that $X = x$ about $\Pr(X = x) = f(x)$ of the time; for example, $X = 1$ about $f(1) = 1/10$ of the time. This can be achieved easily by looking at a table of random numbers (or using a computer) and following this rule: if a two-digit random number equals $00, 01, \ldots, 09$, take $X = 1$; if it equals $10, 11, \ldots, 29$, take $X = 2$; if it equals $30, 31, \ldots, 59$, take $X = 3$; and if it equals $60, 61, \ldots, 99$, take $X = 4$. Clearly, this procedure provides the desired probabilities.

This scheme certainly is easy enough and suggests the following. Think of the graph of the distribution function $F(x)$ as having the jumps at $x = 1, 2, 3$, and 4 filled in with vertical bars; so, in our example, there is a vertical bar at $x = 1$ extending from zero to $1/10$, there is another one at $x = 2$ extending from $1/10$ to $3/10$, and so on, as seen in Figure 3.4. Now let Y have the *uniform distribution* on $0 \le y < 1$ with p.d.f.

$$g(y) = 1, \qquad 0 \le y < 1 .$$

If the observed value of Y is plotted on the y-axis and if a horizontal line is drawn from that point until the line touches this "filled in" $F(x)$, the x value so determined by that intersection is as if it arose from the distribution with $f(x) = x/10$, $x = 1, 2, 3, 4$. For illustration, the probability $\Pr(X = 3) = 0.3$ because, by the process, that x-value will occur if and only if $0.3 < Y \le 0.6$, and the latter has probability of 0.3.

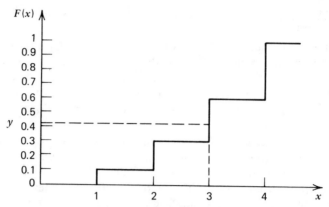

Figure 3.4. Discrete distribution function.

It is interesting that random variables of the continuous type can be generated in exactly the same manner. If we wish X to have the distribution with d.f. $F(x)$ of the continuous type and if Y has the uniform distribution on $0 \le y < 1$, then $Y = F(X)$ or, equivalently, $X = F^{-1}(Y)$ yields a random variable X with d.f. $F(x)$. The distribution function of X generated this way is

$$\Pr(X \le x) = \Pr[F(X) \le F(x)]$$

because $F(\cdot)$ is a nondecreasing function. However, by definition, $Y = F(X)$ and so

$$\Pr(X \le x) = \Pr[Y \le F(x)]$$
$$= \int_0^{F(x)} (1)\, dy = F(x),$$

since $g(y) = 1$, $0 \le y < 1$. That is, the distribution function of X is actually $F(x)$. Since uniform Y are easy to generate with the computer, we can easily generate many X, where $X = F^{-1}(Y)$. See Figure 3.5.

It is an interesting exercise (Exercise 1) to show that the converse of this fact is also true. If X has d.f. $F(x)$, then $Y = F(X)$ has the uniform distribution on $0 \le y < 1$.

Example 1. Suppose we wish to generate a random variable with a Pareto d.f.

$$F(x) = 1 - \frac{\lambda^\alpha}{(\lambda + x)^\alpha}, \qquad 0 \le x < \infty.$$

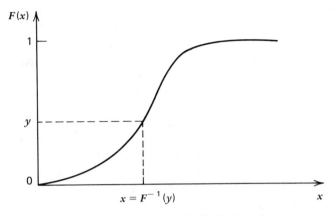

Figure 3.5. Continuous distribution function.

Let Y be the uniform random variable on $0 \le y < 1$. Then, setting

$$Y = 1 - \frac{\lambda^{\alpha}}{(\lambda + X)^{\alpha}}$$

and solving for X in terms of Y, we obtain

$$X = \lambda \left[\frac{1}{(1 - Y)^{1/\alpha}} - 1 \right] = F^{-1}(Y).$$

Thus X defined by this latter expression has the desired Pareto distribution.

In this example, it was easy to find the d.f. $F(x)$ in closed form. This is not always the case; for example, say we desire that X have a gamma distribution with $\alpha = 5/2$ and $\lambda = 4$. Thus numerical methods are needed to find $F(x)$ and $F^{-1}(y)$. In some instances there are special ways of generating certain random variables; for illustration, see Exercise 2 on how to generate normal variables. And sometimes the desired distribution can be approximated closely by one that does have a d.f. in closed form.

Now that we see how to simulate an individual random variable, how about functions of random variables, say $Z = u(X, Y)$? A simple example would be $Z = X + Y$, the sum of the loss amount X and the allocated loss adjustment expense Y resulting from one accident as considered in Section 2.3. For a more complicated illustration, say X is the amount of the final settlement of a claim made Y years ago, possibly in a malpractice case. The value at the time of the claim is $Z = X/(1 + i)^Y$, and even the interest rate i could be treated as a random variable to complicate the situation further. In a few special and relatively simple cases (for example, see Exercise 3), we can work out the distribution of Z. But in most cases the joint distribution of X and Y is too complicated and simulation is needed to approximate the distribution of Z. This is true with many functions of random variables.

Let $Z = u(X, Y)$, where X and Y are independent random variables. Assume that we know something about the respective distribution functions $F(x)$ and $G(y)$ of X and Y, even if it is only a reasonably good ogive estimate of each. Generating a sequence of independent uniform random variables $U_1, U_2, \ldots$ on the interval $0 \le u < 1$, we can use $F(x)$ and $G(y)$—or their ogives—to determine the sequence of independent pairs $(X_1, Y_1), (X_2, Y_2), \ldots, (X_n, Y_n)$, where, for example, in the continuous case, $X_1 = F^{-1}(U_1)$, $Y_1 = G^{-1}(U_2)$, $X_2 = F^{-1}(U_3)$, $Y_2 = G^{-1}(U_4)$, and so on. Immediately, we can compute the sequence

$$Z_1 = u(X_1, Y_1), \qquad Z_2 = u(X_2, Y_2), \ldots, \qquad Z_n = u(X_n, X_n).$$

From these values of $Z_1, Z_2, \ldots, Z_n$, an empirical distribution function, an ogive approximation, and a relative frequency histogram can be determined. In particular, the histogram estimate of the p.d.f. of Z can be very good by increasing the number n of simulations. Obviously, the final solution depends on the accuracy of our knowledge of $F(x)$ and $G(y)$; but, if the latter is very good, we can find strong estimates of the distribution of Z with a relatively small cost of computer time.

Extension of this procedure can be used to handle the situation of functions of more than two random variables. However, if the variables are dependent, as they might be in the example $Z = X/(1 + i)^Y$, then we must generate pairs $(X_1, Y_1), (X_2, Y_2), \ldots, (X_n, Y_n)$ from their joint distribution or from a reasonable approximation of that distribution and thus obtain n values of the function, namely $Z_1, Z_2, \ldots, Z_n$. From these data, we can construct the empirical distribution of Z or some smoothed version of it. A substantial illustration of simulation concerning the distribution of estimators of a parameter is given in Section 3.3. We consider an easier example here.

Example 2. Suppose we are willing to accept that the ogive in Example 1 of Section 3.1 is a reasonable approximation to the distribution of losses caused by heavy winds in 1977. A natural question to ask would concern the distribution of the sum of two independent wind losses, say X_1 and

X_2. The formulas for the four line segments of the ogive are given by

$$\frac{y-0}{x-1.5}=\frac{0.3-0}{2.5-1.5}, \qquad 1.5 \leq x < 2.5,$$

$$\frac{y-0.3}{x-2.5}=\frac{0.675-0.3}{6.5-2.5}, \qquad 2.5 \leq x < 6.5,$$

$$\frac{y-0.675}{x-6.5}=\frac{0.95-0.675}{29.5-6.5}, \qquad 6.5 \leq x < 29.5$$

$$\frac{y-0.95}{x-29.5}=\frac{1-0.95}{49.5-29.5}, \qquad 29.5 \leq x < 49.5.$$

The inverses, which are defined when $0 \leq y < 0.3$, $0.3 \leq y < 0.675$, $0.675 \leq y < 0.95$, and $0.95 \leq y < 1$, respectively, are found very easily by solving for x in terms of y. Suppose two random numbers (y) from the interval $(0, 1)$ are 0.641 and 0.117. The corresponding x values are, using the second and the first expressions, respectively,

$$x_1 = 2.5 + \frac{4}{0.375}(0.641 - 0.3) = 6.14$$

and

$$x_2 = 1.5 + \frac{1}{0.3}(0.117 - 0) = 1.89.$$

Thus the sum of these two losses is $z_1 = 6.14 + 1.89 = 8.03$. This process can be repeated again yielding z_2 and again to obtain z_3 and so on. Thus this procedure produces a sequence of z values, say $z_1, z_2, \ldots, z_m$, from which an ogive and histogram can be constructed. These are estimates of the distribution function and p.d.f. of the sum of two such losses.

Exercises

1. Let X have d.f. $F(x)$ and p.d.f. $f(x) = F'(x)$ of the continuous type. Let $Y = F(X)$.
   (a) Show that the distribution function of Y, $\Pr(Y \leq y) = \Pr[F(X) \leq y] = \Pr[X \leq F^{-1}(y)]$, equals y, $0 \leq y < 1$.
   (b) Show that the m.g.f. of Y, $E[e^{tF(X)}]$, equals $(e^t - 1)/t$, $t \neq 0$, and equals 1, $t = 0$.
   (c) By change-of-variables, show that the p.d.f. of Y equals 1, $0 \leq y < 1$. *Hint:* Recall that $(dx/dy) = 1/(dy/dx) = 1/f(x)$, where $x = F^{-1}(y)$.

2. Let Y_1 and Y_2 be independent uniform random variables, each with p.d.f. $g(y) = 1$, $0 \le y < 1$. Define the *Box-Muller transformation*

$$X_1 = \sqrt{-2 \ln Y_1} \cos (2\pi Y_2)$$
$$X_2 = \sqrt{-2 \ln Y_1} \sin (2\pi Y_2),$$

or, equivalently,

$$Y_1 = \exp \left(-\frac{X_1^2 + X_2^2}{2} \right)$$

$$Y_2 = \frac{1}{2\pi} \arctan \frac{X_2}{X_1}.$$

Show that X_1 and X_2 are independent standard normal random variables. *Hint*: The absolute value of the Jacobian is

$$\frac{1}{2\pi} \exp \left(-\frac{X_1^2 + X_2^2}{2} \right).$$

3. Let X and Y be independent random variables, where X has a lognormal distribution with parameters μ_1 and σ_1^2 and Y is $N(\mu_2, \sigma_2^2)$ with μ_2 large enough so that $\Pr(Y < 0) \approx 0$. Find the distribution of $Z = X/(1 + i)^Y$. *Hint*: Write $\ln Z = \ln X - Y[\ln (1 + i)]$, and first find the distribution of $\ln Z$.

4. Let $y_1 = 0.64$, $y_2 = 0.87$, $y_3 = 0.52$, $y_4 = 0.14$, and $y_5 = 0.35$ be five random numbers. Find the corresponding values (a) from an exponential distribution with distribution function $F(x) = 1 - e^{-x}$, $0 < x < \infty$; (b) from a Pareto distribution with distribution function $F(x) = 1 - 1/(1 + x)^2$, $0 < x < \infty$; (c) from a Burr distribution with distribution function $F(x) = 1 - 1/(1 + x^2)^2$, $0 < x < \infty$.

5. Let X_1 and X_2 be two independent losses with gamma distributions with respective parameters $\alpha_1 = 1$, $\lambda_1 = 0.0002$ and $\alpha_2 = 2$, $\lambda_2 = 0.0002$.
    (a) Find, by theoretical means, the distribution of $Z = X_1 + X_2$.
    (b) If the second gamma distribution had parameters $\alpha_2 = 1$, $\lambda_2 = 0.0001$, how would you solve the problem?

6. Let X be the loss amount and Y be the allocated loss adjustment expense stemming from one accident. Assume that $\ln X$ and $\ln Y$ have a bivariate normal distribution with parameters μ_1, μ_2, σ_1^2, σ_2^2, and ρ. Of course, this means that X and Y have dependent lognormal distributions.

(a) Find the mean and the variance of $Z = X + Y$.

(b) Find the conditional distribution of Y, given $X = x$.

(c) What is $E(Y|X = x)$?

3.3. POINT ESTIMATION

Sections 3.1 and 3.2 deal with the problem of estimating distributions without assuming too much about the underlying distributions, and accordingly the corresponding estimates are referred to as being model-free or distribution-free. In most of the remaining sections in this chapter, we estimate distributions and their parameters after assuming a functional form for the underlying p.d.f. However, in practice, there always must be some doubt about results obtained with a particular model because it probably is not the right one. Of course, we can hope that the model selected is a reasonable approximation to the true state of affairs, and thus the corresponding inferences can be used as a good guide in our decision-making process. As a matter of fact, there is nothing wrong with using a few different models for a given problem and noting the degree of agreement among the various solutions. The better the agreement among them, the more confidence the decision maker should have. However, if there is substantial disagreement, we had better take another hard look at the data before making an important decision about the problem under consideration.

Suppose we assume a model that depends on one or more parameters. For convenience, let us begin with a p.d.f. with one parameter and denote it by $f(x; \theta)$. With a random sample $X_1, X_2, \ldots, X_n$ from the underlying distribution, we want to find an *estimator*, say $u(X_1, X_2, \ldots, X_n)$, of θ. After the sample items have been observed to be equal to $X_1 = x_1$, $X_2 = x_2, \ldots, X_n = x_n$, we wish the *estimate* $u(x_1, x_2, \ldots, x_n)$ to be close to the true parameter θ. There are many procedures for finding workable estimators in applications, and we list some of the important ones through an example.

Example 1. Let $X_1, X_2, \ldots, X_n$ be a random sample from a Pareto distribution with parameters $\alpha = \theta$ and $\lambda = 1$, having p.d.f. $f(x) = \theta(1 + x)^{-(\theta+1)}, 0 < x < \infty$. The *likelihood function* is

$$L(\theta) = \prod_{i=1}^{n} f(x_i) = \theta^n \prod_{i=1}^{n} (1 + x_i)^{-(\theta+1)}.$$

Thus

$$\ln L(\theta) = n(\ln \theta) - (\theta + 1) \sum_{i=1}^{n} \ln (1 + x_i),$$

and

$$\frac{d[\ln L(\theta)]}{d\theta} = \frac{n}{\theta} - \sum_{i=1}^{n} \ln (1 + x_i) = 0$$

yields the *maximum likelihood estimator* of θ:

$$\hat{\theta} = \frac{n}{\sum_{i=1}^{n} \ln (1 + X_i)} = \frac{1}{\ln \left\{ \left[\prod_{i=1}^{n} (1 + X_i) \right]^{1/n} \right\}}.$$

It is written in this last form so that we can clearly see that $\hat{\theta}$ is a function of the *geometric mean* of the quantities $1 + X_1, 1 + X_2, \ldots, 1 + X_n$.

Since the mean of this Pareto distribution (see Section 2.7) is $1/(\theta - 1)$, we can use the *method of moments* to estimate θ; equating the first sample and distribution moments, we have

$$\bar{X} = \frac{1}{\theta - 1}$$

yielding the estimator

$$\bar{\theta} = \frac{1}{\bar{X}} + 1.$$

Sometimes $\hat{\theta}$ is closer to the true θ than is $\bar{\theta}$ and sometimes $\bar{\theta}$ is closer to θ than is $\hat{\theta}$. We will answer which is "best" in the long run after this example, but first consider another estimator.

Suppose, in this example, we have a belief that θ has a prior gamma p.d.f. $g(\theta)$ with parameters α and λ. That is, we feel that θ is about equal to α/λ but with a variance factor of α/λ^2.

Treating $L(\theta)$ as the conditional joint p.d.f. of $X_1, X_2, \ldots, X_n$, given θ, the joint p.d.f. of $X_1, X_2, \ldots, X_n$ and θ is then

$$[L(\theta)] \frac{\lambda^\alpha}{\Gamma(\alpha)} \theta^{\alpha-1} e^{-\lambda\theta}.$$

To find the conditional (*posterior*) p.d.f. of θ, given $X_1 = x_1, \ldots, X_n = x_n$, we integrate out θ in this joint p.d.f. to obtain $h(x_1, x_2, \ldots, x_n)$. Thus this posterior p.d.f. of θ is the joint p.d.f. divided by $h(x_1, x_2, \ldots, x_n)$; that is,

$$\frac{L(\theta)\lambda^\alpha \theta^{\alpha-1} e^{-\lambda\theta}}{\Gamma(\alpha)h(x_1, \ldots, x_n)} \propto L(\theta)g(\theta),$$

where the proportionality is with respect to θ (that is, constants and functions of $x_1, \ldots, x_n$ are included in the constant of proportionality). In this example, the posterior p.d.f. of θ is

$$g(\theta|x_1, \ldots, x_n) \propto \theta^{n+\alpha-1} \exp\left\{-\theta\left[\lambda + \sum_{i=1}^{n} \ln(1 + x_i)\right]\right\}.$$

So the posterior distribution of θ is gamma with parameters $n + \alpha$ and $\lambda + \Sigma \ln(1 + x_i)$.

In a sense, *Bayesian point estimation* is that value of the "random variable" θ which minimizes a certain expected loss. For illustrations, if the loss is the square of the error (deviation), then we use the mean of the posterior distribution; if it is absolute deviation, we use the median of the posterior distribution; and for other losses, we use other appropriate characteristics. (What is the loss associated with the estimator using the mode of the posterior distribution?) For example, using square error loss, we have the *Bayes estimator* that is the mean of the posterior gamma distribution with parameters $n + \alpha$ and $\lambda + \Sigma \ln(1 + x_i)$,

$$\hat{\theta}_B = \frac{(n + \alpha)}{\left[\lambda + \sum_{i=1}^{n} \ln(1 + X_i)\right]}.$$

Note that for small α and small λ this estimator is essentially the same as $\hat{\theta}$, the maximum likelihood estimator because then the prior distribution is very diffuse (noninformative), reflecting indecision about prior beliefs.

To discover which of the estimators, $\hat{\theta}$ or $\bar{\theta}$, is closer to the true but unknown θ most frequently, let us appeal to some asymptotic theory. This type of theory is much like that used to prove the Central Limit Theorem and provides, in practice, certain approximating distributions. Under certain regularity conditions (in particular, we need to be able to differentiate with respect to θ under integral signs so that θ cannot be in the description of the support of the underlying p.d.f.), the maximum likelihood estimator $\hat{\theta}$ has an approximate normal distribution with mean θ and variance

$$\frac{1}{nE\left\{\left[\dfrac{\partial \ln f(X;\theta)}{\partial \theta}\right]^2\right\}} = \frac{-1}{nE\left[\dfrac{\partial^2 \ln f(X;\theta)}{\partial \theta^2}\right]}.$$

This variance is the Rao–Cramér lower bound (HC, 11.1) for the variance of an unbiased estimator of θ; hence the maximum likelihood estimator is said to be asymptotically efficient because its variance equals this lower bound.

In Example 1, we note that

$$\ln f(x;\theta) = \ln \theta - (\theta + 1)\ln (1 + x),$$

$$\frac{\partial \ln f(x;\theta)}{\partial \theta} = \frac{1}{\theta} - \ln (1 + x), \quad \text{and} \quad \frac{\partial^2 \ln f(x;\theta)}{\partial \theta^2} = -\frac{1}{\theta^2}.$$

Therefore, the approximate variance of $\hat{\theta}$ is

$$\frac{-1}{nE\left(-\dfrac{1}{\theta^2}\right)} = \frac{\theta^2}{n}.$$

How does this compare to the approximate variance of $\bar{\theta}$, the estimator by the method of moments? Let us approximate this estimator, $u(\bar{X}) = 1 + 1/\bar{X}$, using two terms (the others can be disregarded in the asymptotic theory) of a Taylor's series about $1/(\theta - 1)$, to obtain

$$u(\bar{X}) \approx u\left(\frac{1}{\theta - 1}\right) + u'\left(\frac{1}{\theta - 1}\right)\left(\bar{X} - \frac{1}{\theta - 1}\right),$$

where

$$u\left(\frac{1}{\theta - 1}\right) = 1 + \frac{1}{1/(\theta - 1)} = \theta$$

and

$$u'\left(\frac{1}{\theta - 1}\right) = \frac{-1}{1/(\theta - 1)^2} = -(\theta - 1)^2.$$

That is,

$$u(\bar{X}) \approx \theta - (\theta - 1)^2\left[\bar{X} - \frac{1}{\theta - 1}\right].$$

From the Central Limit Theorem, $\bar{X}$ is approximately normally distributed with mean $1/(\theta-1)$ and variance $\theta/[(\theta-1)^2(\theta-2)n]$, for $\theta>2$. Thus $\bar{\theta}=u(\bar{X})=1+1/\bar{X}$ is approximately normally distributed with mean θ and variance

$$(\theta-1)^4\frac{\theta}{(\theta-1)^2(\theta-2)n}=\frac{\theta(\theta-1)^2}{(\theta-2)n},$$

since the variance of $\theta-(\theta-1)^2[\bar{X}-1/(\theta-1)]$ equals this latter expression. The ratio of the approximating variance of $\hat{\theta}$ to that of $\bar{\theta}$ is

$$K(\theta)=\frac{\theta^2}{\theta(\theta-1)^2/(\theta-2)}=\frac{\theta(\theta-2)}{(\theta-1)^2}<1.$$

We note that $K(2.1)=21/121$, $K(2.5)=5/9$, $K(3)=3/4$, $K(4)=8/9$, and so on; that is, $\hat{\theta}$ has a smaller asymptotic variance than does $\bar{\theta}$ for all $\theta>2$ and hence is asymptotically more efficient. As a matter of fact, $\bar{\theta}$ does not even have a finite variance when $\theta\leq2$; thus $\hat{\theta}$ has a big advantage in that case.

The above conclusion, of this particular example, is true in general. Under certain regularity conditions, the maximum likelihood estimator is the *best asymptotic normal* (BAN) estimator. It must be emphasized that this is a large sample result and says nothing about the situation when n is small. There have, however, been studies that indicate that the maximum likelihood estimator is better (that is, has a smaller variance) than the method-of-moments estimators even for small sample sizes.

Remark. To emphasize the point that the maximum likelihood estimator is usually better than that found by the method of moments in small samples too, we did the following Monte Carlo experiment. The distribution function of the Pareto distribution in Example 1 is

$$y=F(x)=1-\frac{1}{(1+x)^\theta};$$

so

$$x=\frac{1}{(1-y)^{1/\theta}}-1.$$

Thus, if we generate the random sample $Y_1, Y_2, \ldots, Y_{20}$ of size $n=20$ from the uniform distribution on the interval $(0,1)$, the preceding formula produces the random sample $X_1, X_2, \ldots, X_{20}$ from the Pareto distribution. With $\theta = 1$, we did this 500 times; each time we computed the maximum likelihood estimator $\hat{\theta} = n/[\Sigma \ln (1 + x_i)]$. These 500 observations of $\hat{\theta}$ had mean 1.05494 and variance 0.05855. That is, there seems to be a small positive bias of 0.05494 from the true value $\theta = 1$. Since $E[(\hat{\theta} - \theta)^2] = [E(\hat{\theta}) - \theta]^2 + \text{var}(\hat{\theta}) = (\text{bias})^2 + \text{var}(\hat{\theta})$, we have the estimate of the mean square error (MSE)

$$\text{MSE}(\hat{\theta}) = (0.05494)^2 + 0.05855 = 0.06157.$$

Also, with $\theta = 1$, we did a similar simulation with the method of moments estimator, namely, $\bar{\theta} = 1 + 1/\bar{X}$; the 500 observations of $\bar{\theta}$ had mean 1.30703 and variance 0.04617. Note that the bias is relatively large, 0.30703, and thus the mean square error is

$$\text{MSE}(\bar{\theta}) = (0.30703)^2 + 0.04617 = 0.14044.$$

Using the square error criterion, we find the efficiency of $\bar{\theta}$ as compared to $\hat{\theta}$ here is $0.06157/0.14044 = 0.438$.

This same simulation was repeated with $\theta = 2$ and $\theta = 3$ resulting in Table 1.

Table 1

	$\theta = 1$		$\theta = 2$		$\theta = 3$	
	$\hat{\theta}$	$\bar{\theta}$	$\hat{\theta}$	$\bar{\theta}$	$\hat{\theta}$	$\bar{\theta}$
Mean	1.05494	1.30703	2.10993	2.22764	3.16494	3.25033
Variance	0.05855	0.04617	0.23421	0.24212	0.52699	0.54255
Bias	0.05494	0.30703	0.10993	0.22764	0.16494	0.25033
MSE	0.06157	0.14044	0.24629	0.29394	0.55420	0.60522
Efficiency	0.43841		0.83789		0.91570	

These efficiencies of $\bar{\theta}$ compared to $\hat{\theta}$ are somewhat higher than the asymptotic results (recall that there $\bar{\theta}$ and $\hat{\theta}$ are asymptotically unbiased and the variances can be compared), but this is not surprising.

What about the Bayesian estimator? Clearly, it is somewhat like the maximum likelihood one (even more so using the posterior mode estimator rather than the posterior mean), and thus it should have good properties. As a matter of fact, if the decision maker has a strong belief that θ is in some region (as described by a prior p.d.f.), the Bayes estimator $\hat{\theta}_B$ usually has a smaller *mean square error* than does the maximum likelihood estimator $\hat{\theta}$, provided θ is actually in that region. If, on the other hand, the belief is substantially incorrect, then $\hat{\theta}$ is better than $\hat{\theta}_B$ (see Exercise 1). Of course, when n is large, $\hat{\theta}$ and $\hat{\theta}_B$ are essentially the same unless the decision maker has extremely strong prior convictions.

The concepts introduced here extend to two or more parameters. In maximum likelihood, we must maximize the likelihood function, say $L(\theta_1, \theta_2)$, with respect to two (or more) parameters; usually $\hat{\theta}_1$ and $\hat{\theta}_2$ are found by solving

$$\frac{\partial \ln L(\theta_1, \theta_2)}{\partial \theta_i} = 0, \qquad i = 1, 2.$$

While these solutions with several parameters are more complicated than those with one and frequently involve numerical methods (see Section 3.7), the concepts are nevertheless the same. In particular, we find (see Wilks, 1962) that the maximum likelihood estimators $\hat{\theta}_1$ and $\hat{\theta}_2$ have an approximate joint normal distribution with means θ_1 and θ_2 and variance-covariance matrix $\mathbf{V}$, whose inverse $\mathbf{V}^{-1}$ equals the information matrix $\mathbf{A} = [a_{ij}(\theta_1, \theta_2)]$, where

$$a_{ij}(\theta_1, \theta_2) = -nE\left[\frac{\partial^2 \ln f(X; \theta_1, \theta_2)}{\partial \theta_i \partial \theta_j}\right].$$

Often we approximate a_{ij} by $a_{ij}(\hat{\theta}_1, \hat{\theta}_2)$. If we cannot find the expectation in the expression for a_{ij}, it can also be approximated by

$$a_{ij} \approx -\sum_{k=1}^{n} \frac{\partial^2 \ln f(x_k; \hat{\theta}_1, \hat{\theta}_2)}{\partial \theta_i \partial \theta_j},$$

where $x_1, x_2, \ldots, x_n$ are the observed observations and $\hat{\theta}_1$ and $\hat{\theta}_2$ are the computed estimates.

In the method of moments, we equate the first and second (and possibly more if needed) moments of the sample and the distribution. In Bayesian procedures, we need the joint prior p.d.f. of the several parameters.

In our experience with data sets from the insurance industry, they are usually grouped into classes, say defined by the boundaries c_0, $c_1, \ldots, c_{k-1}, c_k$. Often c_0 is the amount of a deductible and thus claims under or equal to c_0 are never reported and our distribution is *truncated*.

Then, too, c_{k-1} might be an upper limit of a policy. Once it has been established that the claim x is such that $c_{k-1} < x < c_k = \infty$, then c_{k-1} dollars are paid. That is, we know that the claim exceeded c_{k-1} dollars but do not know the exact amount. Such data are said to be *censored*.

In any case, with grouped data, all we have are the frequencies f_1, $f_2, \ldots, f_k$ of the respective classes $(c_0, c_1], (c_1, c_2], \ldots, (c_{k-1}, c_k]$, where $\Sigma_{i=1}^k f_i = n$. Suppose we wish to fit an underlying p.d.f. $f(x; \theta)$ of the continuous type that depends on one or more parameters, represented by θ. The best likelihood function available is proportional to

$$L(\theta) = \left\{ \prod_{i=1}^k \left[\int_{c_{i-1}}^{c_i} f(x; \theta)\, dx \right]^{f_i} \right\} \left[\int_{c_0}^{\infty} f(x; \theta)\, dx \right]^n.$$

denom is b/c it is truncated

The coefficient $(n!)/(f_1!)(f_2!) \ldots (f_k!)$ may be included in this expression for $L(\theta)$. If the distribution function can be written in closed form, say $F(x; \theta)$, then we have

$$L(\theta) = \left\{ \prod_{i=1}^k [F(c_i; \theta) - F(c_{i-1}; \theta)]^{f_i} \right\} [1 - F(c_0; \theta)]^n.$$

This function $L(\theta)$, or its logarithm $\ln L(\theta)$, can be maximized to obtain the best maximum likelihood estimators of these parameters under these circumstances. Patrik (1980) used an analysis similar to this in which c_0 was the primary retention and c_{k-1} was the reinsurer's limit.

Example 2. Suppose we wish to fit a Pareto-type distribution to some reinsurance data; c_0 and c_{k-1} might be numbers like 1,000,000 and 8,000,000, respectively, with $c_k = \infty$. In this case, it might be best to simply subtract c_0 from each claim and thus, in effect, let $c_0 = 0$. Note that here all of the c values will be reduced by c_0. However, this scheme may not be satisfactory for all data sets and careful consideration should be given to the situation at hand. But here let us take $c_0 = 0$. Thus, since

$$F(x) = 1 - \left(\frac{\lambda}{\lambda + x} \right)^\alpha \quad \text{and} \quad f(x) = \frac{\alpha \lambda^\alpha}{(\lambda + x)^{\alpha+1}}, \qquad 0 < x,$$

we have

$$L(\alpha, \lambda) = \prod_{i=1}^k \left[\left(\frac{\lambda}{\lambda + c_{i-1}} \right)^\alpha - \left(\frac{\lambda}{\lambda + c_i} \right)^\alpha \right]^{f_i}$$

and

$$\ln L(\alpha, \lambda) = \sum_{i=1}^{k} f_i \ln \left[\left(\frac{\lambda}{\lambda + c_{i-1}} \right)^{\alpha} - \left(\frac{\lambda}{\lambda + c_i} \right)^{\alpha} \right].$$

We must solve simultaneously, by numerical methods, the two equations

$$\frac{\partial \ln L}{\partial \alpha} = 0 \quad \text{and} \quad \frac{\partial \ln L}{\partial \lambda} = 0$$

to find the maximizing values of α and λ. Numerical solutions of equations like these are discussed in Section 3.7.

While maximum likelihood estimators are extremely attractive, we emphasize that, in the preceding discussion, we had to make some modification in the process to find approximations in the group data situation. Another procedure that is gaining in popularity and is extremely attractive in these cases is *minimum distance estimation*, which was pioneered by Wolfowitz in the 1950s (for example, see Boos, 1981).

The distance considered is that between the empirical distribution function, $F_n(x)$, and the distribution function, $F(x; \theta)$, of the model. Of course, this is the distance used in the popular Kolmogorov–Smirnov statistic (see Section 3.6). However, we use here another important measure, a form of the Cramér–von Mises statistic,

$$\frac{1}{n} \sum_{i=1}^{n} [F_n(x_i) - F(x_i; \theta)]^2$$

where $x_1, x_2, \ldots, x_n$ are the observations. However, since in grouped data we do not know the individual observations, we must make our comparison only on the cell boundaries, obtaining

$$\sum_{i=0}^{k} [F_n(c_i) - F(c_i; \theta)]^2.$$

The Cramér–von Mises distance estimates are found by minimizing this expression with respect to θ, which can be a vector parameter. In addition, it is extremely easy to introduce a weight function, w_i, in case the user wishes to emphasize certain points more (say toward the tails) than others. Thus

$$\min_{\theta} \sum_{i=0}^{k} (w_i)[F_n(c_i) - F(c_i; \theta)]^2$$

gives weighted Cramér–von Mises minimum distance estimates. The very appealing feature about these estimates is that they can be found by any standard nonlinear least squares program (possibly weighted if some $w_i \neq 1$). That is, we are simply fitting the nonlinear function $F(x; \theta)$ to the points $[c_i, F_n(c_i)]$, $i = 0, 1, 2, \ldots, n$, by the method of least squares (possibly weighted).

A third procedure that is extremely good for grouped data, *minimum chi-square estimation*, is explained very well in an article by Moore (1978). If the frequency of the ith cell is

$$f_i = n[F_n(c_i) - F_n(c_{i-1})] \, ,$$

then the chi-square goodness-of-fit statistic is

$$Q = \sum_{i=1}^{k} \frac{\{f_i - n[F(c_i) - F(c_{i-1})]\}^2}{n[F(c_i) - F(c_{i-1})]} \, .$$

These minimum chi-square estimators are found by selecting those values of the parameters in the distribution function F that minimize Q. Note that the parameters appear in the denominator of Q too; and this complicates the problem, the resolution of which can be handled one of two ways:

1. Initial estimates of the parameters can be inserted in the denominator; then it becomes a problem in nonlinear weighted least squares, iterating for a number of steps.
2. The frequency f_i can be used to approximate the denominator, again resulting in a nonlinear weighted least squares problem. With this modification of Q, these modified estimators have the same asymptotic properties as the original minimum chi-square estimators.

We give a number of illustrations of these three procedures in the next chapter.

Remarks. From the study of compounding distributions, it is clear that the tails of distributions will be thinner (and thus the losses will be more predictable) if we consider homogeneous groups with respect to some "intensity" parameter. For illustration, suppose a random loss has a gamma p.d.f. with parameters $\alpha = k$ and $\lambda = \theta$, where the reciprocal of θ is this intensity factor. If we have several random losses with exactly these same parameters k and θ, then the distribution found by combining all observations (*not* summing, but dumping all losses together) is exactly that same gamma p.d.f., the tail of which is of the form $c_1 e^{-\theta x}$. On the other hand, suppose the different losses have different intensity factors; then the tail of the combined distribution is thicker (as in the generalized Pareto case) and thus the next loss is not as predictable due to this extra random element. In particular, if the intensity factor varies according to a gamma p.d.f. with parameters α and λ, we know that the combined p.d.f. of losses is a generalized Pareto with parameters k, α, and λ, the tail of which is of the form

$$c_2 x^{k-1}/(\lambda + x)^{k+\alpha} \approx c_3/(\lambda + x)^{\alpha+1}, \qquad \text{for large } x.$$

This latter tail is certainly thicker than $c_1 e^{-\theta x}$ and hence the loss has more of a chance of being fairly extreme, as measured by some deviation from a middle value.

To the insurance industry, this means that to determine fairer policy rates it is better to group items with similar intensity factors. It does not matter too much whether all of the intensity factors are relatively high or relatively low, just as long as they are about the same (although the low intensity group would obviously have different insurance premiums than would the high group).

Once the items under consideration have been placed in homogeneous groups, it is still necessary to estimate the parameters of these new distributions. Of course, maximum likelihood or minimum distance estimation (or other classical methods) could be used, but possibly the grouping process was such that it is now possible to assign some reasonable—and fairly tight—prior beliefs about the values of the parameters for each group. A Bayesian analysis is then in order, resulting in a posterior distribution of the parameter, say θ. Let us denote the corresponding conditional p.d.f. by $g(\theta|x_1, \ldots, x_n)$. Suppose that an appropriate point estimate of θ is required. This estimate depends on the loss function associated with the process in mind. For example, if the loss is given by $|\theta - \hat{\theta}|$, where θ is the true value and $\hat{\theta}$ is the estimate, to minimize the expected loss $E[|\theta - \hat{\theta}|]$ with respect to $\hat{\theta}$ we would take $\hat{\theta}$ to be the median of the posterior distribution.

This loss function $|\theta - \hat{\theta}|$ can be changed a little to create an interesting modification. For example, consider the loss function depicted in Figure 3.6. We see that errors in which the estimated θ is too large are more costly than those with small estimates. We find the Bayes estimator by minimizing $E[\text{Loss}]$; certainly our intuition would dictate that our estimate would be somewhat lower than the median. In particular, this loss function requires that $\hat{\theta}_B = (33\frac{1}{3})$rd percentile of the posterior distribution. This

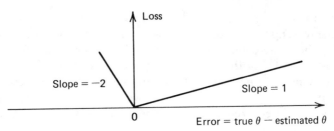

Figure 3.6. Loss function.

generalizes as follows: If the respective slopes of the loss function are proportional to $-(1-p)$ and p, then $\hat{\theta}_B = \hat{\pi}_p$, the $(100p)$th percentile. Since -2 and 1 are proportional to $-\frac{2}{3}$ and $\frac{1}{3}$, we use the percentile corresponding to $(100)(\frac{1}{3}) = 33\frac{1}{3}$.

Of course, in practical applications, there is no need to use artificial loss functions like the square of the error or the absolute value of the error. The actuary could assign the loss function from actual knowledge of the true situation. If the policy is priced too high, the contract might be lost and this costs something. However, if the policy is priced too low and the contract obtained, even more could be lost. Since it is difficult to assess these losses for various errors correctly, there is some tendency to use the standard Bayesian estimates, like the posterior mean and median. However, in important problems, some effort should be made to construct a realistic loss function, even though numerical methods would probably be needed to minimize $E(\text{Loss})$.
$\qquad\qquad\qquad\qquad\qquad\qquad\qquad\quad\;\theta$

Exercises

1. Let $X_1, X_2, \ldots, X_n$ be a random sample from a distribution with p.d.f. $f(x; p) = p^x (1-p)^{1-x}$, $x = 0, 1$.

    (a) Show that both the maximum likelihood and method of moments estimators are the same, namely $\hat{p} = \bar{p} = \Sigma_{i=1}^{n} X_i / n$.

    (b) If p has a beta distribution with parameters α and β, show that the Bayes estimator (with square error loss) equals

    $$\hat{p}_B = \left(\frac{n}{n + \alpha + \beta}\right)\hat{p} + \left(\frac{\alpha + \beta}{n + \alpha + \beta}\right)\left(\frac{\alpha}{\alpha + \beta}\right),$$

    which is a weighted average of $\hat{p}$ and the prior mean $\alpha/(\alpha + \beta)$. Note for small α and β that $\hat{p}_B$ is about the same as $\hat{p}$.

    (c) With $n = 10$, $\alpha = 7$, and $\beta = 3$, show that $\hat{p} = (1/2)\hat{p} + (1/2)(7/10)$ has a smaller mean square error than does $\hat{p}$ in the neighborhood of the prior mean $\alpha/(\alpha + \beta) = 0.7$. That is, find $p_1 < 0.7$ and $p_2 > 0.7$ such that $E[(\hat{p}_B - p)^2] < [E(\hat{p} - p)^2]$, when $p_1 < p < p_2$.

2. Repeat (a) of Exercise 1 when the parameter μ is a mean of a Poisson distribution. Repeat (b) of Exercise 1 where the prior of μ is a gamma distribution with parameters α and λ. Here

$$\hat{\mu}_B = \left(\frac{n}{n+\lambda}\right)(\bar{X}) + \left(\frac{\lambda}{n+\lambda}\right)(\alpha/\lambda),$$

a weighted linear combination of $\hat{\mu} = \bar{X}$ and the prior mean α/λ.

3. With a random sample $X_1, X_2, \ldots, X_n$, find the equations that we need to solve to determine the maximum likelihood estimators $\hat{\theta}_1$ and $\hat{\theta}_2$ for the following distributions: (a) $N(\theta_1, \theta_2)$; (b) gamma with parameters $\alpha = \theta_1$ and $\lambda = \theta_2$; (c) Pareto with parameters $\alpha = \theta_1$ and $\lambda = \theta_2$; (d) Weibull with parameters $c = \theta_1$ and $\tau = \theta_2$. The solutions of (a) can be written in closed form and are $\hat{\theta}_1 = \bar{X}$ and $\hat{\theta}_2 = S^2$. However, note the difficulties with the others, and numerical methods are needed. (e) Could the method of moments provide closed-form solutions in (b), (c), or (d)? If so, find them.

4. Let $Y_1, Y_2, \ldots, Y_n$ be n independent random variables, where Y_i is $N[\alpha + \beta(x_i - \bar{x}), \theta = \sigma^2]$, $i = 1, 2, \ldots, n$, provided $x_1, x_2, \ldots, x_n$ are constants, not all of which are equal to their mean value $\bar{x}$. Let the likelihood function $L(\alpha, \beta, \theta)$ be the joint p.d.f. of $Y_1, Y_2, \ldots, Y_n$ and show that the maximum likelihood estimators of α, β, and θ are

$$\hat{\alpha} = \bar{Y}, \quad \hat{\beta} = \frac{\sum (x_i - \bar{x})Y_i}{\sum (x_i - \bar{x})^2}, \quad \hat{\theta} = \frac{1}{n}\sum_{i=1}^{n}[Y_i - \hat{\alpha} - \hat{\beta}(x_i - \bar{x})]^2.$$

Note: Maximizing L with respect to α and β is equivalent to minimizing the sum of squares

$$\sum_{i=1}^{n}[y_i - \alpha - \beta(x_i - \bar{x})]^2.$$

Thus $\hat{\alpha}$ and $\hat{\beta}$ are also least squares estimators of α and β.

5. Since the wind data of Example 1, Section 3.1, are obviously truncated at 1.5, subtract 1.5 from each value and fit the Weibull p.d.f.

$$f(x; \theta) = \frac{\theta \exp(-\theta x^{1/2})}{2x^{1/2}}, \quad 0 < x < \infty,$$

to the resulting values:
(a) By finding the maximum likelihood estimate $\hat{\theta}$.
(b) By finding a Bayesian estimate (use mean or mode of the posterior distribution) if the prior p.d.f. is gamma with $\alpha = 0.4$ and $\theta = 1$.

(c)   Repeat (a) and (b) using the Weibull p.d.f.

$$(3/2)\theta x^{1/2} \exp\left(-\theta x^{3/2}\right), \quad 0 < x < \infty.$$

3.4. INTERVAL ESTIMATION

In Section 3.1, the importance of the error structure of an estimator was noted in the case in which $\bar{X}$ is used as an estimator of μ. In general, the statistician needs to know something about the reliability of any estimate. If the estimator has an approximate normal distribution with mean equal to the parameter, the variance of the estimator (or an estimate of this variance) is then enough information.

For illustration, $\bar{X}$ has an approximate normal distribution with mean μ and variance σ^2/n. Frequently, σ^2 is unknown, so we suggest the substitution $S^2/(n-1)$ for σ^2/n because

$$E[S^2/(n-1)] = \sigma^2/n.$$

That is, since $E[nS^2/(n-1)] = \sigma^2$, we call $nS^2/(n-1)$ an *unbiased estimator* of σ^2; accordingly, $S^2/(n-1)$ is an unbiased estimator of σ^2/n. If n is large, then, for example, the observed interval

$$\bar{x} \pm 2s/\sqrt{n-1}$$

is an approximate 95% *confidence interval* for the unknown μ. If, however, n is small, we prefer to use the following procedure.

Suppose, for the moment, that the sample arises from the normal distribution $N(\mu, \sigma^2)$. It is well known (HC, 4.8) that (a) $\bar{X}$ is $N(\mu, \sigma^2/n)$, (b) nS^2/σ^2 is $\chi^2(n-1)$, and (c) $\bar{X}$ and S^2 are independent. Thus, from the definition of Student's t, we have

$$T = \frac{\dfrac{\bar{X} - \mu}{\sigma/\sqrt{n}}}{\sqrt{\dfrac{nS^2}{\sigma^2}\Big/(n-1)}} = \frac{\bar{X} - \mu}{S/\sqrt{n-1}}$$

has a t-distribution with $n-1$ degrees of freedom. From t-tables, we can find t_0 so that $\Pr\left(-t_0 < (\bar{X} - \mu)/(S/\sqrt{n-1}) < t_0\right) = 0.95$, say. This is equivalent to

$$\Pr\left(\bar{X} - \frac{t_0 S}{\sqrt{n-1}} < \mu < \bar{X} + \frac{t_0 S}{\sqrt{n-1}}\right) = 0.95.$$

Therefore the observed interval $\bar{x} \pm t_0 s/\sqrt{n-1}$ provides a 95% interval for the unknown mean μ.

Note that the foregoing result is obtained under normal assumptions.

However, even without normality, it has been discovered that $\bar{x} \pm t_0 s/\sqrt{n-1}$ is an approximate 95% confidence interval for μ. Thus, with small n, we suggest the use of t_0 rather than the value 1.96 that comes from the normal table. For illustration, with $n = 15$ so that $n - 1 = 14$, use $\bar{x} \pm 2.145 \, s/\sqrt{14}$ rather than $\bar{x} \pm 1.96 s/\sqrt{14}$. The t_0 value of 2.145 gives us a number larger than 1.96 and thus the wider interval that is needed because we are using $s/\sqrt{n-1}$ as an estimate of $\sigma/\sqrt{n}$.

This idea is used in other instances too. Say $f(x; \theta)$ is such that the maximum likelihood estimator $\hat{\theta}$ must be found by numerical methods (like Newton's method). We know that $\hat{\theta}$ has an approximate normal distribution with mean θ and variance

$$\sigma_{\hat{\theta}}^2 = \frac{1}{nE\left\{\left[\frac{\partial \ln f(X; \theta)}{\partial \theta}\right]^2\right\}} = \frac{-1}{nE\left[\frac{\partial^2 \ln f(X; \theta)}{\partial \theta^2}\right]}.$$

Thus $\hat{\theta} \pm 1.96\sigma_{\hat{\theta}}$ is an approximate 95% confidence interval for θ. Let us say, however, that both expectations in the denominators of the expressions for the variance are difficult to compute or else have a θ in the answer. We can consider W to be one of the two approximations

$$-E\left[\frac{\partial^2 \ln f(X; \theta)}{\partial \theta^2}\right] \approx -\frac{1}{n}\sum_{i=1}^{n}\frac{\partial^2 \ln f(X_i; \hat{\theta})}{\partial \theta^2} = W.$$

or

$$E\left\{\left[\frac{\partial \ln f(X; \theta)}{\partial \theta}\right]^2\right\} \approx \frac{1}{n}\sum_{i=1}^{n}\left[\frac{\partial \ln f(X_i; \hat{\theta})}{\partial \theta}\right]^2 = W.$$

That is, the variance of $\hat{\theta}$ is approximated by $1/(nW)$. Some statisticians feel comfortable quoting $\hat{\theta} \pm t_0\sqrt{1/(nW)}$ as an approximate 95% confidence interval for θ, where t_0 has come from a t-table with $n - 1$ degrees of freedom. Two references for this approximation are Huber (1970) and Sprott (1980).

There are *Bayesian interval estimates* also. Once the posterior p.d.f. $g(\theta|x_1, \ldots, x_n)$ is determined, we can find (from tables or by numerical methods) two points $u = u(x_1, \ldots, x_n)$ and $v = v(x_1, \ldots, x_n)$ such that

$$\Pr(u < \theta < v|x_1, \ldots, x_n) = \int_u^v g(\theta|x_1, \ldots, x_n)d\theta$$

is large, say 0.95. Thus the interval (u, v) provides a Bayes interval estimate with posterior probability of 0.95. Since u and v are not uniquely determined from equating the conditional probability to 0.95, we usually select u and v so that the interval is shortest, if at all possible. This means that the interval contains points having the highest conditional density $g(\theta|x_1, \ldots, x_n)$ such that $\Pr(u < \theta < v|x_1, \ldots, x_n) = 0.95$. Tables or appropriate computer programs can be used in this process. For illustration, the Computer Assisted Data Analysis (CADA) developed at the University of Iowa in 1983, under the direction of Melvin Novick, is excellent for the Bayesian approach to many standard problems and provides these highest density (shortest) intervals.

Example 1. Let $X_1, X_2, \ldots, X_n$ be a random sample from a Weibull distribution with parameters $c = \theta/2$ and $\tau = 2$, having p.d.f. $f(x; \theta) = \theta x \exp(-\theta x^2/2)$, $0 < x < \infty$. Thus

$$L(\theta) = \theta^n (x_1 x_2 \ldots x_n) \exp\left(-\theta \sum_{i=1}^{n} \frac{x_i^2}{2}\right)$$

and

$$\ln L(\theta) = n(\ln \theta) + \ln(x_1 x_2 \ldots x_n) - \frac{\theta \sum_{i=1}^{n} x_i^2}{2}.$$

We have

$$\frac{d[\ln L(\theta)]}{d\theta} = \frac{n}{\theta} - \frac{\sum x_i^2}{2} = 0;$$

so

$$\hat{\theta} = \frac{2n}{\sum X_i^2}.$$

Also

$$\ln f(x; \theta) = \ln \theta + \ln x - \frac{\theta x^2}{2},$$

$$\frac{\partial \ln f(x; \theta)}{\partial \theta} = \frac{1}{\theta} - \frac{x^2}{2}, \quad \text{and} \quad \frac{\partial^2 \ln f(x; \theta)}{\partial \theta^2} = -\frac{1}{\theta^2}.$$

Thus the approximating variance of $\hat{\theta}$ is $\sigma_{\hat{\theta}}^2 = \theta^2/n$, which in turn can be approximated by $\hat{\theta}^2/n$. Finding t_0 in the t-tables with $n-1$ degrees of freedom, we have the approximate confidence interval, $\hat{\theta} \pm t_0 \hat{\theta}/\sqrt{n}$, for θ.

Suppose we do have some prior beliefs in the value of θ that are reflected in the gamma distribution with parameters α and λ. Then the posterior distribution of θ is

$$g(\theta|x_1, \ldots, x_n) \propto \theta^{n+\alpha-1} \exp\left[-\theta\left(\frac{\sum x_i^2 + 2\lambda)}{2}\right)\right]$$

which is gamma with parameters $n + \alpha$ and $(\sum x_i^2 + 2\lambda)/2$. For given n, α, and λ, an interval estimate can be found using incomplete gamma tables. Suppose, however, $n + \alpha$ is large enough that this posterior distribution of θ can be approximated by a normal distribution with respective conditional mean and variance

$$(n+\alpha)\frac{2}{\sum x_i^2 + 2\lambda} \quad \text{and} \quad (n+\alpha)\frac{4}{\left(\sum x_i^2 + 2\lambda\right)^2}.$$

Thus an approximate 95% Bayesian interval estimate of θ is

$$\frac{(n+\alpha)(2)}{\sum x_i^2 + 2\lambda} \pm 1.96\sqrt{n+\alpha}\,\frac{2}{\left(\sum x_i^2 + 2\lambda\right)}.$$

With small α and λ, and large n, note how this is close to

$$\frac{2n}{\sum x_i^2} \pm 1.96\left(\frac{2n}{\sum x_i^2}\right)\Big/\sqrt{n}\,,$$

the interval estimate obtained from the maximum likelihood estimator when n is large enough so that $t_0 = 1.96$. Again, if the decision makers have some good prior beliefs, we encourage them to use Bayesian methods to obtain reasonable inferences.

In Section 3.1, we noted how to estimate the percentiles of a distribution. There is a very easy way of getting a *nonparametric* (model-free) *interval estimate* of the $(100p)$th percentile, π_p, of a distribution of the continuous type with p.d.f. $f(x)$. Here π_p is defined by

$$\Pr(X \le \pi_p) = \int_{-\infty}^{\pi_p} f(x)\,dx = p, \quad 0 < p < 1.$$

Again let $Y_1 \le Y_2 \le \cdots \le Y_n$ be the order statistics of a random sample $X_1, X_2, \ldots, X_n$. Consider the probability

$$\Pr(Y_i \le \pi_p < Y_j), \quad i < j.$$

Say we have "success" if an individual X is less than or equal to π_p. Thus for $Y_i \leq \pi_p$ and $Y_j > \pi_p$, we must have at least i successes and at most $j - 1$ successes in the n independent trials. That is, if we had fewer than i successes, then $Y_i > \pi_p$; and if we had more than $j - 1$ successes, then $Y_j \leq \pi_p$. But the probability of an individual success is p. Hence

$$\Pr\left(Y_i \leq \pi_p < Y_j\right) = \sum_{k=i}^{j-1} \frac{n!}{k!(n-k)!} p^k (1-p)^{n-k} \; ;$$

this binomial probability can be found in binomial tables or can be approximated by either normal or Poisson probabilities, as appropriate. Say this probability is equal to γ. Then the observed interval (y_i, y_j) serves as a $(100\gamma)\%$ confidence interval for π_p.

Example 2. Let $n = 16$ and find a confidence interval for the median $\pi_{1/2}$ of a distribution of the continuous type. If $Y_1 \leq Y_2 \leq \cdots \leq Y_{16}$, then $(Y_8 + Y_9)/2$ is a point estimator for $\pi_{1/2}$ and, for illustration,

$$\Pr\left(Y_5 \leq \pi_{1/2} < Y_{12}\right) = \sum_{k=5}^{11} \frac{16!}{k!(16-k)!} \left(\frac{1}{2}\right)^k \left(\frac{1}{2}\right)^{16-k}$$

$$= 0.9230$$

from binomial tables. To see how well a normal approximation performs here, say W has a binomial distribution with parameters $n = 16$ and $p = 1/2$; so $np = 8$ and $np(1 - p) = 4$. Thus the preceding probability equals

$$\Pr\left(4.5 < W < 11.5\right) \approx \Phi\left(\frac{11.5 - 8}{2}\right) - \Phi\left(\frac{4.5 - 8}{2}\right) = 0.9198 \; .$$

With either probability, we can say the observed interval (y_5, y_{12}) forms a 92% confidence interval for $\pi_{1/2}$.

Example 3. With the wind loss data in 1977 (Example 1, Section 3.1), we note that the 35th order statistic, namely 24 (recorded in millions), is an estimate of the 85th percentile, $\pi_{0.85}$, since $35/(n+1) = 35/41 \approx 0.85$. To find a confidence interval for $\pi_{0.85}$ consider

$$\Pr\left(Y_{30} \leq \pi_{0.85} < Y_{39}\right) = \sum_{k=30}^{38} \binom{40}{k} (0.85)^k (0.15)^{40-k} \; .$$

But a binomial random variable with $n = 40$ and $p = 0.85$ has mean 34 and standard deviation 2.2583; hence we have the approximation

$$\Pr\left(Y_{30} \leq \pi_{0.85} < Y_{39}\right) \approx \Phi\left(\frac{38.5 - 34}{2.2583}\right) - \Phi\left(\frac{29.5 - 34}{2.2583}\right)$$

$$= \Phi(1.99) - \Phi(-1.99) \approx 0.95 .$$

Thus the observed interval ($y_{30} = 9$, $y_{39} = 32$) forms an approximate 95% confidence interval for $\pi_{0.85}$. This is a wide interval, but without additional assumptions this is the best that we can do.

Sometimes we need to estimate functions of parameters. For illustration, most probabilities are functions of parameters, like the tail-end probability $\Pr(X \geq c) = \lambda^{\alpha}(\lambda + c)^{-\alpha}$ of a Pareto distribution is a function of α and λ. Let us denote a function of two parameters by $h(\theta_1, \theta_2)$, and suppose that $u_1 = u_1(X_1, X_2, \ldots, X_n)$ and $u_2 = u_2(X_1, X_2, \ldots, X_n)$ are reasonable estimators of the parameters θ_1 and θ_2 that appear in the joint p.d.f. $f(x; \theta_1, \theta_2)$. Moreover, let us assume that u_1 and u_2 have an approximate joint normal distribution with means $\mu_1 = \theta_1$ and $\mu_2 = \theta_2$, variances σ_1^2 and σ_2^2, and correlation coefficient ρ. First, with h functions having derivatives, we approximate the estimator $h(u_1, u_2)$ of $h(\theta_1, \theta_2)$ by using the constant and linear terms of a Taylor's series about (θ_1, θ_2); in the asymptotic theory, terms of higher order can be disregarded. We obtain

$$h(u_1, u_2) \approx h(\theta_1, \theta_2) + h_1(\theta_1, \theta_2)(u_1 - \theta_1) + h_2(\theta_1, \theta_2)(u_2 - \theta_2) ,$$

where

$$h_i = h_i(\theta_1, \theta_2) = \left[\frac{\partial h(u_1, u_2)}{\partial u_i}\right]_{(\theta_1, \theta_2)}, \qquad i = 1, 2 .$$

This linear function of u_1 and u_2 has an approximate normal distribution with mean $h(\theta_1, \theta_2)$ and variance

$$h_1^2\sigma_1^2 + h_2^2\sigma_2^2 + 2h_1 h_2 \rho \sigma_1 \sigma_2 .$$

Hence $h(u_1, u_2)$ has this same approximate normal distribution.

One important application of this result is the case in which $u_1 = \hat{\theta}_1$ and $u_2 = \hat{\theta}_2$ are the maximum likelihood estimators of θ_1 and θ_2, parameters of $f(x; \theta_1, \theta_2)$. Under certain regularity conditions (see Wilks, 1962), $\hat{\theta}_1$ and $\hat{\theta}_2$ have an approximate joint normal distribution with means θ_1 and θ_2 and variance–covariance matrix $\mathbf{V}$, whose inverse equals $\mathbf{V}^{-1} = (a_{ij})$, where

$$a_{ij} = -nE\left[\frac{\partial^2 \ln f(X; \theta_1, \theta_2)}{\partial \theta_i \partial \theta_j}\right] .$$

Then $h(\hat{\theta}_1, \hat{\theta}_2)$ has an approximate normal distribution with mean $h(\theta_1, \theta_2)$ and variance $\mathbf{h'Vh}$, where $\mathbf{h'} = (h_1, h_2)$. If the unknown parameters θ_1 and θ_2 appear in $\mathbf{h'Vh}$, then that expression is approximated by substituting $\hat{\theta}_1$ and $\hat{\theta}_2$ for those unknown quantities.

Example 4. Again we refer to the data of Example 1 of Section 3.1 involving the $n = 40$ losses due to wind-related catastrophes in 1977. Say our objective in this example is to determine an estimate of the probability that a loss will exceed \$29,500,000; or, in the notation of that example, we wish to estimate $\Pr(X > 29.5)$. Since there were 2 observations that exceeded 29.5, the relative frequency estimate is $2/40 = 0.05$. But let us go further by fitting two models: (1) the truncated exponential with p.d.f.

$$f(x; \theta) = \frac{1}{\theta} e^{-(x-1.5)/\theta}, \qquad 1.5 < x < \infty,$$

where $\theta > 0$, and (2) the truncated Pareto with p.d.f.

$$f(x; \alpha, \lambda) = \frac{\alpha(\lambda + 1.5)^\alpha}{[(\lambda + 1.5) + (x - 1.5)]^{\alpha+1}}, \qquad 1.5 < x < \infty,$$

where $\alpha > 0$, $\lambda > 0$.

The maximum likelihood (and method of moment) estimate of θ is

$$\hat{\theta} = \frac{1}{40} \sum_{i=1}^{40} (x_i - 1.5) = \bar{x} - 1.5 = 9.225 - 1.5 = 7.725.$$

With the exponential model, we have

$$\Pr(X > 29.5) = \int_{29.5}^{\infty} \frac{1}{\theta} e^{-(x-1.5)/\theta}\, dx = e^{-(29.5-1.5)/\theta} = e^{-28/\theta} = h(\theta),$$

which can be estimated by

$$h(7.725) = e^{-28/7.725} = 0.0267.$$

Since $h'(\theta) = e^{-28/\theta}(28/\theta^2)$ and $\sigma_{\bar{x}}^2 = \theta^2/n$, the approximate variance is

$$[h'(7.725)]^2 \sigma_{\bar{x}}^2 = \left[(0.0267)\frac{28}{(7.725)^2}\right]^2 \left[\frac{(7.725)^2}{40}\right] = 0.000234;$$

thus the standard error of the estimate is 0.015. Hence with this model, an approximate 95% confidence interval is the interval from zero to $0.027 + 2(0.015) = 0.057$.

With the Pareto model and the sample characteristics of $\bar{x} = 9.225$ and $s = 10.108$, the method of moments estimators are

$$\tilde{\alpha} = \frac{2s^2}{s^2 - (\bar{x} - 1.5)^2} = 4.809$$

and

$$\tilde{\lambda} + 1.5 = \frac{(\bar{x} - 1.5)[s^2 + (\bar{x} - 1.5)^2]}{s^2 - (\bar{x} - 1.5)^2} = 29.421$$

and $\tilde{\lambda} = 27.921$. The estimate of

$$\Pr(X > 29.5) = \int_{29.5}^{\infty} \frac{\alpha(\lambda + 1.5)^\alpha}{[(\lambda + 1.5) + (x - 1.5)]^{\alpha+1}} \, dx = \left(\frac{\lambda + 1.5}{\lambda + 29.5}\right)^\alpha$$

is equal to 0.040. In Section 3.7, we will find the maximum likelihood estimates $\hat{\alpha}$ and $\hat{\lambda}$ and the corresponding estimate of $\Pr(X > 29.5)$, along with an approximation of its standard error. However, it is interesting to note, with these three estimates of $\Pr(X > 29.5)$, the thicker tailed Pareto model gives a larger estimate than does the tighter tailed exponential model; and, in this example, the Pareto estimate is closer to the relative frequency estimate of 0.05 (this, however, is not always the case).

Exercises

1. Show that $nS^2/(n-1)$ is an unbiased estimator of σ^2. *Hint*: Write $nS^2 = \sum_{i=1}^{n} X_i^2 - n\bar{X}^2$ and take the expected value of each member of the equation. Note that the assumption of normality is not needed.

2. Let $X_1, X_2, \ldots, X_n$ be a random sample from a Burr distribution with parameters $\alpha = \theta$, $\lambda = 1$, and $\tau = 3$, having p.d.f. $f(x; \theta) = 3\theta x^2/[1 + x^3]^{\theta+1}$, $0 < x < \infty$.

    (a) Find a confidence interval for θ using the maximum likelihood estimator.

    (b) Assume that θ has a prior gamma p.d.f. with parameters α and λ, and find point and interval Bayesian estimates.

3. Let $X_1, X_2, \ldots, X_n$ be a random sample from the normal distribution $N(\theta_1, \theta_2)$.

(a) Show that $\hat{\theta}_1 = \bar{X}$ and $\hat{\theta}_2 = S^2$ have an approximate joint normal distribution with means θ_1 and θ_2, variances θ_2/n and $2\theta_2^2/n$, and correlation coefficient $\rho = 0$.

(b) Find the approximate distribution of the estimator $h(\hat{\theta}_1, \hat{\theta}_2)$ of

$$h(\theta_1, \theta_2) = P(X \le c) = \Phi\left(\frac{c - \theta_1}{\sqrt{\theta_2}}\right),$$

where c is a given constant.

4. Recall that the maximum likelihood estimator

$$\hat{\theta} = n \bigg/ \sum_{i=1}^{n} \ln(1 + X_i)$$

of θ in the Pareto p.d.f. $f(x; \theta) = \theta(1 + x)^{-(\theta+1)}$, $0 < x < \infty$, has an approximate normal distribution with mean θ and variance θ^2/n (see Section 3.3). Thus the inequalities $-2 < (\hat{\theta} - \theta)/(\theta/\sqrt{n}) < 2$ could be solved to find an approximate 95% confidence interval for θ. And it is fairly easy in this case: Do it! In more complicated situations, the unknown parameter appearing in the variance can cause problems. Frequently it is approximated by $\hat{\theta}$ and the inequalities solved. But often a function of $\hat{\theta}$ is found that essentially has a variance free of θ (*variance stabilizing transformation*) by considering

$$u(\hat{\theta}) \approx u(\theta) + u'(\theta)(\hat{\theta} - \theta).$$

Then set the variance of this approximating linear function equal to a constant and solve the resulting differential equation for u. In this example, show that $u(\hat{\theta}) = \ln \hat{\theta}$ so that var $(\ln \hat{\theta}) \approx 1/n$.

3.5. TESTS OF STATISTICAL HYPOTHESES

The first four sections of this chapter have treated problems in estimation. In this section, we review the other principal area of statistical inference, tests of statistical hypotheses. Recall that any assertion about the distribution of one or more random variables is a *statistical hypothesis*. A rule, based on sample values, that leads to a decision to accept or to reject that hypothesis is called a *test* of a statistical hypothesis.

For a simple illustration, say $X_1, X_2, \ldots, X_{25}$ is a random sample of size $n = 25$ from $N(\theta, \sigma^2 = 100)$. Suppose the *null hypotheses* is $H_0: \theta = 75$ and the *alternative hypothesis* is H_1: $\theta > 75$. Consider the test that rejects H_0 and accepts H_1 if and only if $\bar{X} \geq 77$; otherwise we do not reject H_0 (some statisticians say we accept H_0 if $\bar{X} < 77$, at least until we have more evidence). We recognize that there are possible errors associated with this procedure: *Type I*, we can reject H_0 when it is true; and *Type II*, we can accept H_0 when it is false. Accordingly, we need to investigate certain probabilities, particularly those of making these errors. To do this we consider the *power function* of the test, which is the probability of rejecting H_0 as a function of θ:

$$K(\theta) = \Pr(\bar{X} \geq 77; \theta).$$

However, $\bar{X}$ is normally distributed with mean θ and variance $100/25 = 4$, so

$$K(\theta) = \Pr\left(\frac{\bar{X} - \theta}{2} \geq \frac{77 - \theta}{2}\right) = 1 - \Phi\left(\frac{77 - \theta}{2}\right).$$

Note that

$$K(75) = 1 - \Phi(1) = 1 - 0.84 = 0.16 = \alpha$$

is the probability of rejecting H_0 when $\theta = 75$; that is, it is the probability of the Type I error and is called the *significance level* α of the test. Also

$$K(80) = 1 - \Phi(-3/2) = 0.93$$

is the probability of a correct decision, namely rejecting H_0 when $\theta = 80$. Thus $1 - K(80) = 0.07$ is a probability of a certain incorrect decision, namely accepting H_0 when $\theta = 80$ (Type II error), and this probability is sometimes denoted by β.

Remark. In modern statistical usage, the *p-value* of a statistical test is usually reported. To explain this, let us refer to the preceding example. Suppose we observe a sample mean of $\bar{x} = 77.8$. We then ask ourselves a question: If the null hypotheses H_0: $\theta = 75$ is true, what is the probability of obtaining a sample mean $\bar{X}$ of at least 77.8? This probability is

$$\Pr(\bar{X} \geq 77.8; \theta = 75) = 1 - \Phi\left(\frac{77.8 - 75}{2}\right) = 1 - \Phi(1.4) = 0.08.$$

Note that this probability is a statistic as it is a function of $\bar{x} = 77.8$ and is called the p-value. That is, here the p-value $= 0.08$ and more generally, it is the tail end probability of the distribution of the test statistic under the null hypotheses. Again referring to the previous example, note that rejecting H_0 if the p-value ≤ 0.16 is equivalent to rejecting H_0 if $\bar{X} \geq 77$. Or, in general, rejecting H_0 if the p-value $\leq \alpha$ provides a test with significance level α.

A *simple hypothesis* is one that completely determines a distribution, for example, H_0 in the previous illustration is a simple hypothesis while H_1 is a *composite hypothesis* (that is, composed of more than one simple hypothesis). The *Neyman–Pearson lemma* (HC, 7.2) provides the best way of testing one simple hypothesis against another simple one and is illustrated in the following example.

Example 1. Suppose the experiment suggests that we have either the gamma distribution H_0: $f(x) = xe^{-x}$, $0 < x < \infty$ or the Weibull distribution H_1: $f(x) = xe^{-x^2/2}$, $0 < x < \infty$. That is, both of these distributions are similar near the origin but the second has a much shorter right tail than the first. The Neyman–Pearson lemma states that we compare the two joint p.d.f.s of the sample items $X_1, X_2, \ldots, X_n$ through a ratio; that is, we reject H_0 and accept H_1 if and only if

$$\frac{(x_1 x_2 \ldots x_n) \exp\left(-\sum x_i\right)}{(x_1 x_2 \ldots x_n) \exp\left(-\sum \frac{x_i^2}{2}\right)} \leq c_1,$$

where c_1 is selected to obtain the desired significance level α. This inequality is equivalent to $\sum x_i^2 - 2 \sum x_i \leq c_2$, where $c_2 = 2 \ln c_1$. This certainly agrees with our intuition: If the sum of squares of the x values is relatively small (compared to $2 \sum x_i$), then we would believe that the sample arose from the shorter tailed Weibull distribution. Incidentally, we would need the distribution of

$$\sum_{i=1}^{n} X_i^2 - 2 \sum_{i=1}^{n} X_i$$

when H_0 is true to be able to determine appropriate values of c_1 and c_2; this is a difficult problem and in practice we would solve it by simulation.

Example 2. Possibly more realistic hypotheses to test, other than those listed in Example 1, are those corresponding to the composite ones given by introducing scale parameters, namely

$$H_0: f(x) = \frac{xe^{-x/\theta}}{\theta^2}, \qquad 0 < x < \infty$$

and

$$H_1: f(x) = \frac{x}{\theta^2} \exp\left(-\frac{x^2}{2\theta^2}\right), \qquad 0 < x < \infty.$$

Under the respective hypotheses the maximum likelihood estimators of θ are (Exercise 1):

$$\hat{\theta} = \frac{\bar{X}}{2} \quad \text{and} \quad \hat{\theta} = \sqrt{\frac{\sum X_i^2}{2n}}.$$

If we modify the Neyman–Pearson lemma by taking the ratios of the maxima of the two joint p.d.f.s, we obtain

$$\frac{\dfrac{(x_1 x_2 \ldots x_n)}{[(\bar{x}/2)^2]^n} \exp\left[-\sum \dfrac{x_i}{(\bar{x}/2)}\right]}{\dfrac{(x_1 x_2 \ldots x_n)}{\left[\left(\sum x_i^2/2n\right)\right]^n} \exp\left[-\dfrac{\sum x_i^2}{2\left(\sum x_i^2/2n\right)}\right]} = \left[\frac{2\left(\sum x_i^2/n\right)}{\bar{x}^2}\right]^n e^{-2n+n} \le c_1.$$

This is equivalent to comparing the average of the square of the x values to the square of the average; that is, reject H_0 and accept H_1 if and only if

$$\frac{\sum x_i^2/n}{\bar{x}^2} \le c_2;$$

this provides a test that again agrees with our intuition. While the distribution of this ratio, under either H_0 or H_1, is difficult to obtain (it probably would be done by simulation in practice), it is free of θ so that c_1 and c_2 do not depend upon the unknown θ in finding an appropriate significance level α.

The modification of the Neyman–Pearson lemma given in Example 2 can be modified again to obtain the well-known *likelihood ratio test*.

Example 3. Let us say that we have two independent Pareto distributions, each with p.d.f. of the form

$$f(z; \theta) = \frac{\theta}{(1+z)^{\theta+1}}, \qquad 0 < z < \infty,$$

but with respective parameters θ_1 and θ_2. We have random samples from each, $X_1, X_2, \ldots, X_m$ and $Y_1, Y_2, \ldots, Y_n$. We wish to test the equality of the two distributions, $H_0: \theta_1 = \theta_2$, against all alternatives, $H_1: \theta_1 \neq \theta_2$. The joint p.d.f. of the random variables is

$$L(\theta_1, \theta_2) = \left[\theta_1^m \theta_2^n \prod_{i=1}^{m} (1+x_i)^{-\theta_1-1} \right] \left[\prod_{i=1}^{n} (1+y_i)^{-\theta_2-1} \right].$$

Under the restricted (assuming H_0 true) parameter space, denoted by ω: $\theta_1 = \theta_2 > 0$, the maximum likelihood estimator of $\theta_1 = \theta_2 = \theta$ is

$$\hat{\theta} = \frac{m+n}{\sum_1^m \ln(1+X_i) + \sum_1^n \ln(1+Y_i)}.$$

In the more general parameter space, denoted by Ω: $\theta_1 > 0$, $\theta_2 > 0$, the maximum likelihood estimators are

$$\hat{\theta}_1 = \frac{m}{\sum_1^m \ln(1+X_i)} \quad \text{and} \quad \hat{\theta}_2 = \frac{n}{\sum_1^n \ln(1+Y_i)}.$$

Taking the ratio of the two maxima of L, one when $(\theta_1, \theta_2) \in \omega$, denoted by $L(\hat{\omega})$, and the other when $(\theta_1, \theta_2) \in \Omega$, denoted by $L(\hat{\Omega})$, we obtain (Exercise 2)

$$\lambda = \frac{L(\hat{\omega})}{L(\hat{\Omega})} = \frac{m^m n^n \left[\sum_1^m \ln(1+X_i) + \sum_1^n \ln(1+Y_i) \right]^{m+n}}{(m+n)^{m+n} \left[\sum_1^m \ln(1+X_i) \right]^m \left[\sum_1^n \ln(1+Y_i) \right]^n} \leq c.$$

This is the likelihood ratio test. By dividing numerator and denominator of λ by $[\sum_1^n \ln(1+Y_i)]^{m+n}$, we see that λ is a function of the ratio

$$F = \frac{\sum_1^m \ln(1+X_i)/2m}{\sum_1^n \ln(1+Y_i)/2n}.$$

Another interesting observation is that, under H_0: $\theta_1 = \theta_2 = \theta$, each of $2\theta \ln(1 + X_i)$ and $2\theta \ln(1 + Y_i)$ has (Exercise 3) a chi-square distribution with two degrees of freedom. Hence the summations in the numerator and denominator, of F, each multiplied by 2θ, are $\chi^2(2m)$ and $\chi^2(2n)$, respectively; thus F actually has an F-distribution with $2m$ and $2n$ degrees of freedom. Now $\lambda \leq c$ is equivalent to $F \leq c_1$ or $F \geq c_2$ for some appropriate c_1 and c_2. Usually, for convenience, these are taken so that, under H_0,

$$\frac{\alpha}{2} = \Pr(F \leq c_1) = \Pr(F \geq c_2),$$

where α is the significance level of the test. The selection of the c values in this manner results in a very slight modification of the actual likelihood ratio test.

In many cases it is difficult to find the distribution of λ (or that of some statistic of which λ is a function), but there is some asymptotic help, first provided by Wilks (1938) and later by Wald (1943). With certain regularity conditions, it is true that, under H_0, $-2 \ln \lambda$ has an approximate chi-square distribution with degrees of freedom equal to the difference of the dimensions of the Ω and ω spaces. In Example 3, since Ω defines a two-dimensional space (here it is the first quadrant), we have dim $(\Omega) = 2$. However, ω is a one-dimensional space (the straight line $\theta_1 = \theta_2$), we have dim $(\omega) = 1$; thus $-2 \ln \lambda$ has an approximate chi-square distribution with $2 - 1 = 1$ degree of freedom. We reject H_0 and accept H_1 if and only if $\lambda \leq c$ or, equivalently,

$$-2 \ln \lambda \geq -2 \ln c = c_3,$$

where c_3 can be found in the chi-square tables for an appropriate significance level α.

Example 4. Using the $n = 40$ observations in the 1977 wind data (see Example 1, Section 3.1), we assume a truncated exponential distribution with p.d.f.

$$f(x; \theta) = \frac{1}{\theta} e^{-(x-1.5)/\theta}, \qquad 1.5 < x < \infty, \quad \theta > 0.$$

We wish to test the hypothesis H_0: $\theta = 9$ against all alternatives, H_1: $\theta \neq 9$. Since ω: $\theta = 9$ consists of one point (so ω has dimension of zero), we have

$$L(\hat{\omega}) = \left(\frac{1}{9}\right)^{40} e^{-\Sigma(x_i - 1.5)/9} = \left(\frac{1}{9}\right)^{40} e^{(-40\bar{x} + 60)/9} .$$

Now Ω is defined by $\theta > 0$ and this is one dimensional. We know $\hat{\theta} = \bar{X} - 1.5$; thus

$$L(\hat{\Omega}) = \left(\frac{1}{\bar{x} - 1.5}\right)^{40} e^{-\Sigma(x_i - 1.5)/(\bar{x} - 1.5)} = \left(\frac{1}{\bar{x} - 1.5}\right)^{40} e^{-40} .$$

Accordingly, the likelihood ratio is

$$\lambda = \frac{L(\hat{\omega})}{L(\hat{\Omega})} = \left(\frac{\bar{x} - 1.5}{9}\right)^{40} e^{-40\{[(\bar{x} - 1.5)/9] - 1\}}$$

and

$$-2 \ln \lambda = -80 \ln \left(\frac{\bar{x} - 1.5}{9}\right) + 80 \left[\frac{\bar{x} - 1.5}{9} - 1\right] .$$

Since $\bar{x} = 9.225$ and $\bar{x} - 1.5 = 7.725$, the observed $-2 \ln \lambda$ equals

$$-2 \ln \lambda = 80(0.1528 - 0.1417) = 0.8907 .$$

Since $-2 \ln \lambda$, under H_0, has an approximate chi-square distribution with d.f. equal to $\dim(\Omega) - \dim(\omega) = 1 - 0 = 1$, we see that 0.8907 is much smaller than the $\alpha = 0.05$ critical value of 3.84. Hence we do not reject the hypothesis that $\theta = 9$. This of course, does not mean that θ is equal to nine, but we go along with it until we have more data.

Exercises

1. Show that the maximum likelihood estimator $\hat{\theta}$ of θ in each of the gamma and Weibull distributions in Example 2 is as listed.

2. In Example 3, find the two maxima $L(\hat{\omega})$ and $L(\hat{\Omega})$ and show that the ratio is equal to the λ given there. *Hint:* Write $(1 + x_i)^{-\theta_1 - 1} = e^{-(\theta_1 + 1) \ln (1 + x_i)}$, etc.

3. Let Z have the Pareto p.d.f. $f(z; \theta) = \theta(1 + z)^{-\theta - 1}$. By the change-of-variables technique, show that $W = 2\theta \ln (1 + Z)$ has a chi-square distribution with 2 degrees of freedom.

4. Let Y have a binomial distribution with $n = 4$ and unknown parameter p. Reject $H_0: p = \frac{1}{2}$ and accept $H_1: p > \frac{1}{2}$ if and only if $Y = 4$.

(a) Find the power function and the significance level of the test.

(b) Find β, the probability of the Type II error, when $p = \frac{3}{4}$.

5. Based upon a random sample $X_1, X_2, \ldots, X_n$, find a test of an exponential p.d.f., H_0: $f(x; \theta) = \theta e^{-\theta x}$, $0 < x < \infty$, against a Pareto p.d.f. H_1: $f(x; \theta) = \theta(1 + x)^{-\theta-1}, 0 < x < \infty$.

6. Let $X_1, X_2, \ldots, X_m$ and $Y_1, Y_2, \ldots, Y_n$ be random samples from two independent gamma distributions with respective parameters $\alpha_1 = \alpha_2 = 3$ and $\lambda_1 = \theta_1$ and $\lambda_2 = \theta_2$.

(a) Find the likelihood ratio λ for testing H_0: $\theta_1 = \theta_2$ against H_1: $\theta_1 \neq \theta_2$.

(b) Show that this λ can be written as a function of a statistic that has an F-distribution under H_0.

7. Use the wind loss data of Example 1, Section 3.1. After subtracting 1.5 from each value (to allow for the truncation), test whether the Weibull p.d.f. with $c = \theta > 0$ and $\tau = 1.5$ or an exponential p.d.f. $\theta e^{-\theta x}$, $0 < x < \infty$, $\theta > 0$ is a better fit by comparing the ratio of the maximums, say $L_1(\hat{\theta})/L_2(\hat{\theta})$, to the number one, where L_1 and L_2 are the respective likelihood functions. Do the same problem except $\tau = 0.5$ in the Weibull distribution. Do these results suggest a constant, decreasing, or increasing failure rate?

3.6. TESTING THE FIT OF MODELS

Let us consider two major ways of testing the fit of models. Suppose, in this first example, we believe that we know the distribution function $F_0(x)$ exactly, and we wish to test that hypothesis; that is, if $F(x)$ is the true d.f., we wish to test H_0: $F(x) = F_0(x)$ against all alternatives.

Example 1. To test H_0: $F(x) = F_0(x)$ we observe a random sample X_1, $X_2, \ldots, X_n$ and count the frequencies of the k classes $(c_0, c_1]$, $(c_1, c_2], \ldots, (c_{k-1}, c_k]$. These classes could be those of the fitted ogive as described in Section 3.1; and, as there, we denote these frequencies by f_1, $f_2, \ldots, f_k$. Since the null hypothesis completely specifies the probabilities of the classes, say $p_i = F(c_i) - F(c_{i-1})$, $i = 1, 2, \ldots, k$, the expected values, under H_0, of the respective frequencies are $np_1, np_2, \ldots, np_k$. We can construct Pearson's *goodness-of-fit* statistic

$$\chi^2 = \sum_{i=1}^{k} \frac{(f_i - np_i)^2}{np_i}.$$

While χ^2 does not have a chi-square distribution, it does have, for large n, an approximate chi-square distribution with $k - 1$ degrees of freedom. If χ^2 is relatively small, then we say the agreement is acceptable and we accept $F_0(x)$ as a reasonable model. If, on the other hand, $\chi^2 \geq c$, where $\Pr[\chi^2(k - 1) \geq c; H_0] = \alpha$, then we reject H_0 at the α significance level.

We observe that there are some subjective decisions in the construction of this goodness of fit statistic. We had to select the number k and also the endpoints $c_0, c_1, \ldots, c_k$ of the classes. The *Kolmogorov–Smirnov* statistic avoids these considerations. Let $F_n(x)$ be the empirical distribution function. Define the K–S statistic by

$$D_n = \max_x [|F_n(x) - F_0(x)|].$$

Since $F_n(x)$ has jumps at the observed sample points $x_1, x_2, \ldots, x_n$, this maximum (actually, a supremum) must occur at or "just before" one of the sample observations, if $F_0(x)$ is of the continuous type. That is,

$$D_n = |F_n(x_i) - F_0(x_i)| \quad \text{or} \quad |F_n(x_i-) - F_0(x_i-)|,$$

for some x_i. Thus, to find the maximum, we must test $2n$ values, although many of these can be ruled out immediately, particularly if $F_n(x)$ and $F_0(x)$ are graphed. Under H_0, D_n has a distribution that is not well known, but it has been tabled in a number of books on statistics; for example, see *Probability and Statistical Inference* (Hogg and Tanis, 1983). Moreover, if we desire a critical value c such that $\Pr(D_n > c; H_0) = \alpha$, then approximate values of c can be found easily by the following table:

α	0.20	0.10	0.05	0.01
c	$1.07/\sqrt{n}$	$1.22/\sqrt{n}$	$1.36/\sqrt{n}$	$1.63/\sqrt{n}$

These approximations are good provided $n \geq 15$.

There is another advantage of the K–S statistic; it can be used to find a confidence band for an unknown d.f. $F(x)$. That is,

$$\Pr[\max_x |F_n(x) - F(x)| \leq c] = 1 - \alpha$$

is equivalent to

$$\Pr[F_n(x) - c \leq F(x) \leq F_n(x) + c, \text{ for all } x] = 1 - \alpha.$$

Moreover, since $F_n(x) - c$ is negative for some x-values and $F_n(x) + c$ is greater than one for other x-values, then $F_L(x)$ and $F_U(x)$ serve as lower and upper bands for $F(x)$, where

$$F_L(x) = \begin{cases} 0 & , & F_n(x) - c \leq 0, \\ F_n(x) - c, & F_n(x) - c > 0, \end{cases}$$

and

$$F_U(x) = \begin{cases} F_n(x) + c, & F_n(x) + c < 1, \\ 1 & , & F_n(x) + c \geq 1. \end{cases}$$

Example 2. Let us again consider the wind loss data first considered in Example 1, Section 3.1. Suppose we believe that a truncated Pareto distribution starting at $x = 1.5$ with parameters $\alpha = 5$ and $\beta = 28.5$ is a reasonably good model. Let us first compute the χ^2 statistics using the four classes (1.5, 2.5), (2.5, 6.5), (6.5, 29.5), and (29.5, 49.5) associated with the ogive and histogram of that example.

Since $\beta + 1.5 = 30$, we have

$$p_1 = 1 - \left(\frac{30}{30 + 1}\right)^5 = 0.151,$$

$$p_2 = \left(\frac{30}{31}\right)^5 - \left(\frac{30}{35}\right)^5 = 0.386,$$

$$p_3 = \left(\frac{30}{35}\right)^5 - \left(\frac{30}{58}\right)^5 = 0.426,$$

$$p_4 = \left(\frac{30}{58}\right)^5 = 0.037,$$

where the probability $\Pr(X > 49.5) = (30/78)^5 = 0.008$ has been included in the fourth cell. The expected (using this model) and observed frequencies are:

Frequencies \ Classes	1	2	3	4
Expected	6.04	15.44	17.04	1.48
Observed	12	15	11	2

Thus the observed chi-square is

$$\chi^2 = \frac{(12-6.04)^2}{6.04} + \frac{(15-15.44)^2}{15} + \frac{(11-17.04)^2}{17.04} + \frac{(2-1.48)^2}{1.48}$$

$$= 5.88 + 0.01 + 2.14 + 0.18$$

$$= 8.21 > 7.81,$$

where 7.81 is the 95th percentile of a chi-square distribution with 3 degrees of freedom. Thus the hypothesis of having this particular Pareto distribution would be rejected at $\alpha = 0.05$ significance level. Incidentally, some statisticians warn about having expected values as low as 1.48; however, this is not of great concern here, particularly when that term contributes so little to χ^2.

To compute the K–S statistic, we observe that the Pareto d.f.

$$F(x) = 1 - \frac{30^5}{[30 + (x-1.5)]^5}, \qquad 0 < x < \infty,$$

has the following values: $F(2) = 0.079$, $F(3) = 0.216$, $F(4) = 0.330$, $F(5) = 0.424$, $F(6) = 0.503$, $F(8) = 0.625$, $F(9) = 0.672$, $F(15) = 0.844$, $F(17) = 0.875$, etc. We compare these to the corresponding values of the observed empirical distribution function $F_{40}(x)$, namely $F_{40}(2) = 12/40 = 0.30$, $F_{40}(3) = 0.40$, $F_{40}(4) = 0.475$, $F_{40}(5) = 0.575$, $F_{40}(6) = 0.675$, etc. That is, the difference $F_{40}(x) - F(x)$ just before $x = 2$ is -0.079 and at $x = 2$ it is 0.221; before and at $x = 3$, they are 0.084 and 0.184, respectively, etc. Without considering all the observed values, it is clear that the $D_n = 0.221$. Comparing this to $1.36/\sqrt{40} = 0.215$, we see that $D_n > 0.215$ and again we reject at the $\alpha = 0.05$ significance level. With both the chi-square and K–S statistics it is clear that the fit is poorer at the lower end, due to the large χ^2 term and value of $F_n(x) - F(x)$ at those points.

Now suppose that the null hypothesis does not completely specify the distribution function but only states that it is a member of some family with certain unknown parameters. For illustration,

$$F_0(x; \alpha, \lambda, \tau) = 1 - [\lambda/(\lambda + x^\tau)]^\alpha, \qquad 0 \le x < \infty$$

is the d.f. of the Burr distribution with unknown parameters α, λ, and τ. The probability of the class $(c_{i-1}, c_i]$ is

$$p_i = \left[\frac{\lambda}{\lambda + c_{i-1}^\tau}\right]^\alpha - \left[\frac{\lambda}{\lambda + c_i^\tau}\right]^\alpha,$$

which depends upon α, λ, and τ, $i = 1, 2, \ldots, k$. Thus

$$\chi^2 = \sum_{i=1}^{k} \frac{(f_i - np_i)^2}{np_i}$$

depends upon α, λ, and τ, and hence it cannot be computed once the frequencies $f_1, f_2, \ldots, f_k$ have been observed. There is a way out of our trouble, however. Let us choose α, λ, and τ to minimize χ^2; that is, find α, λ, and τ to

$$\min_{\alpha, \lambda, \tau} \sum_{i=1}^{k} \frac{(f_i - np_i)^2}{np_i},$$

recalling that p_i is a function of α, λ, and τ. An elegant theory states that if these *minimum chi-square estimators* of α, λ, and τ are substituted in χ^2 to produce that minimum χ^2, then this min χ^2 has an approximate chi-square distribution with $k - 1 - 3 = k - 4$ degrees of freedom. For example, see Cramér (1946). That is, the number of degrees of freedom in the approximating chi-square distribution is reduced one for each parameter estimated by the method of minimum chi-square. This is true not only in this illustration but in general.

There is another problem created, however, because it is usually extremely difficult to estimate by using minimum chi-square. Hence other estimates (maximum likelihood, moments, etc.) are used and accordingly the χ^2 value used is somewhat larger than min χ^2. This makes it a little easier to reject H_0 (and the model) and thus the real significance level is somewhat greater than the quoted α. This means, however, if the model is accepted, then it has passed a tougher test as the probability of the Type II error is less than it would be using min χ^2. An excellent reference is an article on chi-square tests by Moore (1978).

Suppose we wish to use a modified K–S test. As yet, there is no similar theory for the distribution of min D_n. The best recommendation that we can make at present is the following. We must recognize that by estimating parameters, like α, λ, and τ, the D_n that we create is probably much less than that D_n computed from that with specified parameters. Hence, if we used the tabled c-values, it is much harder to reject H_0 and thus the real significance level is smaller than the quoted α. So if H_0 is rejected by this procedure, we can feel very certain that the suggested distribution is not the correct model. However, if H_0 is accepted, we should not feel too comfortable by the resulting fit unless D_n is extremely small. That is, D_n used in this way should be treated only as a guide. For illustration, if the D_n that we get fitting the three-parameter transformed Pareto (Burr) distribution is less than that we get fitting a three-parameter generalized Pareto distribution, then between these two, the transformed Pareto distribution is favored. Incidentally, it should be clear that we can obtain better fits using more parameters, but computational inconveniences and the principle of parsimony frequently dictate fewer parameters.

As we deal with applications in later chapters, other methods (sometimes ad hoc but very useful) of testing fits of models are mentioned. But certainly we have considered in this section two of the major ones: the chi-square and K–S goodness of fit tests. Let us now introduce some new notation and two of these ad hoc tests used by some actuaries.

In Exercise 8, Section 2.7, we defined mean residual life at age x. Here we denote it by $e(x)$; that is,

$$e(x) = \int_x^\infty (w - x) \frac{f(w)}{\Pr(X \ge x)} \, dw,$$

where $f(x)$ is the p.d.f. of the continuous-type random variable X. If the d.f. of X is $F(x) = \Pr(X \le x)$, then, by integrating by parts with $u = x - w$ and $v = 1 - F(w)$, we have

$$e(x) = \frac{\{(x - w)[1 - F(w)]\}_x^\infty + \int_x^\infty [1 - F(w)] \, dw}{1 - F(x)}$$

$$= \frac{\int_x^\infty [1 - F(w)] \, dw}{1 - F(x)},$$

provided

$$\lim_{b \to \infty} (x - b)[1 - F(b)] = 0.$$

When the d.f. is that of the Pareto distribution and thus $1 - F(x) = \lambda^\alpha (\lambda + x)^{-\alpha}$, then, in that exercise, we found that $e(x)$ is a linear function of x,

$$e(x) = \frac{\lambda + x}{\alpha - 1},$$

provided $\alpha > 1$. We now give the mean residual lives for the following distributions; see a paper by Hall and Wellner (1981) for more details.

Exponential (gamma). If $1 - F(x) = e^{-\theta x}$, then it is easy to show that $e(x) = 1/\theta$. Incidentally, when x is large, then the right tail of a gamma distribution is similar to that of an exponential distribution and hence, for large x, $e(x) \approx$ constant for the gamma distribution.

Weibull. We have $1 - F(x) = \exp(-cx^\tau)$, $\tau > 0$. It can be shown that $e(x) \approx 1/cx^{\tau-1} = c_1 x^{-\tau+1}$, for large x.

Lognormal. Here

$$1 - F(x) = \int_x^\infty \frac{1}{\sqrt{2\pi}\sigma w} \exp\left[-\frac{(\ln w - \mu)^2}{2\sigma^2} \right] dw,$$

and after some messy approximations, we obtain

$$e(x) \approx cx/\ln x$$

for large x.

See Figure 3.7 for graphs of some of these functions.

Some knowledge of these functions can be extremely valuable for the

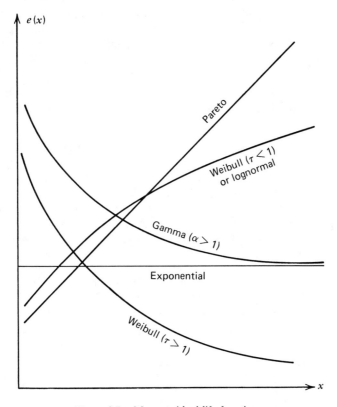

Figure 3.7.   Mean residual life functions.

purpose of modeling. That is, it is relatively easy to compute the empirical mean residual life, say $e_n(x)$, because this is simply the difference of the average of all items greater than or equal to x and x itself. If this seems like a linear function with positive slope, then a Pareto distribution might be an appropriate model. If it is more like a constant for the larger x values, then we might try a gamma fit. Something between these two might suggest a lognormal distribution or Weibull with $0 < \tau < 1$. On the other hand, a decreasing function like $c_1 x^{-\tau+1}$, $\tau > 1$ indicates that a Weibull model should be tried. Then, too, the mean residual life function might seemingly change with various values of x and this would suggest that different densities be used on different parts of the support. Clearly, the use of $e_n(x)$ for this purpose is just another aid in our search for an appropriate model, and it should be used along with other techniques.

Interestingly, there is another ad hoc test that actuaries sometimes use that is closely related to the functions $e(x)$ and $e_n(x)$. This test might be preferred in situations in which the data are censored because then it is impossible to compute $e_n(x)$. We define the expected value of a distribution that has d.f. equal to $F(w)$, when $w \leq x$, and equal to one when $w > x$. That is, we want the mean of the distribution that is the same as that of $F(w)$ when $w \leq x$ but has the probability $1 - F(x)$ at $w = x$. Clearly this is what we must consider if there is censoring at $w = x$. Assuming X is originally a nonnegative random variable of the continuous type the expected value of this distribution is given by

$$E[X; x] = \int_0^x wf(w)\, dw + x[1 - F(x)]$$

and is called the *limited expected value function*. The empirical counterpart, $E_n[X; x]$, is easy to compute for it is simply the average of n values, treating each observation greater than x as though it is equal to x.

What is the relationship between $e(x)$ and $E[X; x]$? Consider

$$\mu = \int_0^\infty wf(w)\, dw = \int_0^x wf(w)\, dw + \int_x^\infty wf(w)\, dw,$$

which leads to

$$\mu = \int_0^x wf(w)\, dw + x\int_x^\infty f(w)\, dw + \int_x^\infty (w - x)f(w)\, dw$$

$$= E[X; x] + e(x)[1 - F(x)].$$

Moreover, dividing each member of this equation by μ, we have

$$1 = \frac{E[X;x]}{\mu} + \frac{e(x)[1-F(x)]}{\mu}$$

$$= \frac{E[X;x]}{\mu} + R(x)[1-F(x)],$$

where $R(x)$ is excess ratio for retention defined in Exercise 8, Section 2.7.

Thus we see that there is a close relationship among $e(x)$, $E[X;x]$, and $R(x)$; and each of them can be used to model or to test underlying distributions. However, due to censoring in which $e_n(x)$ cannot be used, actuaries frequently use the *limited expected value comparison test* of $E[X;x]$ associated with the model d.f. $F_0(x)$ through the vector statistic

$$\frac{E[X;x_i] - E_n[X;x_i]}{E[X;x_i]}, \qquad i = 1, 2, \ldots, n-r,$$

where, for convenience, we assume that the sample items have been ordered $x_1 \le x_2 \le \cdots \le x_{n-r}$, and, due to censoring, the last r have not been observed. If this vector statistic is not close to the vector $(0, 0, \ldots, 0)$, then $E[X;x]$ and thus $F_0(x)$ are not appropriate models. In actuarial circles, there does not seem to be any sampling distribution theory for this vector and subjective testing is used, paying particular attention to the values of the statistic for the larger values of x. It would be worthwhile to have at least some approximating distribution theory for the vector statistic or some function of it (particularly some function of the last few elements of the vector). Applications of the mean residual life and limited expected value functions are discussed later.

Exercises

1. Define 8 cells by $(-\infty, 1]$, $(i-1, i]$, $i = 2, 3, \ldots, 7$, and $(7, \infty)$. We wish to test H_0: $F(x)$ is $N(4, 4)$. If, with a sample of size $n = 200$, the respective frequencies are 10, 25, 35, 40, 43, 25, 12, 10, is H_0 accepted at $\alpha = 0.05$ using the chi-square statistic?

2. Twenty observations of a random variable X yields the following data: 20.1, 16.1, 12.8, 30.6, 22.4, 26.1, 9.8, 18.2, 15.6, 19.1, 17.2, 29.3, 24.1, 33.1, 26.2, 17.3, 19.8, 13.1, 26.2, 18.1. Use the K–S statistic to test, at $\alpha = 0.05$, H_0: $F(x)$ is $N(20, 25)$.

3. We wish to test the fit of the following ogive-type d.f.

$$F(x) = \begin{cases} \dfrac{x}{6}, & 0 < x \le 1, \\[2mm] \dfrac{x}{3} - \dfrac{1}{6}, & 1 < x \le 2, \\[2mm] \dfrac{x}{6} + \dfrac{1}{6}, & 2 < x \le 3, \\[2mm] \dfrac{x}{12} + \dfrac{5}{12}, & 3 < x \le 7. \end{cases}$$

The $n = 16$ observed values are: 0.5, 3.8, 1.8, 1.2, 0.9, 2.1, 1.9, 5.8, 1.6, 1.4, 0.8, 4.2, 2.8, 3.6, 1.8, 1.5. Use the K–S statistic to test, at $\alpha = 0.10$, this fit.

3.7. APPLICATIONS AND ASSOCIATED ALGORITHMS

While most of the remaining part of the book deals with applications, a section making some general remarks about this topic seems appropriate here. Clearly the main purpose of this monograph is to present ways of finding good estimates of probabilities upon which certain important decisions are to be based. Many of these probabilities are associated with the tails of distributions. Without a great deal of data, it is extremely difficult to estimate probabilities in the tails of distributions; and in many instances we simply do not have data in sufficient quantity. Thus we must assume a model and estimate these probabilities by first estimating the parameters of the model. Such estimates should be treated only as guides and not as absolute truth. We recommend, if at all possible, the consideration of more than one model, and then agreement among estimates from the different models should be checked. In this text, we have developed and discussed many models; hence we hope that there might be some justification for selecting one over another, particularly in case the real situation seems to favor the assumptions of that one.

After the selection of a model (or models) we recommend, in most instances, the use of maximum likelihood (or minimum distance or chi-square) estimation because it produces estimators that are usually better than other schemes. However, as with the use of different models, we encourage the computation of more than one estimator for each parameter, checking the agreement or disagreement among them.

For an illustration, suppose we have assumed a Pareto model. In particular, let us say that this model is actually a truncated Pareto p.d.f., beginning at some given point δ (see Exercise 6, Section 2.7). An assumption like this is rather natural in reinsurance work. The p.d.f., with unknown parameters α and λ, is

$$f(x; \alpha, \lambda) = \frac{\alpha(\lambda + \delta)^\alpha}{[(\lambda + \delta) + (x - \delta)]^{\alpha+1}}, \qquad \delta < x < \infty.$$

The likelihood of a random sample $X_1, X_2, \ldots, X_n$ equals

$$L(\alpha, \lambda) = \alpha^n (\lambda + \delta)^{n\alpha} \prod_{i=1}^{n} [(\lambda + \delta) + (x_i - \delta)]^{-\alpha-1}.$$

Thus

$$\ln L(\alpha, \lambda) = n \ln \alpha + n\alpha \ln (\lambda + \delta) - (\alpha + 1) \sum_{i=1}^{n} \ln [(\lambda + \delta) + (x_i - \delta)].$$

If we let $\theta = \lambda + \delta$, the two resulting equations needed to find the maximizing values of α and θ (and hence $\lambda = \theta - \delta$) are

$$\frac{\partial \ln L}{\partial \alpha} = \frac{n}{\alpha} + n \ln \theta - \sum_{i=1}^{n} \ln [\theta + (x_i - \delta)] = 0,$$

$$\frac{\partial \ln L}{\partial \theta} = \frac{n\alpha}{\theta} - \sum_{i=1}^{n} \frac{\alpha + 1}{\theta + (x_i - \delta)} = 0.$$

Clearly these are two nonlinear equations in the unknowns α and θ, and the solution needs to be found by numerical methods. We consider one important algorithm for finding such a solution, Newton's method.

The general problem is this: Determine the solution (or solutions) of k equations in k unknowns. To make the exposition of *Newton's method* easier let us begin with one equation in one unknown, say $g(y) = 0$. Perhaps the easiest way to see the answer is to think of approximating $g(y)$ by a linear function in the neighborhood of a preliminary "guess" y_0 of the solution. That is, using the constant and linear terms of a Taylor's series, we have

$$g(y) \approx g(y_0) + g'(y_0)(y - y_0).$$

Equating the right-hand member to zero and solving for y, we have the one-step approximation

$$y_1 = y_0 - \frac{g(y_0)}{g'(y_0)}.$$

This can be depicted as in Figure 3.8. That is, y_1 is the point at which the tangent line to $g(y)$ at the point $[y_0, g(y_0)]$ crosses the x-axis. The difference $y_0 - y_1$ clearly equals $g(y_0)$ divided by the slope $g'(y_0)$ of that tangent line. Of course, the two-step approximation y_2 can be found using y_1 as the preliminary guess. This iteration can be repeated any number of times until the desired convergence is obtained. It is fairly clear, however, that it is most important, with certain types of functions $g(y)$, that the preliminary guess be reasonably close to the solution or else the procedure might not converge to the correct number.

Let us next consider two equations in two unknowns:

$$g_1(y, z) = 0 \quad \text{and} \quad g_2(y, z) = 0 .$$

Say the preliminary guess is (y_0, z_0). The linear approximations, equated to zero, are

$$g_1(y_0, z_0) + g_{11}(y_0, z_0)(y - y_0) + g_{12}(y_0, z_0)(z - z_0) = 0 ,$$

$$g_2(y_0, z_0) + g_{21}(y_0, z_0)(y - y_0) + g_{22}(y_0, z_0)(z - z_0) = 0 ,$$

where

$$g_{11} = \frac{\partial g_1}{\partial y}, \qquad g_{12} = \frac{\partial g_1}{\partial z}, \qquad g_{21} = \frac{\partial g_2}{\partial y}, \qquad g_{22} = \frac{\partial g_2}{\partial z} .$$

Thus we have two linear equations in the two unknowns (y, z) that can be solved for the one-step approximation (y_1, z_1). In turn, this approximation can be used to find a two-step approximation (y_2, z_2), and so on.

Possibly the display involving two linear functions in two unknowns is enough for us to establish the general algorithm for k equations in k unknowns in matrix notation. Say

$$\mathbf{g}(\mathbf{y}) = \mathbf{0} ,$$

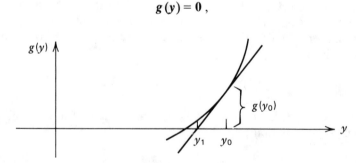

Figure 3.8.   Newton's method.

where $g(y)$ represents a column vector of the k functions $g_1, g_2, \ldots, g_k$ in the k unknowns $y' = (y_1, y_2, \ldots, y_k)$ and $\mathbf{0}$ is the column vector of zeros. Let y_0 represent the preliminary guess and G_0 the $k \times k$ matrix of the first derivatives evaluated at y_0, namely

$$G_0 = \left[\frac{\partial g_i}{\partial y_j}\right]_{y=y_0}.$$

Thus the k linear equations in k unknowns can be written in matrix notation as

$$(G_0)(y - y_0) = -g(y_0).$$

The one-step approximation is

$$y_1 = y_0 - (G_0^{-1})g(y_0).$$

Continuing, the two-step approximation equals

$$y_2 = y_1 - (G_1^{-1})g(y_1),$$

or, in general,

$$y_i = y_{i-1} - (G_{i-1}^{-1})g(y_{i-1}), \qquad i = 1, 2, 3, \ldots.$$

Of course, this can be continued until a certain convergence criterion has been met. However, again we caution the user about the importance of a good preliminary guess, particularly with certain kinds of functions $g(y)$ (for example, if some $|G_j|$ is near zero).

To return to our truncated Pareto illustration, we let our two equations be denoted by

$$g_1(\alpha, \theta) = \frac{\partial \ln L(\alpha, \theta)}{\partial \alpha} = 0,$$

$$g_2(\alpha, \theta) = \frac{\partial \ln L(\alpha, \theta)}{\partial \theta} = 0.$$

We might then use a preliminary guess $(\tilde{\alpha}, \tilde{\theta})$, estimates based on the method of moments. That is, with $Z_i = X_i - \delta$, $\tilde{\alpha}$ and $\tilde{\theta}$ are found equating the first and second moments of the sample and distribution, respectively, to obtain

$$\tilde{\alpha} = \frac{2S_Z^2}{S_Z^2 - \bar{Z}^2}, \qquad \tilde{\theta} = \frac{\bar{Z}(S_Z^2 + \bar{Z}^2)}{S_Z^2 - \bar{Z}^2}, \qquad \text{and} \quad \tilde{\lambda} = \tilde{\theta} - \delta.$$

If the decision maker has some prior notions, some reasonable adjustments might even be made to these estimators before using them as a preliminary guess.

Example 1. In Example 3, Section 3.4, we fitted the wind loss data of Example 1, Section 3.1, to a truncated Pareto ($\delta = 1.5$) distribution by the method of moments to obtain $\tilde{\alpha} = 4.809$, $\tilde{\theta} = 29.421$, and $\tilde{\lambda} = 27.921$. We use the maximum likelihood procedure to obtain

$$\hat{\alpha} = 5.084, \qquad \hat{\theta} = 30.498, \quad \text{and} \quad \hat{\lambda} = 28.998.$$

Thus the maximum likelihood estimate of

$$h(\alpha, \lambda) = \Pr(X > 29.5) = \left(\frac{\lambda + 1.5}{\lambda + 29.5}\right)^\alpha$$

is

$$h(\hat{\alpha}, \hat{\lambda}) = \left(\frac{30.498}{58.498}\right)^{5.084} = 0.036,$$

which is similar to the estimate 0.040 found in Section 3.4 using the method of moment estimators.

What about the accuracy of the estimate 0.036? To determine this, we need to consider

$$\ln f(x; \alpha, \lambda) = \ln \alpha + \alpha \ln(\lambda + 1.5) - (\alpha + 1)\ln(\lambda + x)$$

and

$$\frac{\partial \ln f}{\partial \alpha} = \frac{1}{\alpha} + \ln(\lambda + 1.5) - \ln(\lambda + x), \qquad \frac{\partial \ln f}{\partial \lambda} = \frac{\alpha}{\lambda + 1.5} - \frac{\alpha + 1}{\lambda + x},$$

$$\frac{\partial^2 \ln f}{\partial \alpha^2} = -\frac{1}{\alpha^2}, \qquad \frac{\partial^2 \ln f}{\partial \alpha \partial \lambda} = \frac{1}{\lambda + 1.5} - \frac{1}{\lambda + x},$$

$$\frac{\partial^2 \ln f}{\partial \lambda^2} = \frac{\alpha + 1}{(\lambda + x)^2} - \frac{\alpha}{(\lambda + 1.5)^2}.$$

Since $E[1/(\lambda + X)] = \alpha/(\alpha + 1)(\lambda + 1.5)$ and $E[1/(\lambda + X)^2] = \alpha/(\alpha + 2) \times (\lambda + 1.5)^2$, we have that the matrix

$$
-n \begin{pmatrix} E\left(\dfrac{\partial^2 \ln f}{\partial \alpha^2}\right) & E\left(\dfrac{\partial^2 \ln f}{\partial \alpha \partial \lambda}\right) \\[2ex] E\left(\dfrac{\partial^2 \ln f}{\partial \alpha \partial \lambda}\right) & E\left(\dfrac{\partial^2 \ln f}{\partial \lambda^2}\right) \end{pmatrix} = \begin{pmatrix} \dfrac{n}{\alpha^2} & \dfrac{-n}{(\alpha + 1)(\lambda + 1.5)} \\[2ex] \dfrac{-n}{(\alpha + 1)(\lambda + 1.5)} & \dfrac{n\alpha}{(\alpha + 2)(\lambda + 1.5)^2} \end{pmatrix}.
$$

The inverse of the matrix is the approximate variance-covariance matrix of $\hat{\alpha}$ and $\hat{\lambda}$:

$$
\frac{1}{n} \begin{bmatrix} \alpha^2(\alpha + 1)^2 & \alpha(\alpha + 1)(\alpha + 2)(\lambda + 1.5) \\[2ex] \alpha(\alpha + 1)(\alpha + 2)(\lambda + 1.5) & \dfrac{(\alpha + 1)^2(\alpha + 2)(\lambda + 1.5)^2}{\alpha} \end{bmatrix}.
$$

Replacing α and λ by their maximum likelihood estimates, this matrix is, with $n = 40$, approximately equal to

$$
\begin{pmatrix} 23.918 & 167.065 \\ 167.065 & 1199.317 \end{pmatrix}.
$$

The approximate variance of $h(\hat{\alpha}, \hat{\lambda})$ is determined by considering the function

$$
h(\alpha, \lambda) = \Pr(X > 29.5) = \left(\frac{\lambda + 1.5}{\lambda + 29.5}\right)^{\alpha}
$$

and its partial derivatives

$$
\frac{\partial h}{\partial \alpha} = \left(\frac{\lambda + 1.5}{\lambda + 29.5}\right)^{\alpha} \ln\left(\frac{\lambda + 1.5}{\lambda + 29.5}\right)
$$

and

$$
\frac{\partial h}{\partial \lambda} = \alpha \left(\frac{\lambda + 1.5}{\lambda + 29.5}\right)^{\alpha} \left(\frac{1}{\lambda + 1.5} - \frac{1}{\lambda + 29.5}\right).
$$

The values of these three respective functions at $\hat{\alpha}$ and $\hat{\lambda}$ are

$$
h = 0.036, \qquad h_1 = -0.024, \qquad h_2 = 0.0029.
$$

Hence the approximate variance of $h(\hat{\alpha}, \hat{\lambda})$ is found by computing

$$\left(\frac{\partial h}{\partial \alpha}\right)^2 \mathrm{var}\,(\hat{\alpha}) + \left(\frac{\partial h}{\partial \lambda}\right)^2 \mathrm{var}\,(\hat{\lambda}) + 2\left(\frac{\partial h}{\partial \alpha}\right)\left(\frac{\partial h}{\partial \lambda}\right)\mathrm{cov}\,(\hat{\alpha}, \hat{\lambda}),$$

which equals approximately

$$(-0.024)^2(23.918) + (0.0029)^2(1199.317)$$
$$+ 2(-0.024)(0.0029)(167.065) = 0.000597 \,;$$

thus the corresponding standard deviation is 0.024. Using the fact that $h(\hat{\alpha}, \hat{\lambda})$ has an approximate normal distribution we find that $0.036 \pm 2(0.024)$ or, equivalently, zero to 0.084 serves as an approximate 95% confidence interval for $h(\alpha, \lambda) = \mathrm{Pr}\,(X > 29.5)$.

Clearly, in this day, most, if not all, of the heavy calculations are made on some computer, and each computer system has its own special characteristics. For illustration, to maximize the likelihood function associated with a gamma distribution, namely

$$L(\alpha, \lambda) = \frac{\lambda^{n\alpha}(x_1 x_2 \ldots x_n)^{\alpha-1} e^{-\lambda \Sigma x_i}}{[\Gamma(\alpha)]^n},$$

we definitely need to have the gamma function and/or some of its derivatives available. Some computer systems have these functions; when using those that do not, other schemes (or approximations) must be used. However, we are convinced that if a particular group wants an important problem solved, adequate computer backup will be found.

Remarks. Sometimes, with the sample percentiles (Section 3.1), we can make (preliminary) estimates of parameters, particularly if the distribution function can be written in closed form. For illustration, the d.f. of the Burr distribution is

$$F(x) = 1 - \left(\frac{\lambda}{\lambda + x^\tau}\right)^\alpha, \qquad 0 \le x < \infty.$$

Let $\hat{\pi}_p$, the sample $(100p)$th percentile, be an estimate of the $(100p)$th percentile π_p of the population. With three unknown parameters, we select three p-values, say $p_1 < p_2 < p_3$, and form the three equations

$$p_i = 1 - \left(\frac{\lambda}{\lambda + \hat{\pi}_{p_i}^\tau}\right)^\alpha, \qquad i = 1, 2, 3.$$

We then solve these (frequently by numerical methods) for estimates of α,

λ, and τ. These estimates, of course, depend on the choice of $p_1 < p_2 < p_3$ and these p-values could be varied to see how much the estimates of α, λ, and τ change. Incidentally, these estimators could be looked upon as weighted minimum distance estimators found in the case the weights of one were placed upon the selected percentiles, with zero weights upon the others.

Let $L(\theta)$ be the likelihood function, where θ represents one or more parameters. The maximization of $L(\theta)$ provides extremely good estimates that are best asymptotic normal (BAN) ones, but also extremely satisfactory in small samples. Accordingly, it seems as if the maximization of $L(\theta)g(\theta)$ will provide even better estimates if the weight function $g(\theta)$ associated with θ is, in fact, reasonably accurate; that is, gives relatively high weight to the true but unknown value of θ. If $g(\theta)$ is treated as the prior p.d.f. of θ, then maximizing $L(\theta)g(\theta)$ corresponds to a Bayesian modal estimate since $L(\theta)g(\theta)$ is proportional to the posterior p.d.f. of θ.

While this Bayesian approach is extremely appealing, there are some difficulties associated with it. Possibly it is not used more because, in many instances, it is difficult to assign the weight function (prior p.d.f.) $g(\theta)$, particularly when θ represents two or more parameters. There are some steps being taken to help the user in the selection of a reasonable prior distribution, at least in many fairly standard situations.

The second main objection to these Bayesian procedures might be in the difficulty created in the determination of the maximum. But certainly, with today's computers, this is not as much an obstacle as it once was. Then, too, many times we can honestly select a conjugate prior that reduces these computational difficulties. Let us illustrate this last remark by a very simple example.

Let $X_1, X_2, \ldots, X_{16}$ be a random sample of size $n = 16$ from $N(\mu = \theta$, $\sigma^2 = 25)$. Thus $L(\theta) = (50\pi)^{-8} \exp[-\Sigma(x_i - \theta)^2/50]$. Suppose we believe that θ is in a neighborhood of 70 and, with very high probability, say it is between 67 and 73. Let us construct the positive weight function $g(\theta) = c(\theta - 67)^3(73 - \theta)^3$ on the interval, $67 < \theta < 73$, and let $g(\theta)$ equal zero elsewhere; this $g(\theta)$ is actually like a translated beta p.d.f. Certainly the function $L(\theta)g(\theta)$ can be maximized, but it will require numerical means. However, suppose that we had selected our prior as the normal conjugate p.d.f. $N(70, 1)$ for θ, which accomplishes much the same thing as the previous $g(\theta)$, namely most of the weight is between 67 and 73 with the mean of 70. Then maximization is easy because the posterior distribution for θ is

$$N\left(\frac{\bar{x} + 70(25)/16}{1 + 25/16}, \frac{(25/16)}{1 + 25/16}\right).$$

That is, the value of θ that maximizes $L(\theta)N(70, 1)$ is

$$\frac{\bar{x} + 70(25)/16}{1 + 25/16}$$

(see HC, 6.6).

Not all p.d.f.s have nice conjugate priors, however; for examples, the following do not:

1. *Beta.*

2. *Gamma.* However, if α is known, a conjugate prior for $\theta = \lambda$ is a gamma one. The same remark applies to the *loggamma* distribution.

3. *Weibull.* However, if τ is known, $\theta = c$ has a gamma conjugate prior.

4. *Generalized Pareto* (like the *F*-distribution).

5. *Burr.*

The general problem is this. Let $L(\theta_1, \theta_2, \ldots, \theta_p) = L(\boldsymbol{\theta})$, where $\boldsymbol{\theta} = (\theta_1, \theta_2, \ldots, \theta_p)'$, be the likelihood function that depends upon p parameters. We wish to determine the solution of the p equations in p parameters, namely,

$$S_j(\boldsymbol{\theta}) = \frac{\partial \ln L(\boldsymbol{\theta})}{\partial \theta_j} = 0, \qquad j = 1, 2, \ldots, p,$$

which maximizes $L(\boldsymbol{\theta})$. That is, if $\hat{\boldsymbol{\theta}} = (\hat{\theta}_1, \hat{\theta}_2, \ldots, \hat{\theta}_p)'$ is the vector of those maximum likelihood estimates, then $S_j(\hat{\boldsymbol{\theta}}) = 0, j = 1, 2, \ldots, p$.

To help us find $\hat{\boldsymbol{\theta}}$, let us use $\boldsymbol{\theta}_0 = (\theta_{10}, \theta_{20}, \ldots, \theta_{p0})'$ as a preliminary estimate. Then take the *scores* $S_j(\hat{\boldsymbol{\theta}}), j = 1, 2, \ldots, p$, evaluated at $\hat{\boldsymbol{\theta}}$, and expand them in a Taylor's series about $\boldsymbol{\theta}_0$, retaining only the first power of $\hat{\theta}_j - \theta_{j0}, j = 1, 2, \ldots, p$. Thus we have

$$0 = S_j(\hat{\boldsymbol{\theta}}) \approx S_j(\boldsymbol{\theta}_0) + \sum_{i=1}^{p} (\hat{\theta}_i - \theta_{0i}) \frac{\partial S_j(\boldsymbol{\theta}_0)}{\partial \theta_i},$$

$j = 1, 2, \ldots, p$. Solving these p linear equations for $\hat{\boldsymbol{\theta}} = (\hat{\theta}_1, \hat{\theta}_2, \ldots, \hat{\theta}_p)'$ is essentially *Newton's method*; this clearly does not give $\hat{\boldsymbol{\theta}}$, but only a one-step approximation to the real maximum likelihood estimate $\hat{\boldsymbol{\theta}}$. Call this solution $\boldsymbol{\theta}_1 = (\theta_{11}, \theta_{21}, \ldots, \theta_{p1})'$. This approximation $\boldsymbol{\theta}_1$ can then be used as a preliminary estimate resulting in a two-step approximation, say $\boldsymbol{\theta}_2$. This can be continued until the approximation is sufficiently close to $\hat{\boldsymbol{\theta}}$.

Let us write those p equations in matrix notation, using $\mathbf{0}$ for the column vector of zeros, $S(\boldsymbol{\theta}_0) = [S_1(\boldsymbol{\theta}_0), \ S_2(\boldsymbol{\theta}_0), \ldots, \ S_p(\boldsymbol{\theta}_0)]'$, and the $p \times p$ matrix

$$\mathbf{B}(\boldsymbol{\theta}_0) = \left[\frac{\partial S_j(\boldsymbol{\theta}_0)}{\partial \theta_i} \right].$$

We have

$$\boldsymbol{\theta}_1 = \boldsymbol{\theta}_0 - [\mathbf{B}(\boldsymbol{\theta}_0)]^{-1} S(\boldsymbol{\theta}_0),$$

or, equivalently

$$\boldsymbol{\theta}_1 = \boldsymbol{\theta}_0 - [\mathbf{B}(\boldsymbol{\theta}_0)]^{-1} S(\boldsymbol{\theta}_0),$$

provided that inverse matrix exists. Then using $\boldsymbol{\theta}_1$ in place of $\boldsymbol{\theta}_0$, we obtain $\boldsymbol{\theta}_2$ and so on. That is,

$$\boldsymbol{\theta}_m = \boldsymbol{\theta}_{m-1} - [\mathbf{B}(\boldsymbol{\theta}_{m-1})]^{-1} S(\boldsymbol{\theta}_{m-1}), \qquad m = 1, 2, \ldots,$$

and we continue this until sufficient convergence is obtained.

One final approximation can be made that sometimes improves the convergence immensely. Instead of using

$$\mathbf{B}(\boldsymbol{\theta}_0) = \left[\frac{\partial S_j(\boldsymbol{\theta}_0)}{\partial \theta_i} \right],$$

which depends upon the likelihood $L(\boldsymbol{\theta}_0)$ and thus upon the sample observations, let us replace $\mathbf{B}(\boldsymbol{\theta}_0)$ by its expectation, which is the negative of the information matrix $\mathbf{A}(\boldsymbol{\theta}_0) = [a_{ij}(\boldsymbol{\theta}_0)]$, where

$$a_{ij}(\boldsymbol{\theta}_0) = - E \left[\frac{\partial^2 \ln L(\boldsymbol{\theta}_0)}{\partial \theta_i \partial \theta_j} \right]$$

$$= - nE \left[\frac{\partial^2 \ln f(X; \boldsymbol{\theta}_0)}{\partial \theta_i \partial \theta_j} \right]$$

$$= nE \left[\frac{\partial \ln f(X; \boldsymbol{\theta}_0)}{\partial \theta_i} \frac{\partial \ln f(X; \boldsymbol{\theta}_0)}{\partial \theta_j} \right].$$

With this substitution, we have the equations

$$\boldsymbol{\theta}_m = \boldsymbol{\theta}_{m-1} + [\mathbf{A}(\boldsymbol{\theta}_{m-1})]^{-1} S(\boldsymbol{\theta}_{m-1}), \qquad m = 1, 2, \ldots.$$

The latter scheme is particularly successful with grouped data. Recall, from Section 3.3, that the likelihood function is proportional to

$$L(\boldsymbol{\theta}) = \prod_{r=1}^{k} [P_r(\boldsymbol{\theta})]^{f_r},$$

where $P_r(\boldsymbol{\theta}) = F(c_r; \boldsymbol{\theta}) - F(c_{r-1}; \boldsymbol{\theta})$. Here, in this special case, it can be shown that the information matrix $\mathbf{A}(\boldsymbol{\theta})$ has ijth element

$$a_{ij}(\boldsymbol{\theta}) = n \sum_{r=1}^{k} \frac{1}{P_r(\boldsymbol{\theta})} \left[\frac{\partial P_r(\boldsymbol{\theta})}{\partial \theta_i} \right] \left[\frac{\partial P_r(\boldsymbol{\theta})}{\partial \theta_j} \right],$$

where $n = f_1 + f_2 + \cdots + f_k$. While we have two exercises that illustrate these ideas in the one-parameter case, the reader might want to refer to Chapter 5 of Rao (1965) for a general discussion. In any case, these techniques are illustrated in Chapter 4.

Exercises

1. Show that the estimators, determined by the method of moments, of the gamma distribution are $\tilde{\alpha} = \bar{X}^2/S^2$ and $\tilde{\lambda} = \bar{X}/S^2$.

2. If $x_1 = 3.2$, $x_2 = 1.8$, $x_3 = 8.2$, $x_4 = 2.7$ are four sample values from the Pareto distribution having p.d.f. $f(x; \theta) = 2\theta^2(\theta + x)^{-3}, 0 < x < \infty$, find the maximum likelihood estimate $\hat{\theta}$ of θ. Hint: $\tilde{\theta} = \bar{x}$ is the method of moment estimate.

3. Using the data and the model (p.d.f.) given in Exercise 2, find the maximum likelihood estimate of $h(\theta) = \Pr(X > 8)$. What is the approximate standard deviation of $h(\hat{\theta})$?

4. In addition to the data and the model (p.d.f.) given in Exercise 2, assume that the prior p.d.f. of θ is proportional to $\theta^2 (4 + \theta)^{-5}$, $0 < \theta < \infty$. Find the Bayesian modal estimate of θ.

5. If $f(x; \theta)$ is a p.d.f. of X that depends upon one parameter θ, show, with appropriate assumptions, that

$$E\left\{ \left[\frac{\partial \ln f(X; \theta)}{\partial \theta} \right]^2 \right\} = -E\left[\frac{\partial^2 \ln f(X; \theta)}{\partial \theta^2} \right].$$

Hint: From

$$\int_{-\infty}^{\infty} f(x; \theta) \, dx = 1$$

show that

$$\int_{-\infty}^{\infty} \frac{\partial \ln f(x;\theta)}{\partial \theta} f(x;\theta)\, dx = 0.$$

By differentiating this latter expression, the result can be obtained.

6. With an appropriate constant c, we have, in the grouped data case with our parameter θ, that

$$L(\theta) = c \prod_{m=1}^{k} [P_m(\theta)]^{f_m}$$

and

$$\sum_{(f_1,\ldots,f_k)} L(\theta) = 1.$$

Thus

$$\sum_{(f_1,\ldots,f_k)} \frac{\partial L(\theta)}{\partial \theta} = \sum_{(f_1,\ldots,f_k)} \frac{\partial \ln L(\theta)}{\partial \theta} L(\theta) = 0.$$

Display the preceding equation using

$$\frac{\partial \ln L(\theta)}{\partial \theta} = \sum_{m=1}^{k} \frac{f_m}{P_m(\theta)} \frac{\partial P_m(\theta)}{\partial \theta}.$$

Differentiate a second time with respect to θ to obtain

$$-E\left[\frac{\partial^2 \ln L(\theta)}{\partial \theta^2}\right] = \sum_{m=1}^{k} \sum_{n=1}^{k} \frac{E(f_m f_n)}{P_m(\theta)P_n(\theta)} \left[\frac{\partial P_m(\theta)}{\partial \theta}\right]\left[\frac{\partial P_n(\theta)}{\partial \theta}\right].$$

Substituting $E(f_m f_n) = -nP_m P_n + n^2 P_m P_n$, $m \neq n$, and $E(f_m^2) = nP_m(1 - P_m) + n^2 P_m^2$ and using the fact that

$$\left[\sum_{m=1}^{k} \frac{\partial P_m(\theta)}{\partial \theta}\right]^2 = 0,$$

we obtain

$$-E\left[\frac{\partial^2 \ln L(\theta)}{\partial \theta^2}\right] = n \sum_{m=1}^{k} \frac{1}{P_m(\theta)} \left[\frac{\partial P_m(\theta)}{\partial \theta}\right]^2,$$

which is the 1×1 information matrix in the $p = 1$ case.

CHAPTER 4

Modeling
Loss Distributions

4.1. INTRODUCTION

In this chapter, the techniques introduced in Chapters 2 and 3 for fitting probability models are illustrated. Particular attention is given to the problems created by coverage modifications (truncation and censoring) and data collection procedures (grouping, clustering, and trending). Each section contains an illustration based on actual data. Throughout this chapter we also discuss computational procedures for estimating parameters.

We must emphasize at the beginning that these examples are presented only for illustrative purposes. No attempt is made to claim that the model selected will always be appropriate for the coverage being considered or that the parameters determined are appropriate for an individual insurer's use in ratemaking calculations. We do believe that these examples will provide a guide for the practitioner in solving modeling problems.

The algorithms presented in this chapter were selected to be as general as possible. That is, instead of presenting the best algorithm for finding the maximum likelihood estimator for a lognormal model and then perhaps recommending some other algorithm as being best for a Pareto model, we present one (or two) algorithms which are reasonable for all models. One advantage of this approach is that the reader is not restricted to the distributions presented in this text.

With the examples presented in Sections 4.2 to 4.6 we perform model fitting under a variety of circumstances. Each one illustrates different steps in the fitting procedure. In Section 4.7 we summarize this activity by providing a 'flowchart' that describes the complete process. We advise the reader to take a brief look at that section at this time and then use it as a review after completing the chapter.

Before discussing modeling techniques, we define and then expand on a topic mentioned in Chapter 1. The definition is that of loss. From here on, the *loss* is the value of the actual damage caused by the insured event. It always is represented by the random variable X and its support always is the nonnegative real numbers. The amount paid by the insurer is a function of X determined by the policy. We call this amount the *payment* or the *amount paid*. In most situations we have data on the payments but desire to model the loss.

For the insurer, an important quantity is the severity, the expected payment given that one has been made. When a coverage modification is in effect, another quantity of interest is the expected loss that is eliminated (for the insurer) by the modification. If, for example, the modification is a deductible of d, the expected loss eliminated is

$$E[X; d] = \int_0^d x f_X(x) \, dx + d[1 - F_X(d)] \, ,$$

where $f_X(x)$ and $F_X(x)$ are the p.d.f. and d.f., respectively, of the loss random variable, X. We call this the *limited expected value function* and note that it always exists. (A similar quantity, denoted $E[g(x; k)]$, is given in Miccolis, 1977. Many of the quantities derived in Chapter 5 are also given in that paper.) Another view of $E[X; d]$ is that it is the expected value of $Y = \min(X, d)$, that is, the mean of a random variable censored at d. The *loss elimination ratio* (LER), as introduced in Chapter 1, is the ratio of the expected loss eliminated (from the insurer's viewpoint, as with a deductible or reinsurance) to the expected loss. The LER is then $E[X; d]/E[X]$ provided the expected value in the denominator exists. Formulas for computing $E[X; d]$ for various distributions are given in the appendix.

We can also define an empirical limited expected value function for a sample. It is

$$E_n(d) = \frac{1}{n} \sum_{i=1}^{n} \min(x_i, d) \, .$$

This was essentially the quantity computed in the numerators of the empirical LERs in the examples in Section 1.3.

Before accepting any model as providing a reasonable description of the loss process, we should verify that $E[X; d]$ and $E_n(d)$ are essentially in agreement for all values of d. Since

$$\lim_{d \to \infty} E[X; d] = E[X] \qquad \text{(if it exists)}$$

and

$$\lim_{d \to \infty} E_n(d) = \bar{X},$$

comparing $E[X; d]$ and $E_n(d)$ is like a method of moments approach, only much more restrictive. We ask that not only the means agree, but also the limited expected value functions essentially agree for all values of d.

Discussion of the uses of the limited expected value function is postponed until Chapter 5. For now we will be satisfied to find distributional models.

4.2. UNGROUPED DATA, TRUNCATION FROM BELOW

We begin with the situation that presents the fewest difficulties. Data are ungrouped, that is, the individual values are available. We detail methods of obtaining preliminary parameter estimates and then follow with two formal estimation procedures. The discussion closes with some guidelines for selecting the most appropriate distributional model.

One coverage modification discussed in this section is that of *truncation from below*. This occurs when all losses below a specified amount are not recorded. The most common source of truncation from below is the deductible. There are two methods of recording truncated data. If the losses are merely truncated, the amount recorded is

$$Y = X, \qquad X > d$$

$$Y \text{ not defined}, \qquad \text{otherwise}.$$

If the amount recorded is the actual payment, the variable is

$$W = X - d, \qquad X > d$$

$$W \text{ not defined}, \qquad \text{otherwise}.$$

We refer to Y as X *truncated* at d and to W as X *truncated and shifted* at d. While under insurance with a deductible of d the actual payment always is given by W, the data may be recorded only with truncation. As will be seen later in this chapter, estimation of the distribution of X can proceed from either case.

Table 4.1. Hurricane Values (000 omitted)

Number	Loss	Year	Factor	Trended Loss(x)	$e_{35}(x)$
1.	2,000	1977	1.365	2,730	—
2.	1,380	1971	2.233	3,082	—
3.	2,000	1971	2.233	4,466	—
4.	2,000	1964	3.383	6,766	203,962
5.	2,580	1968	2.761	7,123	209,775
6.	4,730	1971	2.233	10,562	212,784
7.	3,700	1956	3.912	14,474	215,610
8.	4,250	1961	3.612	15,351	221,890
9.	5,400	1966	3.145	16,983	227,853
10.	4,500	1955	4.085	18,383	234,541
11.	5,000	1958	3.806	19,030	242,557
12.	14,720	1974	1.719	25,304	245,371
13.	7,900	1959	3.685	29,112	251,225
14.	13,500	1971	2.233	30,146	260,616
15.	22,697	1976	1.486	33,727	268,210
16.	12,000	1964	3.383	40,596	273,220
17.	8,300	1949	4.989	41,409	285,379
18.	13,000	1959	3.685	47,905	292,827
19.	10,450	1950	4.727	49,397	306,669
20.	12,500	1954	4.208	52,600	320,325
21.	32,300	1973	1.855	59,917	331,420
22.	57,911	1980	1.090	63,123	348,727
23.	23,000	1964	3.383	77,809	356,311
24.	25,200	1955	4.085	102,942	354,833
25.	34,800	1967	2.966	103,217	381,832
26.	32,200	1957	3.841	123,680	391,483
27.	122,070	1979	1.148	140,136	409,121
28.	119,189	1975	1.611	192,013	392,968
29.	97,853	1972	2.028	198,446	429,483
30.	67,200	1964	3.383	227,338	450,665
31.	91,000	1960	3.621	329,511	398,277
32.	100,000	1961	3.612	361,200	427,686
33.	165,300	1969	2.551	421,680	440,647
34.	122,050	1954	4.208	513,586	435,926
35.	129,700	1954	4.208	545,778	538,312
36.	309,950	1970	2.421	750,389	500,552
37.	752,510	1979	1.148	863,881	774,119
38.	500,000	1965	3.276	1,638,000	—

The methods developed in this section are illustrated by a catastrophe process. The event is a single hurricane with the loss being the total damage done by that storm. This is not an insurance example as these losses are not covered under a single insurance contract. The data were compiled by the American Insurance Association from 1949 through 1980 and include only those hurricanes for which total losses exceeded $1,000,000. There were 38 such losses in this 32-year period. The amounts are presented in Table 4.1 along with the year of occurrence.

The first difficulty presented by these data is the long time period covered by the observations. As our goal is to model the process producing losses in the present (and possibly in the future), we need a method of determining the losses in current dollars caused by hurricanes like those observed in the past. To do this, a set of trend factors must be applied. The ones selected are based on the Residential Construction Index prepared by the Department of Commerce. Construction cost appears to be a viable surrogate for the losses due to a certain amount of hurricane damage. The entries in the "factor" column of Table 4.1 are the 1981 value of the index divided by the value for the year of the loss. The trended loss is then the factor times the actual loss. It should be noted that this adjustment does not allow for the increase in losses over time due to increased exposure. Finally, with the maximum factor being 4.989, it was necessary to eliminate all trended losses below $5,000,000. This assures that each hurricane loss was equivalent to at least $1,000,000 in 1949 dollars. This leaves 35 entries for our consideration.

A. Preliminary Estimates

The first step in our determination of a model is to produce some easily obtained descriptions of the sample. Figure 4.1 contains a sample ogive and histogram for the hurricane data. These were constructed by the procedures given in Section 3.1. The intervals were arbitrarily selected to cover ranges where the empirical d.f. is nearly straight.

We must note that due to the truncation at 5,000,000 the figures do not represent the distribution of total hurricane losses. In general, if Y is X truncated at d, we have, for the d.f. of Y,

$$
\begin{aligned}
F_Y(x) &= 0, & x \le d, \\
&= \Pr\left[X \le x \mid X > d\right] \\
&= \frac{F_X(x) - F_X(d)}{1 - F_X(d)}, & x > d.
\end{aligned}
\tag{4.1}
$$

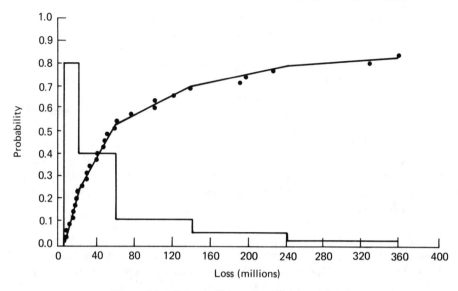

Figure 4.1. Ogive and histogram—hurricane data.

Here, and for the remainder of the text, the subscript on F (or f) indicates the variable for which that function is the distribution function (or p.d.f.). If X is continuous, the p.d.f. of Y is obtained by differentiation:

$$f_Y(x) = 0, \qquad\qquad x \leq d,$$

$$= \frac{f_X(x)}{1 - F_X(d)}, \qquad x > d.$$

If the data are truncated and shifted, we have

$$F_W(x) = 0, \qquad\qquad\qquad\qquad x \leq 0,$$

$$= \Pr[X - d \leq x | X > d]$$

$$= \frac{F_X(d+x) - F_X(d)}{1 - F_X(d)}, \qquad x > 0, \qquad (4.2)$$

and

$$f_W(x) = 0, \qquad\qquad\qquad x \leq 0,$$

$$= \frac{f_X(d+x)}{1 - F_X(d)}, \qquad x > 0.$$

The ogive and histogram provide some indication as to the type of distribution that will model the data. For the hurricane data, it is apparent from Figure 4.1 that the distribution is extremely heavy tailed. It is not clear if it features a strictly decreasing p.d.f. (like the Pareto) or has a nonzero mode as such a mode could be below 5,000,000. A better view might be obtained by taking natural logarithms of the observed values. The transformed ogive and histogram appear in Figure 4.2. The histogram reveals that the transformed distribution is somewhat symmetric, suggesting a lognormal distribution might be appropriate. A final preliminary step is to compute the mean residual life function, $e_{35}(x)$, as outlined in Section 3.6. Values are given in Table 4.1 and plotted in Figure 4.3. The shape of the hand-fitted curve in Figure 4.3 suggests that the Weibull and lognormal distributions may provide good models for these observations (see Figure 3.7).

We are now prepared to fit a model to the data. Throughout Chapter 4, eight families of distributions are considered (actually six since two are special cases of a three-parameter distribution). They are Weibull, Pareto, lognormal, gamma, loggamma, Burr, generalized Pareto, and transformed gamma. These distributions were developed in Chapter 2. The appendix contains relevant functions associated with these families. These include the p.d.f., the d.f., and the moments.

The estimation of parameters is done by five different methods. The first two are crude methods which have the advantage of being easy to do.

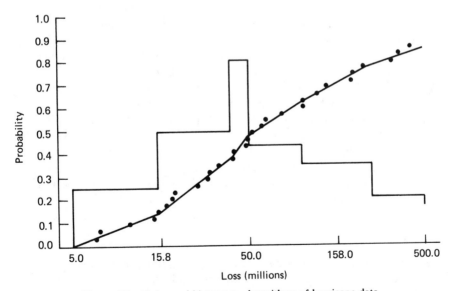

Figure 4.2. Ogive and histogram—logarithms of hurricane data.

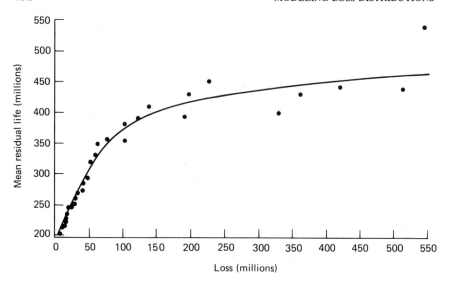

Figure 4.3. Empirical mean residual life—hurricane data.

The penalty is a significant lack of accuracy. These methods are *percentile matching* (pm) and *method of moments* (mm). The other three methods, *minimum distance* (md), *minimum chi-square* (mc), and *maximum likelihood* (ml), are more formal procedures with well-defined statistical properties. They produce reliable estimators but are computationally complex. For each of the eight distributions listed above, iterative procedures are needed to obtain the estimates. The pm and mm estimators provide good starting values for these procedures. Finally, we recommend first working with the five two-parameter distributions. Estimation for the three-parameter models can then begin from the two-parameter estimates, which are special cases of the three-parameter model. We defer discussion of the latter three methods to the second part of this section.

For most distributions, the pm and mm procedures are easy to implement. Recall that with no coverage modifications pm estimation is accomplished by solving the p equations

$$F_X(x_i; \boldsymbol{\theta}) = F_n(x_i), \qquad i = 1, \ldots, p,$$

where $\boldsymbol{\theta}$ is the p-dimensional vector of parameters of the distribution of X. The values $x_1, \ldots, x_p$ are arbitrarily selected from the data. The equations for mm estimation are

$$E[X^i] = \frac{1}{n} \sum_{j=1}^{n} x_j^i, \qquad 1, \ldots, p,$$

where, of course, the expected value on the left-hand side is a function of θ. The appendix gives formulas for solving these equations for a number of different distributions.

When coverage modifications are in effect, the equations take on a more complex form. If truncation is present, the percentiles for pm estimation are from the truncated distribution. The equations are of the form

$$F_Y(x_i) = \frac{F_X(x_i) - F_X(d)}{1 - F_X(d)} = F_n(x_i),$$

since $F_n(x_i)$ is the empirical distribution of a sample from the truncated distribution. This formulation allows us to estimate the distribution of X, the model for untruncated losses. From here on, when fitting models, we drop references to θ when writing the d.f. of X. We must keep in mind that in equations such as the above, the variable is θ.

Consider the hurricane example with a lognormal distribution and comparison points 29,112,000 and 198,446,000. The two equations are

$$\frac{\Phi\left[\frac{\ln (29,112,000) - \hat{\mu}}{\hat{\sigma}}\right] - \Phi\left[\frac{\ln (5,000,000) - \hat{\mu}}{\hat{\sigma}}\right]}{1 - \Phi\left[\frac{\ln (5,000,000) - \hat{\mu}}{\hat{\sigma}}\right]} = \frac{10}{35}$$

and

$$\frac{\Phi\left[\frac{\ln (198,446,000) - \hat{\mu}}{\hat{\sigma}}\right] - \Phi\left[\frac{\ln (5,000,000) - \hat{\mu}}{\hat{\sigma}}\right]}{1 - \Phi\left[\frac{\ln (5,000,000) - \hat{\mu}}{\hat{\sigma}}\right]} = \frac{26}{35}.$$

While the two-dimensional iterative procedure developed in Section 3.7 would yield a solution to these equations, the amount of effort required is not justified by the lack of accuracy of the estimators. One method of reducing the computational effort is to ignore the truncation. The two equations become

$$\Phi[(17.187 - \hat{\mu})/\hat{\sigma}] = 0.28571$$

and

$$\Phi[(19.106 - \hat{\mu})/\hat{\sigma}] = 0.74286.$$

The two-dimensional iteration is now much easier. The formula is given in the appendix and the solutions to this problem are $\hat{\mu} = 18.079$ and $\hat{\sigma} = 1.5753$.

A second approach requires an alternative estimate of one of the parameters. From Table 4.1 we see that the sample median is 59,917,000. Since the median of a lognormal random variable is $\exp(\mu)$ we may approximate μ by $\ln(59,917,000) = 17.908$. The problem reduces to one equation,

$$\Phi((19.106 - 17.908)/\hat{\sigma}) = 0.74286,$$

where we again are ignoring the truncation. From the normal distribution tables we quickly obtain $\hat{\sigma} = 1.8369$.

The same problems occur in mm estimation. The observed kth moment, $(1/n)\sum_{i=1}^{n} y_i^k$, is based on observations from the truncated variable, Y. The population kth moment is

$$E[Y^k] = \int_0^\infty y^k f_Y(y)\, dy$$

$$= \frac{\int_d^\infty x^k f_X(x)\, dx}{1 - F_X(d)}.$$

For the first moment we have

$$E[Y] = \frac{\int_0^\infty x f_X(x)\, dx - \int_0^d x f_X(x)\, dx}{1 - F_X(d)}$$

$$= \frac{E[X] + d[1 - F_X(d)] - E[X; d]}{1 - F_X(d)}$$

$$= d + \frac{E[X] - E[X; d]}{1 - F_X(d)}.$$

The formulas in the appendix for $E[X; d]$ may be used to evaluate this expected value. Similar calculations will provide expressions for the higher moments.

For the lognormal distribution the equation for the first moment is

$$\bar{Y} = E[Y] = \frac{\exp\left(\hat{\mu} + \frac{\hat{\sigma}^2}{2}\right)\left\{1 - \Phi\left[\frac{\ln(d) - \hat{\mu} - \hat{\sigma}^2}{\hat{\sigma}}\right]\right\}}{1 - \Phi\left[\frac{\ln(d) - \hat{\mu}}{\hat{\sigma}}\right]}.$$

Instead of trying to solve two equations, we again substitute the estimate of μ based on the sample median. For the hurricane example with $\bar{Y} = 204,900,000$, $\hat{\mu} = 17.908$, and $d = 5,000,000$, the first moment equation becomes

$$204,900,000 = \frac{\exp\left(17.908 + \frac{\hat{\sigma}^2}{2}\right)\left[1 - \Phi\left(\frac{-2.485 - \hat{\sigma}^2}{\hat{\sigma}}\right)\right]}{1 - \Phi\left(\frac{-2.485}{\hat{\sigma}}\right)}$$

Newton's method provides the solution, $\hat{\sigma} = 1.533$.

B. Formal Estimation

At this stage we have obtained, by either the pm or mm method, preliminary estimates of the parameters. We are now prepared to perform a more formal estimation. Of the three methods discussed in Chapter 3, two of them, minimum distance (md) and maximum likelihood (ml), will be discussed here. The third method, minimum chi-square (mc), is suitable only for grouped data and is presented in Section 4.3.

As introduced in Section 3.3, md estimation is performed by minimizing

$$K = \sum_{i=1}^{n} w(x_i)[F_Y(x_i) - F_n(x_i)]^2 \tag{4.3}$$

where $w(x_i)$ is an arbitrary weight function and $F_Y(x_i)$ is evaluated from Eq. 4.1. If the observations are both truncated and shifted, then $F_W(x_i)$ is used in Eq. 4.3 and is evaluated from Eq. 4.2. A natural choice for the weight function (for truncated data) is

$$w(x) = n/\{F_Y(x)[1 - F_Y(x)]\} \tag{4.4}$$

as this will give each term of the summand an asymptotic $\chi^2(1)$ distribution. If $F_Y(x)$ is the d.f. of Y, then $nF_n(x)$ has a binomial distribution with parameters n and $F_Y(x)$. Therefore, by the Central Limit Theorem, $\sqrt{n}[F_n(x) - F_Y(x)]/\sqrt{F_Y(x)[1 - F_Y(x)]}$ has an asymptotic standard normal distribution and therefore its square has a chi-square distribution with one degree of freedom. However, as the denominator of $w(x)$ must be evaluated using estimated parameters and the terms of the sum in Eq. 4.3 are not independent, the sum will not have a chi-square distribution. Essentially, by using these weights Eq. 4.4 will allow each term to make an equal contribution to the total. A second advantage of using Eq. 4.4 is that the weights will be largest at the ends of the distribution, precisely those places where we want the fit to be best.

For ungrouped observations, as in the hurricane data, we recommend a modification of Eq. 4.3. The empirical d.f. is a step function which takes its jumps at the data points. As Eq. 4.3 measures the distance between these points and the fitted distribution, a good fit will leave most of the empirical d.f. lying below and to the right of the fitted d.f. An appropriate correction is

$$K = \sum_{i=1}^{n} w(x_i)\left[F_Y(x_i) - \frac{n}{n+1}F_n(x_i)\right]^2, \tag{4.5}$$

since the order statistics divide the total probability of one into $n + 1$ equal parts on the average. No correction is needed for grouped data as the d.f.s are evaluated at class boundaries and not at data points.

Obtaining the minimum of Eq. 4.3 or 4.5 is not a trivial task. While it is possible to take derivatives of Eq. 4.5, set them equal to zero, and then use numerical methods to solve the resulting equations, we have elected to use a different approach. Packaged programs which perform numerical minimization without requiring derivatives are widely available. For example, the IMSL subroutine library contains the procedure ZXSSQ which minimizes arbitrary sums of squares. [This routine is available from International Mathematical and Statistical Libraries, Inc., 7500 Bellaire Boulevard, Houston, TX 77036. It uses the Marquardt algorithm (Marquardt, 1963) with a derivative-free algorithm developed by Brown and Dennis (1972).] In particular, if $g(x; \theta_1, \ldots, \theta_p)$ is a function of x and of p parameters, the procedure minimizes $\sum_{i=1}^{n} g(x_i; \theta_1, \ldots, \theta_p)^2$ with respect to the parameters. For our case we write

$$g(x; \theta_1, \ldots, \theta_p) = \sqrt{w(x)}\left[F_Y(x) - \frac{n}{n+1}F_n(x)\right].$$

A second method formulates the problem as a weighted nonlinear least-squares regression. The general problem is to minimize $\sum_{i=1}^{n} w(x_i) \times [y_i - g(x_i; \theta_1, \ldots, \theta_p)]^2$. We then set $y_i = nF_n(x_i)/(n+1)$ and $g(x_i; \theta_1, \ldots, \theta_p) = F_Y(x_i)$. The usual formulation does not allow $w(x_i)$ to be a function of the parameters, in which case $w(x)$ must be based on $F_n(x)$ [or $nF_n(x)/(n+1)$ for ungrouped data] instead of $F_Y(x)$. The SAS procedure

NLIN is an example of this type of program. [This routine is available from The SAS Institute, Box 8000, Cary, NC 27511. It also uses the Marquardt algorithm with a derivative-free algorithm based on Ralston and Jennrich (1978).]

Now consider fitting a lognormal distribution to the hurricane data. We have elected to use weights as in Eq. 4.4 and starting values $\hat{\mu} = 18.079$ and $\hat{\sigma} = 1.5753$. Using the IMSL routine ZXSSQ, the successive iterates are

$\hat{\mu}$	$\hat{\sigma}$
18.079	1.5753
18.084	1.5753
18.079	1.5757
17.626	1.5957
17.174	1.5925
.	.
.	.
.	.
11.588	1.4937
.	.
.	.
.	.
12.973	4.4931
.	.
.	.
.	.
−2.8881	21.714
.	.
.	.
.	.
8.6487	6.1612

Something is not right. Often, by observing the successive iterates it is clear that the starting values are out of line. Here it is more likely that the numbers are too large. From Table 5.1 we see that multiplying all the values of a lognormal variable by a constant leaves σ unchanged and increases μ by the logarithm of that constant. If we multiply the 35 hurricane observations by 0.001, the value of μ is increased by $\ln{(0.001)} = -6.908$. A reasonable starting value is then $18.079 - 6.908 = 11.171$. The iterates are

$\hat{\mu}$	$\hat{\sigma}$
11.171	1.5753
11.174	1.5753
11.171	1.5757
10.993	1.7892
10.937	1.8369
10.920	1.8486
10.922	1.8486
10.920	1.8491
10.919	1.8488
10.921	1.8488
10.916	1.8488
10.919	1.8493
10.919	1.8483
10.919	1.8487

Adding back the 6.908 produces the md estimates $\hat{\mu} = 17.827$ and $\hat{\sigma} = 1.8487$. The value of K is 3.2279. Table 4.2 contains the results of md estimation (as well as those of ml estimation) with $w(x)$ as in Eq. 4.4 for five distributions.

Table 4.2. Parameter Estimates for Hurricane Losses

Distribution Method	Parameter Values			K	$-\ln L$
Lognormal					
md	$\hat{\mu} = 17.827$,	$\hat{\sigma} = 1.8487$		3.2279	454.50
ml	$\hat{\mu} = 17.953$,	$\hat{\sigma} = 1.6028$		7.1355	454.18
Weibull					
md	$\hat{c} = 0.00029732$,	$\hat{\tau} = 0.44835$		4.4032	454.34
ml	$\hat{c} = 0.000074947$,	$\hat{\tau} = 0.51907$		7.0914	454.11
Pareto					
md	$\hat{\alpha} = 0.80251$	$\hat{\lambda} = 39{,}666{,}000$		3.6743	455.19
ml	$\hat{\alpha} = 1.1569$	$\hat{\lambda} = 73{,}674{,}000$		9.1428	454.71
Burr					
md	$\hat{\alpha} = 1.2669$	$\hat{\lambda} = 1{,}965{,}700$	$\hat{\tau} = 0.79901$	3.4871	454.91
ml	$\hat{\alpha} = 3.7697$	$\hat{\lambda} = 610{,}969$	$\hat{\tau} = 0.65994$	7.0133	454.27
Generalized Pareto					
md	$\hat{\alpha} = 0.86482$	$\hat{\lambda} = 60{,}992{,}000$	$\hat{k} = 0.76695$	3.6037	455.10
ml	$\hat{\alpha} = 2.8330$	$\hat{\lambda} = 862{,}660{,}000$	$\hat{k} = 0.33292$	7.9123	454.34

A second estimation method is maximum likelihood. It generally is easier to work with the negative of the natural logarithm of the likelihood function, that is (for truncated data), minimize

$$- \ln L = - \sum_{i=1}^{n} \ln [f_Y(x_i)] = - \sum_{i=1}^{n} \ln [f_X(x_i)] + n \ln [1 - F_X(d)] .$$

In general, this function is more difficult to minimize than Eq. 4.5, because the likelihood surface tends to be flatter than that for the distance function. Once again, we may apply a derivative-free approach to minimization. We reformulate the problem as a sum of squares minimization by setting $g(x; \theta_1, \ldots, \theta_p) = \sqrt{- \ln [f_x(x_i)] + \ln[1 - F_x(d)]}$ Results of the estimation for the hurricane data appear in Table 4.2. Note that the values of $- \ln L$ do not change much from distribution to distribution. Also, changes in the parameters of a model do not greatly affect $- \ln L$. Thus small changes in $- \ln L$ are important in the model selection process.

The third method, minimum chi-square, is not practical for this problem. It requires grouping of the observations; with only 35 observations there would not be enough to fill the groups and yet provide information about the tail. This method is illustrated in the next section.

You will observe that we display results for only five of the eight distributions. It turned out that the gamma distribution and its two transforms proved to be intractable for computational purposes. The appropriate parameters (as estimated by method of moments) were near the limits of our computer's capabilities. That is, α was either too large or too close to zero to allow $\Gamma(\alpha)$ to be computed with reasonable accuracy. The three-parameter families also can be troublesome as the parameters are related. The function to be minimized contains a ridge with major changes in two of the parameters producing little change in the distribution. The numerical procedures may end up traveling along such a ridge and never locate the minimum.

C. Model Selection

The procedures outlined to this point enabled us to select a model from a particular family of distributions. The final task is to select one model from among the fitted distributions. Our decision is based on two considerations. First, the objective function used in parameter estimation provides a measure of fit. The model producing the smallest value of K or of $- \ln L$ must be judged to be superior, at least under the criterion that defines the method.

One problem with using the objective function is that the three-parameter models must always produce smaller values than their two-parameter counterparts. However, if the improvement is slight, parsimony requires that we prefer the simpler model. The likelihood ratio test (Section 3.5) provides a formal test. As the sample size approaches infinity, twice the difference of the negative loglikelihoods has a chi-square distribution with one degree of freedom when testing a three-parameter model against the more special one having two parameters.

For the hurricane model we can test the adequacy of the Pareto distribution versus its three-parameter generalizations. With respect to the Burr distribution the test statistic is $2(454.71 - 454.27) = 0.88$ and, with one degree of freedom, the p-value (Section 3.5) is only 0.35. For the generalized Pareto the values are 0.74 and 0.39. Clearly the accuracy gained by the addition of the third parameter is not significant. We reject the two three-parameter models in favor of the simpler description.

The second consideration in model selection is agreement between the empirical and fitted limited expected value functions. As mentioned earlier, this function is crucial to the determination of the effects of coverage modifications.

For the hurricane example, the Pareto model is rejected due to its relatively inferior performance on both the distance and likelihood measures. As the lognormal and Weibull models are each superior by one method, we use the limited expected value functions to make the final decision. They are presented, along with the empirical function, in Table 4.3. Once again, as we are observing the truncated variable Y, we must compare the empirical values to their counterparts for a truncated distribution. $F_Y(x)$ is computed from Eq. 4.1 while $E[Y; x]$ is

$$
\begin{aligned}
E[Y; x] &= \int_d^x y f_Y(y)\, dy + x[1 - F_Y(x)] \\
&= \frac{\int_d^x y f_X(y)\, dy + x[1 - F_X(x)]}{1 - F_X(d)} \\
&= \frac{\int_0^x y f_X(y)\, dy - \int_0^d y f_X(y)\, dy + x[1 - F_X(x)]}{1 - F_X(d)} \\
&= \frac{E[X; x] - E[X; d] + d[1 - F_X(d)]}{1 - F_X(d)} \\
&= d + \frac{E[X; x] - E[X; d]}{1 - F_X(d)}
\end{aligned}
\tag{4.6}
$$

Table 4.3. Hurricane Data (000,000 omitted)

			Lognormal (md)		Weibull (ml)	
x	$E_n(x)$	$F_n(x)$	$E[Y;x]$	$F_Y(x)$	$E[Y;x]$	$F_Y(x)$
5	5.00	0.0000	5.00	0.0000	5.00	0.0000
10	9.82	0.0571	9.77	0.0894	9.75	0.0928
25	22.39	0.2286	22.00	0.2626	22.02	0.2545
50	38.75	0.4571	38.23	0.4226	38.61	0.4044
100	61.71	0.5714	62.52	0.5858	63.85	0.5683
250	107.07	0.7714	108.04	0.7708	110.39	0.7743
500	153.14	0.8571	150.63	0.8708	149.42	0.8925
1000	186.67	0.9714	195.95	0.9351	181.56	0.9629
2500	204.90	1.0000	251.34	0.9783	202.83	0.9957
5000	204.90	1.0000	284.46	0.9918	206.64	0.9996
∞	204.90	1.0000	336.90	1.0000	207.13	1.0000

Visual inspection reveals that the Weibull distribution stays closer to the empirical limited expected value function than does the lognormal. We select the Weibull distribution as estimated by maximum likelihood to be our model for hurricane losses. In Chapter 5 we use this distribution and these values to solve various problems related to this coverage. They include the probability and frequency of large losses ("How large a loss can be expected once in 10 years? 100 years?"), confidence intervals for the losses, and the effects of inflation on the distribution of losses.

4.3. GROUPED DATA, MIXTURE OF MODELS

In most insurance situations the data are grouped. This may be forced upon the analyst due to the use of grouping by the organization supplying the data. Or the data may be so extensive that it is too costly to perform estimation using the individual values.

A second estimation problem is the *mixture of models*. This occurs naturally if losses are of more than one type, each with a unique distribution. These distributions would need to be combined by the probability with which each occurs.

The methods discussed in this section are illustrated with experience under Homeowners 02 policies. Data were supplied by the Insurance Services Office (ISO) from experience in California during accident year 1977. Losses were developed to 27 months and include only policies with

Table 4.4. Homeowners Physical Damage

i	c_i	Fire		Theft		Fire and Theft	
		$F_n(c_i)$*	$\bar{x}_i$**	$F_n(c_i)$	$\bar{x}_i$	$F_n(c_i)$	$\bar{x}_i$
1	100	0.00000	117	0.00000	115	0.00000	116
2	125	0.01075	141	0.01797	140	0.01663	140
3	150	0.03889	154	0.06012	154	0.05612	154
4	156	0.04393	167	0.06875	166	0.06407	166
5	175	0.06544	191	0.10465	192	0.09726	192
6	200	0.10101	207	0.16881	206	0.15604	206
7	211	0.11362	233	0.18825	232	0.17419	232
8	250	0.16313	278	0.25216	277	0.23538	277
9	300	0.22299	328	0.32258	327	0.30382	327
10	350	0.28086	378	0.38390	377	0.36449	377
11	400	0.33316	452	0.43462	452	0.41550	452
12	500	0.42448	555	0.52066	567	0.50254	565
13	600	0.50345	715	0.62146	713	0.59922	714
14	850	0.62012	974	0.75517	972	0.72972	972
15	1,100	0.69153	2,256	0.82848	1,997	0.80268	2,060
16	5,100	0.91001	7,135	0.98814	6,870	0.97342	6,990
17	10,100	0.94173	16,419	0.99695	14,354	0.98655	15,796
18	25,100	0.96974	35,486	0.99975	30,430	0.99410	35,107
19	50,100	0.98792	78,278	1.00000	—	0.99772	78,278
		$n = 7,534$	$\bar{x} = 3,094$	$n = 32,451$	$\bar{x} = 795$	$n = 39,985$	$\bar{x} = 1,228$

*Proportion observed less than or equal to c_i.
**Average of losses between c_i and c_{i+1}.
n = Total number of losses.
$\bar{x}$ = Average of all losses.

a \$100 deductible. The losses were tabulated in 19 classes of varying lengths. The class boundaries, $c_1, c_2, \ldots, c_{19}$, were determined by the ISO so we must use them as given. Both the number of observations and the average loss are recorded for each class. Values for losses under fire, theft, and fire and theft combined are presented in Table 4.4.

Once again we begin by graphing the ogive and histogram for the observations. It is apparent from Figure 4.4 that there is a substantial difference between fire and theft experience. Also, even with the log transformation there is still some skewness to the right in the histogram suggesting a model with a tail heavier than lognormal, possibly the loggamma.

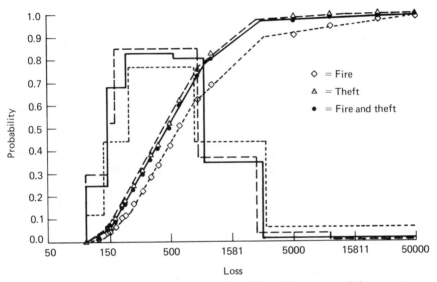

Figure 4.4. Ogive and histograms—logarithms of homeowners' data.

A. Grouped Data

Most of the analyses presented in the previous section can be used with grouped data. for example, pm estimation is unchanged except that the comparisons must be done at the class boundaries. For mm estimation, higher order moments must be approximated (unless they were supplied separately). If class means are available, we may approximate the hth moment by

$$\sum_{i=1}^{k} [F_n(c_{i+1}) - F_n(c_i)]\bar{x}_i^h$$

where $\bar{x}_i$ is the class average. If $\bar{x}_i$ is unavailable, the midpoint of the interval may be used. Since we are only trying to obtain starting values for subsequent procedures, this lack of accuracy is not a problem.

With the class means available, it is also possible to compute the empirical mean residual life function at the class boundaries. A recursive relationship is

$$e_n(c_i) = \frac{\sum\limits_{x > c_i} (x - c_i)}{n[1 - F_n(c_i)]} = \frac{\sum\limits_{x > c_i} x}{n[1 - F_n(c_i)]} - c_i$$

$$= \frac{\sum\limits_{c_i < x \le c_{i+1}} x + \sum\limits_{x > c_{i+1}} x}{n[1 - F_n(c_i)]} - c_i$$

$$= \frac{\bar{x}_i[F_n(c_{i+1}) - F_n(c_i)] + [e_n(c_{i+1}) + c_{i+1}][1 - F_n(c_{i+1})]}{1 - F_n(c_i)} - c_i .$$

The procedure begins with $e_n(c_k) = \bar{x}_k - c_k$, where c_k is the lower boundary of the last class. Figure 4.5 shows the values of this function for the three data sets along with a hand-fitted curve. It appears that the Pareto distribution will provide a good model for the individual perils as both empirical functions follow a straight line. However, the combined set does not produce a curve representative of one of our standard families.

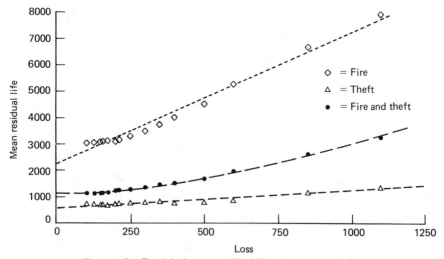

Figure 4.5. Empirical mean residual life—homeowners' data.

For md estimation there is no change except that the distance can only be measured at the interior class boundaries. For ml estimation we use the grouped data formula given in Section 3.3. For a truncated variable, the negative loglikelihood is

$$
\begin{aligned}
- \ln L &= -n \sum_{i=1}^{k} [F_n(c_{i+1}) - F_n(c_i)] \ln [F_Y(c_{i+1}) - F_Y(c_i)] \\
&= -n \sum_{i=1}^{k} [F_n(c_{i+1}) - F_n(c_i)] \ln \left[\frac{F_X(c_{i+1}) - F_X(c_i)}{1 - F_X(d)} \right] \\
&= -n \sum_{i=1}^{k} [F_n(c_{i+1}) - F_n(c_i)] \ln [F_X(c_{i+1}) - F_X(c_i)] + n \ln [1 - F_X(d)],
\end{aligned}
\tag{4.7}
$$

where, as before, d is the truncation point.

In addition to minimization by writing the loglikelihood as a sum of squares (as outlined in Section 4.2), the ml estimates may be obtained by the method presented at the end of Section 3.7. In the notation of that section we have

$$
P_i(\boldsymbol{\theta}) = \frac{F_X(c_{i+1}; \boldsymbol{\theta}) - F_X(c_i; \boldsymbol{\theta})}{1 - F_X(d; \boldsymbol{\theta})}
$$

where $\boldsymbol{\theta} = (\theta_1, \theta_2, \ldots, \theta_p)'$ is the vector of parameters. The rsth element of the information matrix $\mathbf{A}(\boldsymbol{\theta})$ is

$$
a_{rs}(\boldsymbol{\theta}) = n \sum_{i=1}^{k} \frac{\partial P_i(\boldsymbol{\theta})}{\partial \theta_r} \frac{\partial P_i(\boldsymbol{\theta})}{\partial \theta_s} \frac{1}{P_i(\boldsymbol{\theta})}.
$$

The general form of the partial derivative is

$$
\frac{\partial P_i(\boldsymbol{\theta})}{\partial \theta_r} =
$$

$$
\frac{[1 - F_X(d; \boldsymbol{\theta})] \left[\dfrac{\partial F_X(c_{i+1}; \boldsymbol{\theta})}{\partial \theta_r} - \dfrac{\partial F_X(c_i; \boldsymbol{\theta})}{\partial \theta_r} \right] + [F_X(c_{i+1}; \boldsymbol{\theta}) - F_X(c_i; \boldsymbol{\theta})] \dfrac{\partial F_X(d; \boldsymbol{\theta})}{\partial \theta_r}}{(1 - F_X(d; \boldsymbol{\theta}))^2}
$$

$$
= \frac{\dfrac{\partial F_X(c_{i+1}; \boldsymbol{\theta})}{\partial \theta_r} - \dfrac{\partial F_X(c_i; \boldsymbol{\theta})}{\partial \theta_r} + P_i(\boldsymbol{\theta}) \dfrac{\partial F_X(d; \boldsymbol{\theta})}{\partial \theta_r}}{1 - F_X(d; \boldsymbol{\theta})}.
$$

The iterative step is

$$\hat{\boldsymbol{\theta}}_{m+1} = \hat{\boldsymbol{\theta}}_m + \mathbf{A}(\hat{\boldsymbol{\theta}}_m)^{-1}\mathbf{S}(\hat{\boldsymbol{\theta}}_m)$$

where

$$S_r(\boldsymbol{\theta}) = \frac{\partial \ln L(\boldsymbol{\theta})}{\partial \theta_r} = \sum_{i=1}^{k} f_i \frac{\partial P_i(\boldsymbol{\theta})}{\partial \theta_r} \frac{1}{P_i(\boldsymbol{\theta})}, \qquad r = 1, \ldots, p,$$

with

$$f_i = n[F_n(c_{i+1}) - F_n(c_i)].$$

All that is required for successful implementation of this approach is the partial derivatives of the distribution function with respect to the parameters. For four of the eight distributions we have been considering (Weibull, Pareto, lognormal, and Burr), these derivatives are easily obtained. The other four require approximate integration plus evaluation of the gamma and digamma functions. Formulas for the derivatives are given in the appendix.

If the number of classes is small, this method can be done by hand. Consider the following reduced version of the theft losses in Table 4.4:

i	c_i	$F_n(c_i)$
1	100	0.00000
2	200	0.16881
3	350	0.38390
4	600	0.62146
5	1100	0.82848
6	∞	1.00000

Using pm with the boundaries 350 and 1100 yields $\hat{\mu}_0 = 6.1298$ and $\hat{\sigma}_0 = 0.92095$ as preliminary estimates for the lognormal distribution. For the first iteration we calculate:

i	f_i	$F_X(c_i; \boldsymbol{\theta})$	$\partial F/\partial \mu$	$\partial F/\partial \sigma$	$P_i(\boldsymbol{\theta})$	$\partial P/\partial \mu$	$\partial P/\partial \sigma$
1	5478	0.04891	−0.11004	0.18217	0.14130	−0.20365	0.10910
2	6980	0.18330	−0.28818	0.26019	0.21094	−0.15745	−0.10444
3	7709	0.38392	−0.41472	0.12243	0.24203	−0.02865	−0.20903
4	6718	0.61411	−0.41534	−0.12047	0.22540	0.12008	−0.10566
5	5566	0.82849	−0.27633	−0.26202	0.18033	0.26968	0.31003
6	—	1.00000	0.00000	0.00000	—	—	—

We then have

$$\ln L(\hat{\mu}_0, \hat{\sigma}_0) = \sum_{i=1}^{5} f_i \ln P_i(\boldsymbol{\theta}) = -52,062 ,$$

$$S_1(\hat{\mu}_0, \hat{\sigma}_0) = -2115.0 , \qquad S_2(\hat{\mu}_0, \hat{\sigma}_0) = 535.93 ,$$

$$a_{11}(\hat{\mu}_0, \hat{\sigma}_0) = 28,612 , \qquad a_{12}(\hat{\mu}_0, \hat{\sigma}_0) = a_{21}(\hat{\mu}_0, \hat{\sigma}_0) = 11,449 ,$$

$$a_{22}(\hat{\mu}_0, \hat{\sigma}_0) = 29,174 ,$$

$$\begin{bmatrix} \hat{\mu}_1 \\ \hat{\sigma}_1 \end{bmatrix} = \begin{bmatrix} 6.1298 \\ 0.92095 \end{bmatrix} + \begin{bmatrix} 0.000041461 & -0.000016271 \\ -0.000016271 & 0.000040662 \end{bmatrix} \begin{bmatrix} -2115.0 \\ 535.93 \end{bmatrix}$$

$$= \begin{bmatrix} 6.0334 \\ 0.97716 \end{bmatrix} .$$

The new computed loglikelihood using the revised estimates is $-51,949$, a definite improvement. Subsequent iterations produce the following:

$\hat{\mu}$	$\hat{\sigma}$	$\ln L$
6.0261	0.97814	$-51,949$
6.0261	0.97812	$-51,949$
6.0261	0.97812	$-51,949$

After the fourth, and final, iteration, the inverse of the information matrix is calculated to be

$$\begin{bmatrix} 0.000058221 & -0.000029453 \\ -0.000029453 & 0.000053720 \end{bmatrix} .$$

As indicated in Section 3.3, this is an estimate of the variance–covariance matrix of the maximum likelihood estimator. (It is an estimate because expectations were computed assuming the ml estimates were the true parameters.) We then have that the standard deviation of $\hat{\mu}$ is approximately 0.0076303 and of $\hat{\sigma}$ is approximately 0.0073294. The correlation between these estimates is approximately $-0.000029453/(0.0076303)(0.0073294) = -0.55025$. If desired, we could obtain confidence intervals for μ and σ and even a joint confidence region by using the bivariate normal distribution.

Two points should be noted about this procedure. First, since $F_X(c_i; \boldsymbol{\theta}) = 1$ at $c_i = \infty$, the partial derivatives are always zero (see line six in the above example). Second, if there is no deductible, $F_X(d; \boldsymbol{\theta}) = 0$ and we have

$$\frac{\partial P_i(\boldsymbol{\theta})}{\partial \theta_r} = \frac{\partial F_X(c_{i+1}; \boldsymbol{\theta})}{\partial \theta_r} - \frac{\partial F_X(c_i; \boldsymbol{\theta})}{\partial \theta_r}.$$

We have found this method easy to set up on the computer, especially for the four distributions with pleasant derivatives. The only external computation required was a routine for providing the standard normal distribution function. These are widely available. The only drawback we have observed is a need for starting values close to the solution. Some trial and error may be required if the preliminary estimates are not sufficiently close for convergence.

With grouped data we are also able to perform minimum chi-square (mc) estimation. As described in Section 3.3, the function to minimize is

$$Q = \sum_{i=1}^{k} \frac{(O_i - E_i)^2}{E_i},$$

where

$$O_i = n[F_n(c_{i+1}) - F_n(c_i)]$$

and

$$E_i = n[F_Y(c_{i+1}) - F_Y(c_i)]$$
$$= \frac{n[F_X(c_{i+1}) - F_X(c_i)]}{1 - F_X(d)}.$$

The IMSL routine ZXSSQ may be used to perform this minimization. In each case the sum of squares is created by taking the square root of the summand. For mc estimation, computation is easier if O_i replaces E_i in the denominator. This modified estimator is asymptotically equal to the true mc estimator (Moore, 1978). This modification also allows the minimization to be accomplished by non-linear weighted least squares. Finally, we note that the ml and mc estimators are asymptotically equal, provided the same class boundaries are used (Moore, 1978).

We now apply each of the three estimation methods to the theft loss data. In Table 4.5, md estimates are given for all eight distributions. We begin with md estimation because our experience has been that convergence is more likely to occur here. That is, the md procedure tolerates less accurate starting values. It is clear that only the first three distributions are reasonable candidates for the model.

Table 4.5. md Fit of Theft Loss Data

Distribution	Parameter Values			K
Loggamma	$\hat{\alpha} = 43.409$	$\hat{\lambda} = 7.0886$		696.2
Burr	$\hat{\alpha} = 1.0417$	$\hat{\lambda} = 32595$	$\hat{\tau} = 1.7136$	825.9
Generalized Pareto	$\hat{\alpha} = 1.5840$	$\hat{\lambda} = 10.968$	$\hat{k} = 50.022$	853.8
Lognormal	$\hat{\mu} = 6.0577$	$\hat{\sigma} = 1.0013$		1,433.6
Transformed gamma	$\hat{\alpha} = 19.309$	$\hat{\lambda} = 4200.6$	$\hat{\tau} = 0.20507$	2,500.3
Pareto	$\hat{\alpha} = 3.5491$	$\hat{\lambda} = 650.1$		2,660.0
Weibull	$\hat{c} = 0.01955$	$\hat{\tau} = 0.64622$		6,732.6
Gamma	$\hat{\alpha} = 0.14803$	$\hat{\lambda} = 0.00044353$		10,915.8

To continue our search for the best choice we obtain mc and ml estimates. We use the md estimates as starting values for mc estimation and then use the mc estimates as starting values for ml estimation. The results are presented in Table 4.6.

Table 4.6. Further Fit of Theft Loss Data

Distribution	Parameter Values			Value
	Minimum Chi-Square			*Q*
Loggamma	$\hat{\alpha} = 42.607$	$\hat{\lambda} = 6.9730$		1,077.4
Burr	$\hat{\alpha} = 1.1396$	$\hat{\lambda} = 19,826$	$\hat{\tau} = 1.6187$	1,177.0
Generalized Pareto	$\hat{\alpha} = 1.6680$	$\hat{\lambda} = 19.055$	$\hat{k} = 30.652$	1,136.1
	Maximum Likelihood			$-\ln L$
Loggamma	$\hat{\alpha} = 43.416$	$\hat{\lambda} = 7.0882$		83,604
Burr	$\hat{\alpha} = 1.0954$	$\hat{\lambda} = 26,670$	$\hat{\tau} = 1.6694$	83,669
Generalized Pareto	$\hat{\alpha} = 1.6592$	$\hat{\lambda} = 13.048$	$\hat{k} = 44.585$	83,644

With the loggamma "winning" all three contests it appears to be the model of choice. The other two distributions are equally good second choices. It should not surprise us that the results for mc and ml estimation are similar. Although it did not win, an advantage of selecting the Burr distribution is that its d.f. can be computed without resort to numerical approximations. The large value of alpha in the loggamma model makes approximation especially difficult.

In Table 4.7 we compare the three ml estimates by presenting the number of observations in each class and the limited expected value function. For grouped, truncated data we have

Table 4.7. Values of Truncated Distributions Fitted by Maximum Likelihood

| Class | Number of Observations | | | | Limited Expected Value[a] | | | |
| | Observed | Expected | | | Empirical | Loggamma | Burr | Generalized Pareto |
		Loggamma	Burr	Generalized Pareto				
100.01–125	583	1080	1171	783	125	125	125	125
125.01–150	1368	1247	1244	1108	149	148	148	149
150.01–175	1445	1331	1284	1323	172	171	171	172
175.01–200	2082	1356	1297	1435	194	193	192	194
200.01–250	2705	2651	2553	2920	233	233	233	234
250.01–300	2285	2450	2413	2730	269	269	269	271
300.01–350	1990	2201	2217	2423	302	302	302	303
350.01–400	1646	1952	2000	2104	331	331	332	331
400.01–500	2792	3237	3368	3371	384	382	383	380
500.01–600	3271	2516	2632	2508	428	424	424	420
600.01–850	4339	4203	4335	3968	505	502	501	494
850.01–1100	2379	2465	2448	2212	556	555	552	544
1100.01–5100	5181	5457	5081	5001	747	735	733	754
5100.01–10100	286	250	288	377	778	756	767	804
10100.01–25100	91	51	96	146	794	764	790	845
25100.01–	8	4	22	43	795	765	811	895

[a]Computed at the upper boundary of each class.

$$E_n[Y; c_i] = \frac{1}{n} \sum_{d < x < c_i} x + c_i[1 - F_n(c_i)]$$

$$= \sum_{j=1}^{i-1} \bar{x}_j[F_n(c_{j+1}) - F_n(c_j)] + c_i[1 - F_n(c_i)]$$

or

$$E_n[Y; c_{i+1}] = \sum_{j=1}^{i-1} \bar{x}_j[F_n(c_{j+1}) - F_n(c_j)] + \bar{x}_i[F_n(c_{i+1}) - F_n(c_i)]$$

$$+ c_i[1 - F_n(c_i)] - c_i[1 - F_n(c_i)] + c_{i+1}[1 - F_n(c_{i+1})]$$

$$= E_n[Y; c_i] + (\bar{x}_i - c_i)[F_n(c_{i+1}) - F_n(c_i)]$$

$$+ (c_{i+1} - c_i)[1 - F_n(c_{i+1})]$$

with $E_n[Y; c_0] = c_0 = d$.

For the fitted distributions, we again use Eq. 4.6 to compute the limited expected values of the truncated random variables. The similarity is evident. The major difference is in the tail with the generalized Pareto putting more probability on the large values and the loggamma the least. The Burr distribution provides the best fit in the tails according to the limited expected values. This confirms the Burr distribution as the best choice for modeling the theft losses.

We now turn to the fire loss data. A similar analysis produced the Burr distribution as a clear choice for the model. The ml values of the parameters are 0.29113, 4,622,100 and 2.7692.

We close this part by recalling the inference drawn from the plot of $e_n(x)$ that the Pareto distribution would provide the best fit. Our subsequent analysis failed to uphold this prediction. Aside from demonstrating the unreliability of this method it allows us to see how similar these models are. In Figure 4.6 we plot the $e(x)$ function for the Pareto, loggamma, and Burr models as fitted to the theft loss data by maximum likelihood. The similarity is evident. In Chapter 5 these models are used to illustrate the effects of inflation and of a change in the deductible on the severity of losses.

B. Mixture of Models

Suppose our goal had been to model theft and fire losses combined. Perhaps we have a policy which insures against both perils and are interested in the size of a random loss. One approach would be to combine the two samples into one and repeat the model selection procedure. Here we must assume that the relative frequency with which

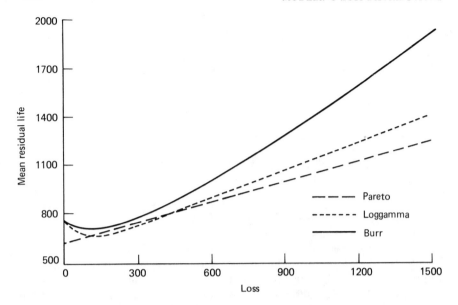

Figure 4.6. Mean residual life—theft loss models.

losses are due to fire (as opposed to theft) is accurately reflected in the sample sizes.

A second approach is the *mixture of models*. If $F_1(x)$ and $F_2(x)$ are d.f.s for two types of loss and if p is the probability that a loss is of the first type, then the d.f. for total losses is given by

$$F(x) = pF_1(x) + (1-p)F_2(x). \qquad (4.8)$$

The value of p should be easy to estimate from prior experience.

For the homeowners data, the best fit to the combined sample is provided by a generalized Pareto distribution with ml estimates $\hat{a} = 1.4390$, $\hat{\lambda} = 9.3145$, and $\hat{k} = 55.661$. For the mixture we have $F_1(x)$ as the loggamma distribution for theft, $F_2(x)$ as the Burr distribution for fire, and $p = 32,451/39,985 = 0.81158$. Table 4.8 provides a comparison of the two models where both are truncated at 100. For the mixture, the truncation is performed after the distributions have been mixed.

A comparison of the two indicates that the mixture provides a slightly better fit. In particular, the weighted sum of squares is 657.7 versus 708.7 and chi-square is 1088 versus 1126.

In this setting, the nature of the mixture was obvious. In the next section we will also fit a mixture of models but do so with no prior basis for doing so.

Table 4.8. Two Models for Combined Theft and Fire

x	Observed	$F(x)$ from Eq. 4.8	$F(x)$ from Generalized Pareto
100	0.00000	0.00000	0.00000
125	0.01663	0.03017	0.02453
150	0.05612	0.06545	0.05797
175	0.09726	0.10364	0.09698
200	0.15604	0.14310	0.13866
250	0.23538	0.22144	0.22248
300	0.30382	0.29492	0.30044
350	0.36449	0.36140	0.36975
400	0.41550	0.42051	0.43025
500	0.50254	0.51852	0.52828
600	0.59922	0.59459	0.60249
850	0.72972	0.72158	0.72342
1,100	0.80268	0.79647	0.79372
5,100	0.97342	0.97495	0.97187
10,100	0.98665	0.98857	0.98915
25,100	0.99410	0.99508	0.99702
50,100	0.99772	0.99725	0.99889

4.4. TRUNCATED AND SHIFTED DATA, MIXTURE OF MODELS

In this section only one new topic is introduced, estimation from truncated and shifted observations. As noted in Section 4.1, this occurs when the amount recorded on a claim is the loss less the deductible, that is, the actual payment. The second part of this section presents another application of the mixture of models.

The techniques discussed in this section are illustrated with data from group long-term disability insurance. Instead of measuring the loss in dollars, it is measured in time. In particular, the loss on a disability coverage is related to the duration of the disability. The loss is recorded as the number of months from the incident of disability to the earlier of recovery or death. The data cover experience from 1962 to 1976 and are from the 1978 *Reports of Mortality and Morbidity Experience* (published by the Society of Actuaries, pp. 273 and 284). They are displayed in Table 4.9. The values are from the empirical d.f. computed at the class boundaries. The relationships between the empirical d.f. $F_n(c_i)$ and the crude

Table 4.9. Duration of Disability—Empirical Distributions

Duration (months)	3-Month Elimination Age at Disablement		6-Month Elimination Age at Disablement	
	30–39	40–49	30–39	40–49
3	0.00000	0.00000	—	—
4	0.11380	0.09160	—	—
5	0.22644	0.18553	—	—
6	0.31895	0.26046	0.00000	0.00000
7	0.38856	0.31659	0.04410	0.03550
8	0.43637	0.36272	0.09715	0.07524
9	0.46805	0.39959	0.14591	0.11158
10	0.49321	0.42730	0.18605	0.14241
11	0.52017	0.45078	0.22105	0.16882
12	0.54445	0.47110	0.25563	0.19401
13	0.56481	0.48755	0.28772	0.21714
14	0.58065	0.50123	0.31265	0.23765
15	0.59646	0.51330	0.33395	0.25587
16	0.61256	0.52532	0.35440	0.27112
17	0.62496	0.53648	0.37448	0.28497
18	0.63423	0.54552	0.39068	0.29856
19	0.63993	0.55297	0.40384	0.30943
20	0.64515	0.55900	0.41416	0.31751
21	0.65182	0.56430	0.42312	0.32556
22	0.65938	0.57013	0.43529	0.33352
23	0.66680	0.57546	0.44851	0.34159
24	0.67593	0.58090	0.46102	0.35232
36	0.73987	0.64016	0.56132	0.43788
48	0.76295	0.66963	0.60800	0.47925
60	0.77987	0.68327	0.63791	0.50695
72	0.78788	0.69426	0.65906	0.53097
84			0.68442	0.55625
96			0.70888	0.58021
	$n = 1501$	$n = 2797$	$n = 1765$	$n = 3647$

termination rates q_{c_i} as given in the report are

$$q_{c_i} = \frac{F_n(c_{i+1}) - F_n(c_i)}{1 - F_n(c_i)},$$

and

$$F_n(c_i) = 1 - (1 - q_{c_1})(1 - q_{c_2}) \ldots (1 - q_{c_{i-1}}).$$

Data are presented for two age groups and two elimination periods. The elimination period is the time the insured must wait before disability payments begin. It is, in this setting, identical to a deductible.

A. Estimation from Truncated and Shifted Data

The data in Table 4.9 are presented in truncated form. We first attempted to fit models by the same methods used in the previous section. The ogive and related histogram (Figure 4.7) for ages 30–39 with a three-month elimination period indicate how rapidly the probabilities fall off in the truncated distribution. However, the extra 20% of probability beyond 72 months indicates that the tail stretches out a long way.

It is very difficult to fit from this truncated sample. As a matter of fact, we were unable to get any of our fitting routines to converge. To do so requires extrapolation for the first three months as well as for the tail. The problems in fitting any of our standard distributions are caused by the sharp decrease in probability after three months. None of the eight distributions drops off that rapidly from a point beyond zero while leaving a large probability in the tail. There are two options available at this point. The first is to fit a model to truncated and shifted observations. The second is to fit a mixture of models; this approach is discussed in the second part of this section.

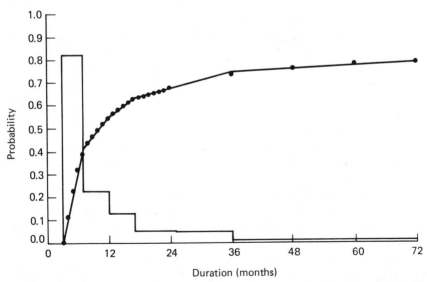

Figure 4.7. Ogive and histogram—duration of disability (3-month elimination, ages 30–39).

When data have been truncated and shifted, the observations begin at zero. They appear the same as a sample from an unmodified distribution. The major drawback is that we cannot recover the underlying loss distribution from the fitted model. To do so requires an estimate of $F_X(d)$. The fitted model will be useful provided we are interested in losses equal to or greater than the deductible.

For the LTD data we subtracted 3 or 6 from each observation as appropriate and then fitted each of the standard distributions. With no truncation to consider, there was no difficulty in providing this fit. In all four cases the Burr distribution was superior to the others. For the six-month elimination period the generalized Pareto distribution was equally good and both of them were superior to the Pareto distribution. The parameters are given in Table 4.10.

Table 4.10. Burr Parameters for LTD Data

Elimination Period:	3 months		6 months	
Age at Disablement:	30–39	40–49	30–39	40–49
$\hat{\alpha}$	0.23694	0.16582	0.30963	0.23085
$\hat{\lambda}$	1.5416	1.3167	6.2821	5.7438
$\hat{\tau}$	1.6766	1.7839	1.2870	1.2153

It may, at first glance, be surprising to observe that none of these distributions has a mean. A possible explanation is that there is too little information about the tail. Observation ended after eight years at which time a reasonably large number were still disabled. Our information does not allow the effects of old age on survivorship to be taken into account. This is a good reminder of the dangers of extrapolation.

B. Mixture of Models

In the previous section it was clear that two distributions were being mixed. Here there are no identifiable subsets, yet such a mixture may well provide a superior fit. It allows us to combine two characteristics (e.g., a nonzero mode and a heavy right tail as in the LTD data) into one model. A successful use of this technique is illustrated in Hewitt and Lefkowitz (1979).

A drawback to this approach is that the eight distributions lead to 36 pairs of distributions to be considered. The number of parameters to estimate may be as many as seven. In addition, estimation of p in Eq. 4.8

is very difficult because the minimization must be done with the restriction $0 < p < 1$. Without this restriction a global minimum may be at a value of p outside this range, in which case $F(x)$ might not be a distribution function. We reduce the problem by restricting attention to two-parameter distributions. In addition, we examine only a few values of p, doing each minimization holding that value fixed. There is no inherent difficulty in the minimization; all three of the estimation methods (md, mc, ml) require only that we be able to compute $F(x)$ or its derivative.

With four parameters to estimate, good starting values are important. Considerable trial and error may be required before a good set of starting values is found. By having the minimization routine print out the successive iterates, it is possible to see what corrections are needed. For example, in fitting a mixture of two Pareto distributions the starting values might be $\hat{\alpha}_1 = 0.15$, $\hat{\lambda}_1 = 10$ and $\hat{\alpha}_2 = 1.5$, $\hat{\lambda}_2 = 3$. After five iterations of the routine ZXSSQ the values are $\hat{\alpha}_1 = -0.1525$, $\hat{\lambda}_1 = 30.214$, $\hat{\alpha}_2 = -0.0214$, and $\hat{\lambda}_2 = 4.3163$. This suggests that the starting values $\hat{\alpha}_1$ and $\hat{\alpha}_2$ be lowered while $\hat{\lambda}_1$ and $\hat{\lambda}_2$ are raised.

Eleven models were fitted to the disability data at ages 30–39 with a three-month elimination period. The Pareto was used to supply a heavy tail while the lognormal was selected to provide a distribution with a nonzero mode. The results of maximum likelihood estimation are presented in Table 4.11. As the data are truncated, the distribution function must be modified as in Eq. 4.1. This modification was done after the distributions were mixed. The best fit is provided by the mixture of two Pareto distributions with $p = 0.1$. Several of the other mixtures provide models that are almost as good. The likelihood value for the best mixed model (4093.6) is not as good as that for the best shifted model (4091.1) found earlier. We prefer the truncated model as it models the process during the elimination period.

Another technique that may successfully model "two-part" distributions is based on using a different distribution for the different regions. For the LTD data we might select one Pareto distribution for the interval from zero to six and a second one for the interval from six to infinity. The two p.d.f.s would need to be properly scaled so the total probability is one. A method of md estimation for this type of model is given in von Lanzenauer and Wright (1977).

We should also note that in many cases we have a large number of small losses, but little information about the tail. In such cases it may be reasonable to use the empirical distribution as is for the small losses and then to fit a shifted parametric model in the tail. The Pareto distribution provides a convenient model as its p.d.f. is strictly decreasing. An example of this procedure is presented in Exercise 6 of Section 5.4.

Table 4.11. Fit of Mixed Distributions to LTD Data

		Pareto-Pareto			
p	$\hat{\alpha}_1$	$\hat{\lambda}_1$	$\hat{\alpha}_2$	$\hat{\lambda}_2$	$-\ln L$
0.10	0.056788	13.389	1.2549	3.4499	4093.6
0.25	0.27521	4.7217	2.4872	8.0694	4093.9
0.50	0.32010	0.62964	3.8800	13.881	4094.5

		Lognormal-Lognormal			
p	$\hat{\mu}_1$	$\hat{\sigma}_1$	$\hat{\mu}_2$	$\hat{\sigma}_2$	$-\ln L$
0.10	1.5514	0.69775	-4.5178	5.2505	4094.8
0.25	1.3854	0.93973	-3.3809	5.6721	4094.1
0.50	1.3398	0.98624	1.1489	4.2564	4094.1

		Pareto-Lognormal			
p	$\hat{\alpha}_1$	$\hat{\lambda}_1$	$\hat{\mu}_2$	$\hat{\sigma}_2$	$-\ln L$
0.10	0.98538	40.052	0.77912	1.5429	4094.2
0.25	0.27564	7.4188	1.1853	1.1233	4093.8
0.50	0.28607	0.53447	1.3137	1.0164	4093.9
0.75	0.36734	0.38709	1.5490	0.72158	4094.2
0.90	0.44225	0.44733	1.6653	0.36733	4093.8

In Chapter 5 we use the models to show how comparisons may be made between distributions and to illustrate the effects of introducing nonstandard deductibles.

4.5. CLUSTERING, TRUNCATION FROM ABOVE, COMBINING SAMPLES

Until this point we assumed that the observations correctly reflected the underlying loss process. Any difficulties were created by the manner in which the data were recorded, not by the losses themselves. In particular, we had to deal with data which were truncated from below and/or grouped. There is one additional problem: the settlement process may produce payments that are not consistent with the actual damages produced by the event. The tendency is for a few, popular, values to appear more frequently than would be expected from a continuous model. In this section we use the selection of class boundaries to minimize this problem.

The second topic is estimation when the data are truncated from above. This occurs, for instance, when the policy has an upper limit on the amount that the insurance will provide. If the number of claims which exceed the limit are recorded, the effect is one of *censoring* and produces no new problems. We merely place these claims in a class with lower boundary equal to that limit and an upper boundary of infinity. If no record is made of such losses, the data are said to be *truncated*. The analysis is similar to that used in Sections 4.2 and 4.3.

The final topic is the combination of several data sets. This can be a problem if different class boundaries are used for the various sets. One way this happens is when the loss data are collected on policies having different deductibles or limits. The methods of minimum chi-square and maximum likelihood estimation may easily be adapted to this situation.

The methods developed in this section are illustrated with data provided by the ISO on automobile bodily injury losses. The losses were collected nationwide and occurred in the accident year ending June 30, 1979. They were developed until September 30, 1981. The policies had no deductible but a variety of limits. The limits selected for our example are 5000, 10,000, 25,000, 50,000, and 100,000.

A. Clustering

The process of settling losses tends to produce payments which cluster about particular values. Reasons for this include: (1) a natural tendency to work with round numbers, (2) adjusters being permitted to settle losses up to a fixed amount on their own authorization, and (3) losses incurred but not yet settled requiring an estimation (of the eventual payment) that is likely to be a popular number. In Table 4.12 we present the data as they were compiled by the ISO except that all losses above $25,000 are placed in one class. The losses are only from policies with a $25,000 limit.

The clustering at 5000, 10,000, 20,000, and 25,000 is apparent; no continuous random variable can successfully model this behavior. Also, the mc and ml methods of estimation cannot deal with classes of width zero. Any model we select must necessarily spread these values over the neighboring points providing a better reflection of the true losses. To fit such a model this spreading must be done prior to fitting the model. For example, we could combine the clustered values with the groups on either side to form a larger interval. In Table 4.12 we spread the cluster at 5000 over its neighbors to create a single interval from 4001 to 6000 with 120 observations. Similar adjustments are in order at the other cluster points. It will now be possible to use any of the three estimation methods to obtain a smooth model.

Table 4.12. Automobile Bodily Injury Losses ($25,000 limit)

Interval	Number	Amount
1–250	660	75,420
251–500	268	101,558
501–1,000	311	236,068
1,001–2,000	282	425,042
2,001–3,000	170	437,265
3,001–4,000	94	333,232
4,001–4,999	49	220,878
5,000–5,000	25	125,000
5,001–6,000	46	256,168
6,001–7,000	31	204,257
7,001–8,000	46	332,649
8,001–9,000	27	233,143
9,001–9,999	9	85,411
10,000–10,000	18	180,000
10,001–11,000	5	53,475
11,001–12,000	7	80,838
12,001–14,000	26	340,215
14,001–15,000	13	194,393
15,001–16,000	5	77,756
16,001–17,000	3	49,576
17,001–18,000	5	88,431
18,001–19,000	2	37,000
19,001–19,999	3	58,629
20,000–20,000	5	100,000
20,001–21,000	3	62,651
21,001–22,000	6	128,055
22,001–23,000	2	45,000
23,001–24,000	2	48,000
24,001–24,999	4	97,864
25,000–25,000	34	850,000
25,001–	29	1,491,943
Total	2,190	7,049,917

We still may have doubts about the model's utility. None of the eight distributional models we have been using will account for clustering. A loss of, say, 4998 is just as likely as one of 5000. Also, for insurance calculations, it is not the actual damage which is relevant, but the amount paid by the insurer. If, however, clustering results from both increases and decreases in actual damage values, the effect of removing the clustering on the pure premium will be small. As in previous sections, this may be verified by comparing the limited expected value function from the model to the empirical function. An additional check can be provided by comparing the observed number in the enlarged classes to that predicted by the fitted model.

An additional problem is created when policies have payment limits. Occasionally, the amount paid by the insurance will exceed the limit (this happened 29 times in the automobile data). In liability coverages this can occur if a court rules that the insurer did not defend the insured in an appropriate manner. The insurance company is then liable for the entire amount. These values are not likely to be indicative of the actual loss. As well, the 34 observations which were censored at the limit were from

Table 4.13. Automobile Bodily Injury Losses—Empirical Distribution Functions

Upper Limit	5,000	10,000	25,000	50,000	100,000
250	0.31857	0.32524	0.30137	0.30488	0.25407
500	0.47708	0.47179	0.42374	0.44095	0.38034
1,000	0.61849	0.57837	0.56575	0.56194	0.50561
2,000	0.74463	0.70611	0.69452	0.68549	0.63509
3,000	0.81430	0.77900	0.77215	0.75610	0.71780
4,000	0.85366	0.82367	0.81507	0.80745	0.77073
6,000	0.87283	0.89028	0.86986	0.86425	0.83531
7,000		0.90674	0.88402	0.87644	0.85245
8,000		0.92006	0.90502	0.89730	0.87244
9,000		0.93025	0.91735	0.90725	0.88348
11,000		0.93966	0.93196	0.92908	0.90371
12,000			0.93516	0.93261	0.90970
14,000			0.94703	0.93806	0.91944
16,000			0.95525	0.94961	0.92981
19,000			0.95982	0.95764	0.93782
21,000			0.96484	0.96502	0.94436
23,000			0.96849	0.96727	0.94640
30,000			0.97123	0.97593	0.96120
35,000				0.97818	0.96558
40,000				0.98042	0.96928
45,000				0.98267	0.97212
55,000				0.98556	0.97952
60,000					0.98168
70,000					0.98409
80,000					0.98723
100,000					0.99143
	$n = 3,861$	$n = 1,276$	$n = 2,190$	$n = 3,116$	$n = 16,212$

losses at 25,000 and above. The only reasonable solution is to place all 63 observations in a class with a lower limit of 25,000 and an upper limit of infinity.

There is one more adjustment to be made. After spreading the clustered observations there are still many classes with a small number of observations. Combining them into larger classes will speed the calculations and may also improve the estimation. This is especially true for minimum chi-square estimation where the denominator values should not be too small, in particular, classes with less than five expected observations are to be avoided if possible.

In Table 4.13 the empirical distribution functions are presented for each of the five sets of automobile losses. All of the foregoing adjustments were implemented by just leaving out the entries from selected values in the original empirical d.f. The last entry in each column is the empirical d.f. evaluated at the policy limit, not at the indicated value.

With no truncation from below, the values in Table 4.13 are ready for direct use in md, mc, and ml estimation. Starting values are easy to obtain and the fitting routines converge rapidly. In Table 4.14 the ml estimates are presented for each of the five samples. Only the three models which provided good fits for all five samples are listed.

Table 4.14. Maximum Likelihood Estimates—Automobile Bodily Injury

		Limit		
5,000	10,000	25,000	50,000	100,000
Lognormal				
$\hat{\mu} = 6.3717$	6.4229	6.5538	6.5506	6.8404
$\hat{\sigma} = 1.8491$	1.9186	1.9172	1.9755	1.9716
$-\ln L = 7{,}133.5$	2,662.0	4,854.3	7,087.3	39,450
Burr				
$\hat{\alpha} = 0.98289$	6.2743	2.2244	2.2596	1.7477
$\hat{\lambda} = 313.88$	369.48	240.47	208.45	272.88
$\hat{\tau} = 0.92004$	0.57880	0.67760	0.65348	0.71001
$-\ln L = 7{,}132.5$	2,617.8	4,851.4	7,085.8	39,446
Generalized Pareto				
$\hat{\alpha} = 0.82414$	1.5331	1.1791	1.1610	1.0507
$\hat{\lambda} = 518.18$	3,889.5	2,336.1	2,586.2	2,363.7
$\hat{k} = 0.88433$	0.48011	0.55614	0.52014	0.59345
$-\ln L = 7{,}132.8$	2,619.9	4,852.1	7,088.9	39,457

Table 4.15. Evaluation of Models—25,000 Limit

Upper Limit	Empirical f_i	Empirical $E_n[X;x]$	Lognormal f_i	Lognormal $E[X;x]$	Burr f_i	Burr $E[X;x]$	Pareto f_i	Pareto $E[X;x]$
250	660	209	646	207	661	202	661	200
500	268	369	295	365	265	360	257	359
1,000	311	623	314	610	303	610	304	611
2,000	282	994	294	961	303	971	311	973
3,000	170	1,266	149	1,216	159	1,232	162	1,232
4,000	94	1,474	93	1,418	99	1,435	100	1,433
6,000	120	1,790	111	1,726	117	1,742	117	1,734
7,000	31	1,915	36	1,849	38	1,862	37	1,852
8,000	46	2,014	28	1,957	29	1,967	29	1,955
9,000	27	2,105	23	2,054	24	2,060	23	2,046
11,000	32	2,255	35	2,220	36	2,218	34	2,202
12,000	7	2,322	14	2,293	14	2,286	13	2,269
14,000	26	2,440	22	2,421	22	2,405	21	2,388
16,000	18	2,539	17	2,531	17	2,508	16	2,491
19,000	10	2,667	19	2,672	19	2,637	18	2,621
21,000	11	2,743	10	2,753	9	2,710	9	2,697
23,000	8	2,808	8	2,825	8	2,776	7	2,765
25,000	6	2,869	7	2,890	6	2,835	6	2,827
∞	63		68		62		65	

Note: f_i = number of observations in class (expected number for fitted models).

In the appendix, examples of the density functions for each of the eight families are presented. The first density illustrated in each case has the parameters set approximately equal to the estimates from the automobile policies with a 25,000 limit. Examination of these graphs can provide additional insight into the differences between these models.

To compare the three choices we examine the limited expected value functions. We also want to verify that the clustering problem has been handled in an acceptable manner. In Table 4.15 a detailed analysis is presented for the 25,000 limit. For each of the three models the limited expected values and the expected number of claims for each class are presented.

All three models do a good job of describing the observations. In particular, the expected number of observations for the groups with upper limits of 6000 and 11,000 closely agree with the observed numbers. This indicates that the clustering is adequately accounted for by spreading the observations to the adjoining classes. We prefer the Burr model because it has the smallest negative loglikelihood and the best correspondence of the limited expected value function. The latter observation is based on an examination of Table 4.15, not on any formal statistical test procedure.

B. Truncation from Above

Suppose in the automobile example there was no record of the number of losses at or above the liability limit. The data are then said to be *truncated from above* and a minor adjustment is required. The expression relating the d.f. for the observed values, Y, to the d.f. for all losses, X, is, for truncation at u,

$$F_Y(x) = \frac{F_X(x)}{F_X(u)}.$$

Note the similarity to Eq. 4.1. The corresponding relationship for the p.d.f. is then

$$f_Y(x) = \frac{f_X(x)}{F_X(u)}.$$

Estimation now follows routinely with the model, X, being converted to Y before estimation begins. For example, ml estimation for grouped data requires minimization of

$$-\ln L = -n \sum_{i=1}^{k} [F_n(c_{i+1}) - F_n(c_i)] \ln [F_X(c_{i+1}) - F_X(c_i)] + n \ln F_X(u).$$

This is similar to Eq. 4.7, the negative loglikelihood for observations which are truncated from below.

For the automobile data truncated at 25,000, the best Burr fit is given by $\hat{\alpha} = 2.2686$, $\hat{\lambda} = 240.45$, and $\hat{\tau} = 0.67494$. It is not surprising that these values are close to those obtained from the censored data; we have lost less than 3% of the observations.

C. Combining Samples

Suppose we have collected data from policies which differ only in the amount of the deductible or limit. If we believe that the distribution of losses (prior to imposing the deductible or limit) is the same for all these policies, it would be reasonable to use a single model estimated from the combined sample. Of the three estimation methods we have been using, both mc and ml estimation can be adapted to this situation.

To specify the needed modifications, let $F_{n_i}(x)$ be the empirical d.f. for the sample from the ith policy type, $i = 1, \ldots, m$. With grouped observations, let $c_{i0} < c_{i1} < \cdots < c_{ik_i}$ be the class boundaries for the ith sample. One way to perform mc estimation would be to treat the m samples separately. We then minimize

$$Q = \sum_{i=1}^{m} \sum_{j=1}^{k_i} \frac{(O_{ij} - E_{ij})^2}{E_{ij}},$$

where

$$O_{ij} = n_i\{F_{n_i}[c_{i(j+1)}] - F_{n_i}(c_{ij})\},$$

and

$$E_{ij} = n_i\{F_X[c_{i(j+1)}] - F_X(c_{ij})\}$$

with n_i being the number of observations in the ith sample and $F_X(x)$ the common fitted d.f. If the ith sample is truncated from above or below, $F_X(x)$ should be adjusted accordingly. If desired, the number of terms in the sum could be reduced by combining the O and E values for any two classes with identical boundaries.

A simple example can be constructed from the automobile data. In Table 4.16, observed values are given for expanded classes from the two low limit policies. In addition, the d.f. for a Burr distribution with parameters $\hat{\alpha} = 0.98164$, $\hat{\lambda} = 302.89$, and $\hat{\tau} = 0.90219$ is given. This was the model fitted to the data from policies with a $5000 limit. It is a good place to start an iteration for fitting a model to the combined sample.

Table 4.16. Low Limit Automobile Data

| c_{ij} | Sample 1, 5,000 Limit | | Sample 2, 10,000 Limit | | Burr d.f. |
	$F_1(c_{1j})$	O_{1j}	$F_2(c_{2j})$	O_{2j}	$F(x)$
0	0.00000	2388	0.00000	738	0.00000
1,000	0.61849	756	0.57837	256	0.62004
3,000	0.81430	226	0.77900	142	0.81328
5,000	0.87283	491			0.87288
6,000			0.89028	63	0.88983
10,000			0.93966	77	0.92713
∞	1.00000	—	1.00000	—	1.00000

The first version of mc estimation would have nine terms in the sum. The first term would have $O = 2388$ and $E = 3861(0.62004 - 0) = 2394$ and the final term would have $O = 77$ and $E = 1276(1 - 0.92713) = 93$. Combining terms from classes with common boundaries reduces the sum to seven terms. The first term would have $O = 2388 + 738 = 3126$ and $E = 5137(0.62004 - 0) = 3185$. The second term would have $O = 756 + 256 = 1012$ and $E = 5137(0.81328 - 0.62004) = 993$. The remaining five terms would be identical to the corresponding terms from the sum with nine entries.

Once the specific form for Q is set out, the actual minimization can be performed by the same routines used for single-sample estimation. For the above example the nine-term formula produces $\hat{\alpha} = 3.7752$, $\hat{\lambda} = 209.21$, and $\hat{\tau} = 0.59001$. For the seven-term formula the mc estimates are $\hat{\alpha} = 3.8539$, $\hat{\lambda} = 211.08$, and $\hat{\tau} = 0.58789$. The similarity of the estimates is apparent.

The modification for ml estimation proceeds along similar lines. In this case there will be no advantage to merging classes with common boundaries. The negative loglikelihood is

$$- \ln L = - \sum_{i=1}^{m} \sum_{j=1}^{k_i} n_i \{F_{n_i}[c_{i(j+1)}] - F_{n_i}(c_{ij})\} \ln \{F_X[c_{i(j+1)}] - F_X(c_{ij})\}.$$

We are merely adding the m individual negative loglikelihoods using the common fitted distribution. For the complete set of automobile data, the ml estimates of the Burr parameters are $\hat{\alpha} = 1.8692$, $\hat{\lambda} = 232.16$, and $\hat{\tau} = 0.69007$. The value of the negative loglikelihood is 61,277. The lognormal model did slightly better. With $\hat{\mu} = 6.6957$ and $\hat{\sigma} = 1.9700$ the negative loglikelihood is 61,273.

Even though it is always possible to fit models to combined data sets, it may not always be appropriate to do so. A common model should be used only if the individual data sets are actually from the same loss distribution. In Section 5.5 we present a method for testing this assumption.

4.6. A BIVARIATE MODEL

In some instances a single policy covers two types of loss. If only one type of loss can occur with a given claim, the mixture of models as discussed in Section 4.3 is appropriate. In this section we study the situation in which a single event produces both types of loss. We will model this with a bivariate random variable, (X, Y) where X and Y are the individual losses. The quantity of interest is the total loss, $S = X + Y$. If X and Y are independent, there is little difficulty. However, if X and Y are dependent, additional problems are created. We attack this problem by estimating the marginal distribution of X and the conditional distribution of Y given X. Together, these two models provide the necessary information.

The development of a bivariate model is illustrated with data on hospital professional liability losses. The data, provided by the ISO, are based on incidents occurring in 1974 and were developed to March 31, 1980 at which time 86% of the claims were closed. While data were available at a number of policy limits, we restrict attention to just one. The values in Table 4.17 are from 2988 claims on policies with a limit of $1,000,000. This limit was both per claim and per year. Of these claims, 1856 were settled for zero loss. The ISO had divided the observations into 118 subintervals (classes). Many classes contained no observations and others had zero widths. For example, one class contained losses of exactly $10,000. To enlarge the numbers in the classes and to smooth out the concentrations at certain amounts, we selected 25 classes, with boundaries spanning popular values. The empirical d.f. is based on the 1132 nonzero losses.

The bivariate model for liability losses consists of X, the actual damages awarded, and Y, the *allocated loss adjustment expenses* (ALAE). In most casualty coverages, expenses are of two kinds. The first are general expenses which are spread over all policies. These include acquisition costs, taxes, licenses, and fees, and general overhead (e.g., salaries, property costs, and general claims department expenses). The remaining expenses are the ALAE and are those specifically associated with settling individual claims. They include attorney's fees, payments to expert witnesses, medical examination expenses, and other costs involved in investigating the claim. The ISO data give the average ALAE for losses in each of the intervals. These are also presented in Table 4.17. Since there is a great variety of choices for bivariate models and forms in which data are recorded, we will not attempt to provide a general solution to the problem. Instead, we devote the remainder of this section to finding a model describing hospital professional liability losses.

Our goal, then, is to find a model for the total cost, $S = X + Y$, where X is the amount of the loss, given that a nonzero loss occurred, and Y is the ALAE. We separate from the analysis all claims settled for a payment

Table 4.17.   Hospital Malpractice Experience

i	c_i	f_i	$F_n(c_i)$	Average Loss[a]	Average ALAE[a]
1	0	1856	—	0	1,030
2	100	42	0.03710	49	244
3	250	49	0.08039	191	563
4	500	58	0.13163	408	678
5	1,000	84	0.20583	838	1,269
6	2,000	108	0.30124	1,561	1,628
7	4,000	140	0.42491	2,951	2,265
8	6,000	102	0.51502	5,124	3,445
9	9,000	74	0.58039	7,646	3,131
10	12,000	107	0.67491	10,197	5,967
11	16,000	72	0.73852	14,325	6,375
12	22,000	48	0.78092	19,564	6,370
13	30,000	80	0.85159	25,731	7,802
14	40,000	36	0.88339	35,457	17,337
15	55,000	30	0.90989	49,586	10,106
16	70,000	10	0.91873	62,147	9,598
17	90,000	17	0.93375	77,500	10,087
18	130,000	34	0.96378	106,548	10,237
19	180,000	19	0.98057	151,500	15,729
20	230,000	6	0.98587	202,500	9,799
21	280,000	4	0.98940	256,250	18,715
22	340,000	2	0.99117	312,500	5,708
23	420,000	5	0.99558	370,000	16,561
24	500,000	1	0.99647	500,000	14,486
25	750,000	2	0.99823	601,130	10,738
26	1,000,000	2	1.00000	890,431	50,727

[a] Average for losses greater than c_{i-1} and less than or equal to c_i.

of zero. They are considered when analysis of this example is concluded in Section 5.6. However, we have far from complete information: neither the marginal distribution of Y nor the joint distribution of X and Y is available. We do have information about the marginal distribution of X and the conditional mean of Y, given X.

To make the model more accessible, let $f(x)$ be the p.d.f. of the marginal distribution of X and $g(y|x)$ be the conditional p.d.f. of Y, given $X = x$. The joint p.d.f. of X and Y is given by $f(x)g(y|x)$. Later in this section, two methods for obtaining the distribution of S from the joint distribution of X and Y are presented.

The marginal distribution of X may be estimated by the methods previously demonstrated. Once again we use md, mc, and ml in sequence to fit each of the eight distributional models. It should again be noted that the model is being applied only to those claims settled for positive amounts. The best fit was provided by a Burr distribution with parameters $\hat{\alpha} = 2.2878$, $\hat{\lambda} = 1502.2$, and $\hat{\tau} = 0.72744$ as estimated by maximum likelihood.

We now turn to the conditional distribution of Y, given $X = x$. The values given in Table 4.17 enable us to estimate the conditional mean $E[Y|X = x]$. Each pair of values in the last two columns represents an average Y value calculated from a sample based on f_i values taken from observations whose losses (X) were in the ith class. To conveniently model the relationship we must assume a functional form for the conditional distribution. We begin with a simple model:

$$Y|X = x: a_1 + b_1 x + e, \tag{I}$$

where the colon indicates that the random variable on the left-hand side (in this case a conditional random variable) has the same probability distribution as the random variable on the right-hand side (in this case a function of the random variable e). Specification of this model is completed by assigning to the variable e a normal distribution with mean zero and variance σ^2. This is the standard model for simple linear regression (HC, 8.6). Recall, however, that we do not observe individual values of Y. We only have the average of f_i observations in the ith class, $i = 1, 2, \ldots, k$, where k is the number of classes. Averaging over all the observations in the jth class gives

$$\bar{Y}_i|\bar{X}_i = \bar{x}_i: a_1 + b_1\bar{x}_i + \bar{e}_i,$$

where $\bar{e}_i$ is the average of f_i independent observations of e and thus has a normal distribution with mean zero and variance σ^2/f_i. Note that this model also assumes that the conditional variance of Y is the same for each x. This is not likely to be true, but we do not have sufficient information to further assess this assumption. To do so would require the availability of the individual ALAEs.

Estimators of a_1, b_1, and σ^2 are provided by the method of maximum likelihood; those for a_1 and b_1 are also least squares estimates. For model I they are

$$\hat{b}_1 = \frac{\displaystyle\sum_{i=1}^{k} f_i(\bar{x}_i - \bar{x})(\bar{y}_i - \bar{y})}{\displaystyle\sum_{i=1}^{k} f_i(\bar{x}_i - \bar{x})^2},$$

$$\hat{a}_1 = \bar{y} - \hat{b}_1\bar{x},$$

and

$$\hat{\sigma}^2 = \frac{1}{k}\sum_{i=1}^{k} f_i(\bar{y}_i - \hat{a}_1 - \hat{b}_1\bar{x}_i)^2$$

$$= \frac{1}{k}\sum_{i=1}^{k} f_i(\bar{y}_i - \bar{y})^2 - \frac{1}{k}\sum_{i=1}^{k} \hat{b}_1 f_i(\bar{x}_i - \bar{x})(\bar{y}_i - \bar{y}),$$

where

$$\bar{y} = \frac{1}{n}\sum_{i=1}^{k} f_i\bar{y}_i$$

and

$$\bar{x} = \frac{1}{n}\sum_{i=1}^{k} f_i\bar{x}_i.$$

In our example, $\bar{x}_i$, $\bar{y}_i$, and f_i are found in Table 4.17 and $k = 25$ is the number of intervals. These provide the estimates

$$\hat{a}_1 = 3688.0, \qquad \hat{b}_1 = 0.050169, \quad \text{and} \quad \hat{\sigma}^2 = 496{,}880{,}000.$$

A measure of the success of this model in describing the relationship between Y and X is provided by the correlation coefficient. It is computed as

$$r = \frac{\displaystyle\sum_{i=1}^{k} f_i(\bar{x}_i - \bar{x})(\bar{y}_i - \bar{y})}{\sqrt{\displaystyle\sum_{i=1}^{k} f_i(\bar{x}_i - \bar{x})^2}\ \sqrt{\displaystyle\sum_{i=1}^{k} f_i(\bar{y}_i - \bar{y})^2}}.$$

For model I, the value is $r = 0.09155$, an unacceptably low value. We must search for an improved formula. The skewed nature of the loss values indicates that their logarithms may provide a better argument for the linear regression formula. This produces

$$Y|X = x: a_2 + b_2 \ln x + e, \qquad (II)$$

where again the variable e has a normal distribution with mean zero and variance σ^2. The model for $\bar{Y}_i$ also takes on a simple form:

$$\bar{Y}_i | \overline{\ln x_i}: a_2 + b_2 \overline{\ln x_i} + \bar{e}_i.$$

Here $\overline{\ln x_i}$ is the arithmetic mean of the logarithms of the losses in the ith class. From this point on we will use $\mathbf{X}_i$ to represent the vector of x-observations in the ith group. The right-hand side will indicate the precise manner in which Y depends on $\mathbf{X}_i$. For model II we rewrite the above as

$$\bar{Y}_i | \mathbf{X}_i: a_2 + b_2 \overline{\ln x_i} + \bar{e}_i.$$

We do not have access to values of $\overline{\ln x_i}$ and so an approximation is needed. For each x-value in the ith group we substitute $\bar{x}_i$, the group mean. Since the x-values are all within the boundaries of the ith group this should make little difference. Model II is then approximately

$$\bar{Y}_i | \mathbf{X}_i: a_2 + b_2 \ln \bar{x}_i + \bar{e}_i.$$

For this version of the model the maximum likelihood estimators are given by the same formulas used for model I. The only change is that $\bar{x}_i$ is replaced by $\ln \bar{x}_i$. The estimates for our example are

$$\hat{a}_2 = -11{,}685, \qquad \hat{b}_2 = 1940.8, \qquad \hat{\sigma}^2 = 332{,}130{,}000, \quad \text{and} \quad r = 0.80699.$$

The improvement in fit as measured by r is substantial.

There is still one unpleasant aspect to this model. With e having a normal distribution, Y also has a normal distribution. This means that the distribution of Y is symmetric about $a_2 + b_2 \ln x$ and, in particular, that negative values are possible. Although we have no data on the distribution of Y, given X, we are more inclined to believe that it is skewed and takes on only positive values. While a number of distributions with this property are available, we confine attention to the lognormal distribution. This is done solely because maximum likelihood estimators are readily available. The model is

$$\ln Y|X = x: a_3 + b_3 \ln x + e, \qquad \text{(III)}$$

where the variable e has a normal distribution with mean zero and variance σ^2. Exponentiating both sides gives

$$Y|X = x: \exp(a_3)x^{b_3} \exp(e).$$

Thus $Y|X = x$ is equal to a constant times a random variable with a lognormal distribution, producing another lognormal distribution (this fact is established in Section 5.2).

However, we are interested in $\bar{Y}_i$. It is

$$\bar{Y}_i|\mathbf{X}_i: \frac{1}{f_i} \exp(a_3) \sum_{j=1}^{f_i} x_j^{b_3} \exp(e_j).$$

Once again we replace each x_j in class i by $\bar{x}_i$ so that the corresponding factor can be taken outside the summation. The model is then

$$\bar{Y}_i|\mathbf{X}_i: \exp(a_3)\bar{x}_i^{b_3} \overline{\exp(e_i)}. \qquad (4.9)$$

Taking logarithms, we obtain

$$\ln \bar{Y}_i|\mathbf{X}_i: a_3 + b_3 \ln \bar{x}_i + \ln \left[\overline{\exp(e_i)}\right].$$

Unfortunately, the mean of lognormal random variables does not have a lognormal distribution and therefore $\ln \left[\overline{\exp(e_i)}\right]$ does not have a normal distribution. We cannot use the least squares formula to obtain maximum likelihood estimates of the parameters. There is a way, however, to approximate the solution.

In particular, we can approximate $E[\ln \bar{Y}_i|\mathbf{X}_i]$ by employing an analysis similar to that used at the end of Section 3.4. For any random variable Z and function $h(z)$ possessing all derivatives, the Taylor series expansion gives, with $\mu = E[Z]$,

$$E[h(Z)] = E[h(\mu) + (Z - \mu)h'(\mu) + (Z - \mu)^2 h''(\mu)/2 + \cdots]$$

$$= h(\mu) + \mathrm{Var}(Z)h''(\mu)/2 + \cdots.$$

In our case, with $h(z) = \ln(z)$ and $Z = \bar{Y}_i|\mathbf{X}_i$,

$$E[\ln \bar{Y}_i|\mathbf{X}_i] = \ln (\mu) - \text{Var} (\bar{Y}_i|\mathbf{X}_i)/2\mu^2 + \cdots . \tag{4.10}$$

To evaluate Eq. 4.10, we need, using Eq. 4.9,

$$\mu = E[\bar{Y}_i|\mathbf{X}_i] = \exp (a_3)\bar{x}_i^{b_3} E[\overline{\exp (e_i)}]$$

$$= \exp (a_3)\bar{x}_i^{b_3} E[\exp (e)]$$

$$= \exp (a_3)\bar{x}_i^{b_3} \exp (\sigma^2/2) ,$$

and

$$\text{Var} (\bar{Y}_i|\mathbf{X}_i) = \exp (2a_3)\bar{x}_i^{2b_3} \text{Var} [\overline{\exp (e_i)}]$$

$$= \exp (2a_3)\bar{x}_i^{2b_3} \text{Var} [\exp (e)]/f_i$$

$$= \exp (2a_3)\bar{x}_i^{2b_3}[\exp (2\sigma^2) - \exp (\sigma^2)]/f_i .$$

Substituting these two expressions into Eq. 4.10 and dropping all terms of higher order, we have

$$E[\ln \bar{Y}_i|\mathbf{X}_i] \approx a_3 + b_3 \ln \bar{x}_i + \sigma^2/2 - [\exp (\sigma^2) - 1]/2f_i$$

$$\approx a_3 + b_3 \ln \bar{x}_i + \sigma^2/2$$

with the equality holding as f_i goes to infinity, provided all moments exist. The appropriate model to fit, therefore, is

$$\ln \bar{Y}_i|\mathbf{X}_i: (a_3 + \sigma^2/2) + b_3 \ln \bar{x}_i + \bar{e}_i$$

$$= a_4 + b_3 \ln \bar{x}_i + \bar{e}_i .$$

We can successfully estimate a_4, b_3, and σ^2 by maximum likelihood using the least squares formulas with both $\bar{x}_i$ and $\bar{y}_i$ replaced by their logarithms. The values for the data in Table 4.17 are

$$\hat{a}_4 = 3.5753 , \qquad \hat{b}_3 = 0.52472 , \qquad \hat{\sigma}^2 = 2.3235 , \quad \text{and} \quad r = 0.97532 .$$

The fit, as measured by r, is outstanding. The model for Y is based on $\hat{a}_3 = 3.5753 - 2.3235/2 = 2.4135$. We use this model for the remainder of this section.

With these assumptions and fits, we have now completely specified the approximate joint distribution of X and Y. The distribution of $S = X + Y$ is, using a convolution formula similar to the one discussed in Section 2.5, given by

$$F_S(s) = \Pr[S \le s] = \Pr[X + Y \le s]$$

$$= \int_0^s \Pr[X + Y \le s | X = x] f_X(x)\, dx$$

$$= \int_0^s \Pr[Y \le s - x | X = x] f_X(x)\, dx$$

$$= \int_0^s \Pr[\ln Y \le \ln (s - x) | X = x] f_X(x)\, dx$$

$$= \int_0^s \Phi\left[\frac{\ln (s - x) - a_3 - b_3 \ln (x)}{\sigma}\right] f_X(x)\, dx, \qquad (11)$$

where $f_X(x)$ is the p.d.f. of the fitted Burr distribution and $\Phi(x)$ is the d.f. of a standard normal random variable. Exact evaluation of this integral is not possible. We are left with two choices. The first is approximate integration. Use of a composite Simpson's rule (Kellison, 1975, p. 174) over the interval $(0, s)$ with a large number of intervals coupled with a good approximation for $\Phi(x)$ should produce reasonable results. Accuracy will depend on the number of intervals into which the range is split.

The second method is simulation. Our goal is to generate a random sample from the distribution of S. This is done in two steps. First, generate a claim amount, x, from the Burr distribution. Then use this amount to obtain $z = \exp(a_3) x^{b_3}$. Finally, obtain e, a value from a normal distribution with parameters 0 and σ^2, exponentiate it, multiply it by z, and add the product to x. The result is a random observation of S. Formulas for x, z, e, and s are given below where u_1, u_2, and u_3 are independent observations from a uniform distribution on the unit interval.

For x:

$$u_1 = 1 - \left(\frac{\lambda}{\lambda + x^\tau}\right)^\alpha$$

$$x = \{\lambda[(1 - u_1)^{-1/\alpha} - 1]\}^{1/\tau}$$

$$= \{1502.2[(1 - u_1)^{-0.43710} - 1]\}^{1.3747}$$

(see Section 3.2). Then

$$z = \exp(2.4135) x^{0.52472}$$

$$= 11.173 x^{0.52472}.$$

For e:

$$\ln e = \sqrt{-2 \ln u_2} \cos (2\pi u_3)1.5243$$

(from problem 3.2.2). Finally,

$$s = x + ze .$$

We used the method outlined above to generate 10,000 values of s. The empirical distribution $F_n(s)$, with $n = 10,000$, is presented at selected points in Table 4.18. We also used Eq. 4.11 with 1000 intervals and a composite Simpson's rule to obtain additional estimates of these probabilities. They are also presented in Table 4.18.

Remark. The integrand in Eq. 4.11 goes to infinity as x goes to 0 when the third parameter (τ) in the Burr distribution is less than 1. To approximate the integral near zero, observe that for small x, the argument of $\Phi(x)$ in the integrand will be large and therefore $\Phi\{[\ln (s - x) - a_3 - b_3 \ln x]/\sigma\}$ will be close to 1. We found the value of x that made this argument equal to 3.5 (call it r) and then approximated the integral from 0 to r by setting $\Phi(x)$ equal to 1. The remaining factor is just the Burr p.d.f., and so the integral from 0 to r is approximated by $F_X(r)$, the Burr d.f. The integral from r to s is then approximated by 500 applications of Simpson's rule.

In Table 4.18 we also present some evidence for the success of the regression model in providing reasonable values of Y. For each simulated value of X the group into which it belongs was noted and the corresponding Y value (ze, above) was assigned to that group. The arithmetic means of the Y were computed for each group and their logarithms are recorded in Table 4.18. Also appearing are the logarithms of the sample (arithmetic) means from Table 4.17. The close correspondence between the two arithmetic means is reassuring.

A final cautionary note is in order. Neither the close correspondence between the two distributions presented in Table 4.18 nor the agreement of the means is justification for the validity of model III. While we are convinced that this model reproduces the given data, we still have no information about the distribution of Y and can only hope that our assumption of a lognormal distribution with constant variance is a reasonable one.

In Section 5.6, this example is continued with a discussion of the effects of inflation and censoring on the distribution of S. In particular, we want

Table 4.18. Distribution of Losses plus ALAE

s	Approximation by Simpson's Rule	Simulation			Predicted[a] $\ln \bar{y}_i$	Observed[b] $\ln \bar{y}_i$
		f_i	$F_n(s)$	$\ln \bar{y}_i$		
100	0.0191	203	0.0203	5.277	5.617	5.497
250	0.0433	223	0.0426	6.376	6.331	6.333
500	0.0777	365	0.0791	6.542	6.730	6.519
1,000	0.1345	569	0.1360	6.928	7.107	7.146
2,000	0.2225	885	0.2245	7.328	7.434	7.395
4,000	0.3470	1297	0.3542	7.669	7.768	7.725
6,000	0.4351	862	0.4404	7.973	8.057	8.145
9,000	0.5302	942	0.5346	8.182	8.267	8.049
12,000	0.5988	698	0.6044	8.342	8.418	8.694
16,000	0.6658	634	0.6678	8.496	8.597	8.760
22,000	0.7353	755	0.7433	8.672	8.760	8.759
30,000	0.7956	564	0.7997	8.950	8.904	8.962
40,000	0.8437	474	0.8471	9.100	9.072	9.761
55,000	0.8875	416	0.8887	9.094	9.248	9.221
70,000	0.9142	270	0.9157	9.415	9.367	9.169
90,000	0.9364	228	0.9385	9.542	9.483	9.219
130,000	0.9603	249	0.9634	9.456	9.650	9.234
180,000	0.9745	133	0.9767	10.364	9.834	9.663
230,000	0.9820	68	0.9835	9.921	9.987	9.190
280,000	0.9865	34	0.9869	9.784	10.110	9.837
340,000	0.9899	30	0.9899	9.929	10.214	8.650
420,000	0.9927	25	0.9924	10.209	10.303	9.715
500,000	0.9945	14	0.9938	10.590	10.461	9.581
750,000	0.9971	31	0.9969	10.655	10.558	9.282
1,000,000	0.9982	14	0.9983	9.359	10.764	10.834
∞	1.0000	17	1.0000	10.602	—	—

[a] $\ln \bar{y}_i = 3.5753 + 0.52472 \ln(\bar{x}_i)$, where $\bar{x}_i$ is from Table 4.17. [b] $\ln \bar{y}_i$, where $\bar{y}_i$ is from Table 4.17.

to know the expected value of S when losses (but not ALAE) are limited to $1,000,000 and what the effects of inflation are on this value.

4.7.   A REVIEW OF THE MODELING PROCESS

Throughout this chapter we have presented an approach to fitting continuous probability models to data. Each illustration began with the data set and concluded with a fitted probability distribution. In this section we use a "flow-chart" to review the steps in this procedure. This should prove especially useful to those readers who want to set up a computer system to perform the model-fitting operation.

The notation used is as follows:

X	The model random variable.
θ	A vector of parameters which determines the distribution of X.
Y	The amount paid random variable. It is a function of X (usually used to incorporate a deductible, a limit, or both).
$F_Y(x; \theta)$	The d.f. of Y.
$F_n(x)$	The empirical d.f. It is considered to be based on a random sample from Y. For individual data it has jumps at each data point. For grouped data it has jumps at class boundaries.

Flow-Chart

1. Collect data, record as $F_n(x)$.
2. Select distributional model.
   Use two-parameter models at first. Use histograms and $e_n(x)$ as guides.
3. Note coverage modifications, obtain $F_Y(x; \theta)$.
4. Obtain preliminary estimates by pm or mm.
5. Select an estimation technique (md, mc, or ml).
6. Write the objective function (K, Q, or L, as appropriate).
7. Iterate to minimize objective function.
   Marquardt algorithm
   Nonlinear weighted least-squares
   Scoring (grouped ml only)
   Write iterates to check for convergence. If divergence, try new starting values.
8. Record estimated parameters and value of objective function.
9. Return to Step 5 and try another estimation technique. (optional)

10. Return to Step 2 and try another distributional model. It may be appropriate to try a three-parameter generalization of a previously fitted model. (optional)

11. Select one or more models which had low values of the objective function. For each, display $F_Y(x; \boldsymbol{\theta})$ and $E[Y; x]$ along with the empirical values.

12. Select the model that provides the best fit in terms of all the values presented in Step 11.

CHAPTER 5

Applications of
Distributional Models

5.1. INTRODUCTION

In Chapter 4 we obtained models which described a variety of loss processes. As indicated in Chapter 1, there are a number of uses for these models. In this chapter we illustrate several of them. They include (1) effects of inflation, (2) evaluation of deductibles, limits, and layers, (3) comparisons of distributions, and (4) estimation of percentiles. In each section of this chapter examples are provided which use the model developed in the corresponding section of Chapter 4.

5.2. INFLATION, PERCENTILE ESTIMATION

The first two problems concern inflation and percentile estimation. The first relates to the increase in losses due to inflation. The model must often be adjusted to bring it up to the current level of loss experience since, in general, the model was estimated from observations made several years in the past. In addition, we may desire a projection to reflect losses anticipated in some future period.

The second problem relates to estimation of points from the loss distribution. Chapter 4 was devoted to obtaining such point estimators. In this section we obtain interval estimates for these values. Solutions to both problems will be illustrated with the model for hurricane losses developed in Section 4.2.: a Weibull distribution with parameters $c = 0.000074947$ and $\tau = 0.51907$.

A. Effects of Inflation

Whether we are interested in updating models based on values from the past or in projecting models into the future, the problem is the same. If X is the random variable which models the losses, we desire the distribution of $Z = (1 + r)X$, where r is the inflation rate over the period of concern. The expression relating the d.f. of Z to that of X is

$$F_Z(z) = \Pr\,[Z \le z]$$

$$= \Pr\left[\frac{Z}{1+r} \le \frac{z}{1+r}\right] \qquad (5.1)$$

$$= F_X\left(\frac{z}{1+r}\right).$$

In addition, if X is a continuous random variable, we have the following relationship between the two p.d.f.s:

$$f_Z(z) = \frac{d}{dz}\,F_Z(z)$$

$$= \frac{f_X\left(\dfrac{z}{1+r}\right)}{1+r}. \qquad (5.2)$$

For seven of the eight distribution families studied in Chapter 4, multiplication by a constant produces another member of that family. Results for these distributions are presented in Table 5.1. You are asked to verify these results in Exercise 1.

Table 5.1. Effect of Inflation on Parameters

Family	Parameters of X	Parameters of $Z = (1 + r)X$
Lognormal	μ, σ	$\mu + \ln(1 + r), \sigma$
Pareto	α, λ	$\alpha, (1 + r)\lambda$
Burr	α, λ, τ	$\alpha, \lambda(1 + r)^\tau, \tau$
Generalized Pareto	α, λ, k	$\alpha, \lambda(1 + r), k$
Gamma	α, λ	$\alpha, \lambda/(1 + r)$
Transformed gamma	α, λ, τ	$\alpha, \lambda/(1 + r), \tau$
Loggamma	α, λ	Not loggamma
Weibull	c, τ	$c/(1 + r)^\tau, \tau$

For the hurricane example, if the construction cost index for 1982 was 1.12 times that for 1981, the appropriate model for 1982 losses is a Weibull distribution with parameters

$$c = 0.000074947/1.12^{0.51907} = 0.000070665 \quad \text{and} \quad \tau = 0.51907 \,.$$

We are now prepared to perform any subsequent analysis on the inflated distribution. In later sections we will be especially interested in the effects of inflation on frequency and severity when the policy has a deductible, a limit, or both.

B. Percentile Estimation

With a distributional model in hand, we might be interested in the probability that there will be an insured event which produces losses in excess of a specified amount. Given that there is a loss, we use the distribution function to provide a point estimate. In this section the estimation procedure will be illustrated with the Weibull model. Recall that the d.f. and p.d.f. are, respectively,

$$F_X(x) = 1 - \exp(-cx^\tau)$$

and

$$f_X(x) = c\tau x^{\tau-1} \exp(-cx^\tau) \,.$$

For 1981, the probability that a given hurricane produces over \$1 billion in losses is estimated by

$$\begin{aligned}
\Pr[X > 10^9] &= 1 - F_X(10^9) \\
&= \exp[-c(10^9)^\tau] \\
&= \exp[-0.000074947(10^9)^{0.51907}] \\
&= 0.02964 \,.
\end{aligned}$$

Since c and τ were estimated by maximum likelihood, this too is a maximum likelihood estimator. We recognize, however, that this value is an estimate based on sample information and as such might well be in error. A more descriptive estimate is provided by the construction of a confidence interval. As the point estimator is a function of maximum likelihood estimates, the theory presented in Section 3.4 may be used to estimate the confidence interval. The example that follows uses the

Weibull distribution; in Exercise 4 you are asked to do similar calculations for the lognormal distribution.

We begin by estimating **A**, the inverse of the asymptotic variance-covariance matrix of the maximum likelihood estimators of the Weibull parameters. The elements of this 2×2 matrix are, for the Weibull distribution,

$$a_{11} = -\sum_{i=1}^{n} \frac{\partial^2 \ln f(x_i; c, \tau)}{\partial c^2} = \sum_{i=1}^{n} \frac{1}{c^2} = \frac{n}{c^2},$$

$$a_{12} = a_{21} = -\sum_{i=1}^{n} \frac{\partial^2 \ln f(x_i; c, \tau)}{\partial c \partial \tau} = \sum_{i=1}^{n} x_i^\tau \ln x_i,$$

and

$$a_{22} = -\sum_{i=1}^{n} \frac{\partial^2 \ln f(x_i; c, \tau)}{\partial \tau^2} = c \sum_{i=1}^{n} x_i^\tau (\ln x_i)^2 + \frac{n}{\tau^2}.$$

For the hurricane data, using $n = 35$, $c = 0.000074947$, and $\tau = 0.51907$, the estimators are

$$a_{11} = 6{,}231{,}025{,}630\,,$$

$$a_{12} = a_{21} = 10{,}989{,}823.5\,,$$

and

$$a_{22} = 16{,}040.723\,.$$

Note that the matrix **A** is the same as the information matrix presented in Section 4.3. For grouped data, the estimate developed in that section can be used for this analysis. The method then proceeds as outlined below.

We next obtain the elements of the vector (h_1, h_2), the two first partial derivatives of the function $h(c, \tau)$ that we are trying to estimate. In this example,

$$h(c, \tau) = \exp(-cx^\tau)\,.$$

And so

$$h_1(c, \tau) = -x^\tau \exp(-cx^\tau)$$

and

$$h_2(c, \tau) = -cx^\tau (\ln x) \exp(-cx^\tau).$$

At $x = 10^9$ and with c and τ replaced by their estimates, we obtain

$$h_1 = -1391.46063 \quad \text{and} \quad h_2 = -2.16114235.$$

Finally, the asymptotic variance of the probability estimate is $\mathbf{h}'\mathbf{A}^{-1}\mathbf{h} =$ 0.00028504 and the standard deviation is 0.016883. An approximate 90% confidence interval is then

$$0.02964 \pm 1.645(0.016883) \quad \text{or} \quad (0.00187, 0.05741).$$

We may ultimately be interested in the probability of having a hurricane that causes losses exceeding $1 billion in a one-year period or in the number of years which can be expected to pass between such losses. To do so requires knowledge of the frequency of losses. For illustrative purposes, assume that the number of losses in one year which exceed $5 million has a Poisson distribution with parameter $35/32 = 1.09375$ (based on observing 35 such losses in 32 years). The probability of observing a loss in excess of 5,000,000 is estimated by

$$\exp[-0.000074947(5{,}000{,}000^{0.51907})] = 0.79860.$$

We can then estimate the expected number of losses of any amount as $1.09375/0.79860 = 1.36958$ per year. Using the point estimate developed above, the number of losses in excess of $1 billion in one year will have a Poisson distribution with parameter $1.36958(0.02964) = 0.04059$. The probability of at least one such loss in a year is one minus the Poisson probability of no losses, that is, $1 - \exp(-0.04059) = 0.03978$. Under a Poisson process the expected time between events is equal to the reciprocal of the parameter. Thus we can expect a billion-dollar hurricane every $1/0.04059 = 24.64$ years. We must keep in mind that these losses are in constant (1981) dollars. With continued inflation, the expected time to the next (actual) billion-dollar loss would be less than 24.64 years.

Exercises

1. Use Eq. 5.1 or 5.2 to verify the entries in Table 5.1.

2. Suppose we are interested in hurricane losses for 1984. Further suppose inflation continues at an annual rate of 12%.
   (a) What are the Weibull parameters of the model for 1984 losses?

(b) What is the point estimate of the probability that a 1984 hurricane will produce a loss in excess of $1 billion?

(c) What is the standard deviation of the estimate in part (b)? *Hint*: Only the function $h(c, \tau)$ and its derivatives change. Remember that the point estimator $h(c, \tau)$ must be expressed in terms of the values of c and τ obtained from the original, 1981, data. The matrix **A** is unchanged.

3. The estimate of a billion-dollar hurricane every 24.64 years was based on three estimated quantities. It was found as $h = a_3/a_1a_2$ where a_1 is the frequency of losses in excess of $5 million and a_2 and a_3 are the probabilities of losses exceeding $1 billion and $5 million respectively. Both a_2 and a_3 are functions of the estimated parameters c and τ. Assuming a_1 is estimated without error as 1.09375, what is a 90% confidence interval for the expected time between billion-dollar losses. As in Exercise 2, **A** is unchanged.

4. In Chapter 4 we found that the hurricane losses in 1981 dollars could also have been modeled by a lognormal random variable with parameters $\mu = 17.953$ and $\sigma = 1.6028$ as estimated by maximum likelihood.

(a) What are the parameters if inflation increases losses by 12%?

(b) What is the probability of a loss exceeding $1 billion in the original (1981) distribution?

(c) Find a 90% confidence interval for the estimate in (b).

5. A related question is one of how large a loss can be expected every n years. Use the 1981 Weibull model to find the magnitude of hurricane loss which can be expected once every 10 years. This can be done by reversing the development at the end of Part B of this section.

6. (a) Consider a mixture of two Pareto distributions with d.f.

$$F(x) = 1 - p\left(\frac{\lambda_1}{\lambda_1 + x}\right)^{\alpha_1} - (1-p)\left(\frac{\lambda_2}{\lambda_2 + x}\right)^{\alpha_2}.$$

Show that the distribution of $Y = (1 + r)X$ is also a mixture of two Pareto distributions and express the parameters of Y in terms of the parameters of X.

(b) Show that, in general, if multiplication by a constant produces another member of the original distributional family, the same will be true for a mixture of random variables from that family.

7. Suppose X has a transformed gamma distribution with parameters k, θ, and τ. Further suppose that θ also has a transformed gamma

distribution with parameters α, $\lambda^{1/\tau}$, and τ. Use the p.d.f. as given in the appendix and the compounding technique as illustrated in Section 2.7 to show that X has p.d.f.

$$f(x) = \frac{\Gamma(\alpha + k)\tau\lambda^{\alpha}x^{\tau k-1}}{\Gamma(\alpha)\Gamma(k)(\lambda + x^{\tau})^{\alpha+k}}.$$

This has been called the transformed beta distribution (Venter, 1983). Show that the following are special cases:

$$k = 1 \qquad \text{Burr}$$

$$\tau = 1 \qquad \text{generalized Pareto}$$

$$k = \tau = 1 \qquad \text{Pareto}.$$

The following is an application of the above development; see Venter (1983) for details and an example. Suppose 1981 losses have a transformed gamma distribution with parameters k, η, and τ where all three values are fixed. Let the random variable, R, be the currently unknown inflation rate. From Section 5.2 we know that 1982 losses will have a transformed gamma distribution with parameters k, $\theta = \eta/(1 + R)$, and τ. Now assume R is distributed so that θ is transformed gamma with parameters α, $\lambda^{1/\tau}$, and τ. Then 1982 losses will have a transformed beta distribution. As an exercise, let $k = 1$, $\eta = 1.1288 \times 10^{-8}$, and $\tau = 0.51907$ (this gives the Weibull model for 1981 hurricane losses). Instead of setting $r = 0.12$, let $\theta = 1.1288 \times 10^{-8}/(1 + R)$ be distributed transformed gamma with parameters $\alpha = 4$, $\lambda^{1/\tau} = 576{,}140{,}000$, and $\tau = 0.51907$ (so $\lambda = 35{,}264$). These values were selected so that the expected values [(a) below] match. Let Z be the resulting transformed beta distribution ($k = 1$, $\alpha = 4$, $\lambda = 35{,}264$, and $\tau = 0.51907$). This is actually a Burr distribution and is a model for 1982 hurricane losses with uncertain inflation. We want to compare it to Y, the Weibull model ($c = 0.000070665$, $\tau = 0.51907$) for 1982 losses developed in this section.

(a) Verify that $E[Y] = E[Z] = 185{,}631{,}421$.

(b) What are the standard deviations of Y and Z?

(c) Compute $\Pr(Y > 500{,}000{,}000)$ and $\Pr(Z > 500{,}000{,}000)$.

Formulas for the probabilities and moments are given in the appendix. Use $\Gamma(0.14696) = 6.3558$, $\Gamma(2.0735) = 1.0333$, $\Gamma(2.9265) = 1.8709$, $\Gamma(4) = 6$, and $\Gamma(4.8530) = 19.280$. Your answers to (b) and (c) should verify that the distribution with uncertain inflation has a much heavier right tail.

5.3. DEDUCTIBLES, LEVERAGING

The first topic for discussion in this section is the influence of a deductible on frequency and severity. In particular, we are interested in the effect on the pure premium of a change in the deductible. Even if the deductible is kept unchanged, the pure premium will be affected by inflation. However, the effect will not be equal to the inflation rate as losses which were formerly below the deductible may, with inflation, exceed it. This effect is called *leveraging* and is discussed in the second part of this section.

In all of the analyses we must assume that changing the deductible does not affect the loss process. That is, persons who purchase insurance at one level of deductible will produce the same level of losses as those who purchase a different deductible. In the next two sections we discuss methods of testing this assumption.

These problems are illustrated with the theft loss model developed in Section 4.3. The observations were from policies with a hundred-dollar deductible. The model of choice was a Burr distribution with parameters $\alpha = 1.1613$, $\lambda = 20{,}854$, and $\tau = 1.6175$.

A. Deductibles

When a deductible is put into effect or an existing deductible is altered we are interested in both the distribution of the amount paid and the severity. For a deductible of d the payment is given by the truncated and shifted (see Section 4.2) random variable, W, given by

$$W = X - d, \qquad X > d$$

$$W \text{ not defined}, \qquad \text{otherwise}.$$

The deductible has two effects. It eliminates some losses $(X \le d)$ and reduces (to $X - d$) the rest. For continuous loss distributions the d.f. and p.d.f. of W are, from Section 4.2,

$$
\begin{aligned}
F_W(x) &= 0, && x \le 0 \\
&= \frac{F_X(x+d) - F_X(d)}{1 - F_X(d)}, && x > 0
\end{aligned}
\tag{5.3}
$$

and

$$
\begin{aligned}
f_W(x) &= 0, && x \le 0 \\
&= \frac{f_X(x+d)}{1 - F_X(d)}, && x > 0.
\end{aligned}
\tag{5.4}
$$

To estimate the severity, we return to a quantity introduced in Section 4.1, $E[X; d]$, the limited expected value function. The severity is the expected value (if it exists) of the truncated and shifted loss variable, W:

$$
\begin{aligned}
E[W] &= \int_0^\infty x f_W(x)\, dx = \int_0^\infty \frac{x f_X(x+d)}{1 - F_X(d)}\, dx \\
&= \int_d^\infty \frac{(y-d) f_X(y)\, dy}{1 - F_X(d)} \\
&= \frac{\int_0^\infty y f_X(y)\, dy - \int_0^d y f_X(y)\, dy - d[1 - F_X(d)]}{1 - F_X(d)} \\
&= \frac{E[X] - E[X; d]}{1 - F_X(d)} \, ,
\end{aligned}
\tag{5.5}
$$

where d is the deductible. This expression is the expected loss less the expected amount eliminated by the deductible conditioned on losses which exceed the deductible.

If the frequency of a loss (prior to imposing the deductible) is p, then with a deductible of d the frequency will be $p[1 - F_X(d)]$. The new pure premium will be frequency times severity:

$$
\frac{p(1 - F_X(d))(E[X] - E[X; d])}{1 - F_X(d)} = p(E[X] - E[X; d]). \tag{5.6}
$$

The pure premium for policies with a deductible of d would then be $(E[X] - E[X; d])/E[X]$ as a percentage of $pE[X]$, the pure premium with no deductible.

This ratio is also called the *excess pure premium ratio*. It is used in Worker's Compensation Insurance where d is viewed not as a deductible but as a policy limit. In this setting it is the relative part of the pure premium which is not paid due to the policy limit. Writing the ratio as $1 - E[X; d]/E[X]$ we see that it is also one minus the loss elimination ratio (LER), as discussed in Section 4.1.

Finally, if the deductible is to be raised from d to d', the new pure premium as a percentage of the old one is, for the fitted and empirical distributions respectively,

$$
(E[X] - E[X; d'])/(E[X] - E[X; d]) \tag{5.7}
$$

and

$$
(\bar{X} - E_n[X; d'])/(\bar{X} - E_n[X; d]) \, .
$$

Each of the two formulas has advantages. The empirical distribution uses only the data, and as such best represents the observations. In addition, $\bar{X}$ always exists while $E[X]$ may not (as was the case for the LTD model in Section 4.4). One method of dealing with the nonexistence of $E[X]$ is to replace it by $E[X; m]$, where m is a suitably large number. On the other hand, as pointed out in Section 1.4, the data may not accurately represent the loss process. In addition, exact computation of $\bar{X}$ and $E_n[X; d]$ requires all of the data values. If, for grouped data, only the number in each class is available, the class means would have to be estimated. The fitted, continuous model has the advantage of smoothing any irregularities in the data. It allows for the calculation of class averages and factors for deductibles at values not equal to class boundaries. Fitting a distribution also provides extrapolation into the tail. By emphasizing models which produce values of $E[X; d]$ close to $E_n[X; d]$, as was done throughout Chapter 4, the differences in using the two formulas should be small.

We now want to obtain the LERs for the theft loss model when the deductible is raised from 100 to d. We could calculate them as one minus the quantity in (5.7), or we may want to use the values of $E[Y; d]$ given in Table 4.7. From Eq. 4.6, replacing d by 100 and x by d, we have,

$$E[X; d] = (E[Y; d] - 100)[1 - F_X(100)] + E[X; 100]$$

and

$$E[X] = (E[Y] - 100)[1 - F_X(100)] + E[X; 100].$$

Substituting these in Eq. 5.7 and replacing d by 100 and d' by d, and noting that $E[Y; 100] = 100$, gives

$$(E[Y] - E[Y; d])/(E[Y] - 100)$$

as the ratio of the new pure premium to the one with a deductible of 100. Note the similarity to (5.7). The value of $E[Y]$ is given in the last line of Table 4.7. The LER is the complement of the preceding ratio,

$$(E[Y; d] - 100)/(E[Y] - 100). \tag{5.8}$$

To see that this is an LER in the sense of Chapter 1, consider the random variable W introduced earlier. We have, with W based on a hundred-dollar deductible,

$$E[W; d] = E[Y; d + 100] - 100$$

(you are asked to prove this in Exercise 4). The ratio in (5.8) becomes $E[W; d - 100]/E[W]$. Increasing the deductible from 100 to d is therefore the same as instituting a deductible of $d - 100$ in the truncated and shifted distribution, W. The same approach will provide LERs based on the empirical distribution. Here, the distribution of X is not available, but we can use (5.8) with the empirical values in Table 4.7. The LERs under both models for selected deductible levels are presented in Table 5.2.

Table 5.2. Loss Elimination Ratios for Increases in a $100 Deductible—Theft Loss Data

Increased Deductible	Using Empirical d.f.	Using Fitted d.f.
100	0.00000	0.00000
150	0.07050	0.06828
200	0.13525	0.13229
250	0.19137	0.18919
500	0.40863	0.40114

B. Leveraging

We now turn our attention to the leveraging problem introduced at the beginning of this section. The deductible amount is held fixed, but the random variable is changed from X to $Z = (1 + r)X$, and the amount paid by the insurance is changed from $W = Y - d$ to V, where $V = Z - d$, if $Z > d$, and is undefined otherwise.

The frequency after inflation is, using Eq. 5.1,

$$p[1 - F_Z(d)] = p\left[1 - F_X\left(\frac{d}{1+r}\right)\right].$$

Since the d.f. of X is nondecreasing, the frequency is not decreased (most likely increased) when $r > 0$. The severity for V is

$$E[V] = \int_0^\infty z f_V(z)\, dz$$

$$= \int_d^\infty \frac{(z - d)f_Z(z)\, dz}{1 - F_Z(d)}$$

$$= \int_d^\infty \frac{(z - d)f_X[z/(1 + r)]\, dz}{(1 + r)[1 - F_Z(d)]}$$

$$= \int_{d/(1+r)}^{\infty} \frac{[(1+r)x - d]f_X(x)\,dx}{1 - F_Z(d)}$$

$$= \frac{(1+r)\left\{\left(E[X] - \int_0^{d/(1+r)} x f_X(x)\,dx\right) - \frac{d}{1+r}\left[1 - F_X\left(\frac{d}{1+r}\right)\right]\right\}}{1 - F_Z(d)}$$

$$= \frac{(1+r)\left\{E[X] - E\left[X; \frac{d}{1+r}\right]\right\}}{1 - F_Z(d)}.$$

The pure premium after inflation is then

$$p(1+r)\left(E[X] - E\left[X; \frac{d}{1+r}\right]\right).$$

Note that when the random variable is changed from X to $Z = (1+r)X$ and the deductible is raised from d to $(1+r)d$, the pure premium becomes

$$p(1+r)(E[X] - E[X; d]).$$

Keeping the deductible at d must then cause the pure premium to increase by a factor greater than the inflation rate. This is the leveraging effect; pure premiums on policies with a constant deductible increase faster than the rate of inflation.

Calculations of the new pure premium are easily handled for fitted models, although it usually is not possible to do so on an empirical basis. If all policies are sold with a deductible, no losses below the smallest deductible will be observed so it will not be possible to compute $E_n[X; d/(1+r)]$. Even if untruncated observations are available, $d/(1+r)$ is unlikely to be a class boundary, making exact empirical calculations impossible for grouped data.

For the theft loss data with the Burr model, the pure premium will increase, assuming a 10% inflation rate, from $p(738 - 97) = 641p$ to $p(1.1)$ $(738 - 88) = 715p$ where the numbers are obtained from the distribution of X. The relative increase is 11.54%.

Exercises

1. Suppose the loss random variable X has the mixture p.d.f. $f_X(x) = \exp(-2x) + \exp(-x)/2$ for $x > 0$ and 0 elsewhere.

    (a) What is $E[X; d]$?

(b)   What is the pure premium with a deductible of 0.25?

(c)   What will the pure premium be with 5% inflation if the deductible remains at 0.25?

2.   Suppose losses have a Pareto distribution with parameters $\alpha = 1.5$ and $\lambda = 2500$.

(a)   What is the pure premium if the deductible is $50,000? (Note that at this level the coverage is more likely to be called excess insurance if X is the loss on one claim or stop-loss reinsurance if X is the total loss on a policy or group of policies. The term deductible is used only when the amount is small.)

(b)   What is the LER if the retention (the term for the deductible in the reinsurance setting) is increased to $100,000?

3.   Losses have a transformed gamma distribution with parameters $\alpha = 3.7$, $\lambda = 0.14$, and $\tau = 0.27$. The frequency is 0.026. Below are some values of $F_X(x)$ and $E[X; d]$. Use them to compute the following:

(a)   The expected value of X and the pure premium.

(b)   The severity, frequency, and pure premium for a deductible of 250.

(c)   The proportional reduction in the pure premium if a deductible of 250 is instituted.

(d)   The proportional increase in pure premium caused by 10% inflation assuming the deductible remains at 250.

x	$F_X(x)$	$E[X; x]$
227.27	0.30912	183
250.00	0.32470	198
9,090.91	0.93302	1,865
10,000.00	0.94063	1,922
25,000.00	0.98542	2,370
∞	1.00000	2,659

4.   Let Y be a random variable with support (t, b) and let $W = Y - t$. Show that $E[W; d] = E[Y; d + t] - t$. Hint: $F_W(x) = F_Y(x + t)$ for $0 < x < b - t$.

5.   A random sample of 25 losses produced the following values:

5	11	16	57	65	103	112	302	316
343	344	426	430	430	520	576	585	666
691	722	926	1000	1142	1521	2612

(a) Consider only exponential models $f_X(x) = \lambda \exp(-\lambda x)$. Find the maximum likelihood estimate of λ.

(b) Using your estimate from (a), obtain $E[X; x]$ for $x = 100$ and $x = 250$. Compare them to the values of $E_{25}[X; x]$.

(c) What are the LERs for deductibles of 100 and 250? By what fraction can the pure premium be reduced if the deductible is raised from 100 to 250? Compute these for both the fitted and empirical models.

(d) Fix the deductible at 100. If inflation increases losses by 15%, by what percent is the pure premium increased?

6. Show that $E[X; x] = E[X] - [1 - F_X(x)]e(x)$.

5.4. OTHER DEDUCTIBLES, COMPARISONS OF DISTRIBUTIONS

The formulas and illustrations in Section 5.3 dealt with the simplest form of the deductible, which we now call the *straight deductible*. In this section, two forms introduced in Section 1.2 are considered. The first is the *franchise deductible*. Under this agreement, any loss that exceeds the deductible is paid in full. It satisfies one of the major objectives of the straight deductible: the insurer is spared the expense of processing small claims. However, unlike the straight deductible, the franchise deductible does not provide any incentive for the insured to reduce the magnitude of losses. The insured will be more likely to report losses which barely exceed the deductible, or, if possible, to influence losses to exceed the deductible. A compromise is provided by the *disappearing deductible*. With it, the amount paid by the insured is a decreasing function of the total loss with the amount eventually reaching zero. Here the deductible is waived only if it is inconsequential with respect to the total loss.

The second problem addressed in this section concerns comparison of loss distributions. That is, does the distribution of losses (prior to deducting the deductible) differ among policyholders who purchase different levels of deductible? If there is no difference, we can use the model obtained from the experience under one deductible to obtain pure premiums for other levels or types of deductible.

The formulas and methods for solving these problems will be illustrated with the long-term disability models developed in Section 4.4. Although the term deductible is rarely used in the context of disability insurance, it should be clear that the elimination period is another form of the straight deductible. Instead of being measured in dollars, the deductible is the number of months of disability during which no benefits are paid.

A. Other Deductibles

As in Section 5.3, let W be the amount paid by the insurer. The type of deductible determines the relationship between W and X, the total loss caused by the event. For the three types of deductible it is, with W undefined when $X \le d$,

Straight:

$$W = X - d, \qquad X > d$$

Franchise:

$$W = X, \qquad X > d$$

Disappearing:

$$W = \frac{d^*(X - d)}{d^* - d}, \qquad d < X \le d^*$$

$$= X \qquad\qquad X > d^*.$$

For all three deductibles the frequency is $p[1 - F_X(d)]$. For the franchise deductible, W is simply X truncated at d. The d.f. and p.d.f. as given in Section 4.2 are

$$F_W(x) = \frac{F_X(x) - F_X(d)}{1 - F_X(d)}, \qquad x > d$$

and

$$f_W(x) = \frac{f_X(x)}{1 - F_X(d)}, \qquad x > d.$$

The severity with a franchise deductible of d is

$$E[W] = \int_d^\infty x f_W(x)\, dx$$

$$= \int_d^\infty \frac{x f_X(x)\, dx}{1 - F_X(d)}$$

$$= \frac{E[X] - \int_0^d x f_X(x)\, dx}{1 - F_X(d)}$$

$$= \frac{E[X] - E[X; d] + d(1 - F_X(d))}{1 - F_X(d)}$$

$$= d + \frac{E[X] - E[X; d]}{1 - F_X(d)}.$$

The pure premium is then

$$pd[1 - F_X(d)] + p(E[X] - E[X; d]).$$

The first term is the extra cost produced by the franchise deductible. It is the amount (d) of the additional payment times the frequency with which such payments are made. You are asked to perform the same calculations for the disappearing deductible in Exercise 1.

As an illustration, consider the mixture of Pareto distributions used in Section 4.4 to model the number of months of disability. The distribution function for ages 30–39 with a three-month elimination period was found to be

$$F_X(x) = 1 - 0.1[13.389/(13.389 + x)]^{0.056788}$$
$$- 0.9[3.4499/(3.4499 + x)]^{1.2549}. \qquad (5.9)$$

Thus if the deductible is changed from straight to franchise, the expected additional number of months of disability payments per policy is

$$(p)(3)[1 - F_X(3)] = 1.4722p.$$

B. Comparisons

In the past two sections we used data collected from experience on policies with one level or type of deductible to obtain pure premiums for other levels or types of deductible. We cannot, however, be assured that the experience will be unchanged. For example, switching from a straight to a franchise deductible for disability insurance may increase losses beyond the amount predicted. This would happen if insureds who are near recovery at the end of the elimination period "elect" to remain disabled for a short period in order to collect the retroactive payment. Or consider homeowners' theft insurance. Those who purchase policies with larger deductibles may engage in better theft prevention practices since they have more to lose. It is not our purpose to speculate on the cause of such differences. What we desire is a method for detecting the presence of such differences.

There are two ways to phrase the comparison question:

1. Can the observations from the various policies each be considered as a random sample from the same distribution?
2. Can the observations from one policy be considered as a random sample from the model fitted to observations from a different policy?

Discussion of the first question is postponed until Section 5.5. In this section we develop methods for answering the second question. To formalize the second question let $F_{Y*}(y)$ be the d.f. for observations from policy 2 based on the model fitted to experience under policy 1. For example, if policy 1 has a deductible of 100 and policy 2 a deductible of 250, then

$$F_{Y*}(y) = \frac{F_X(y) - F_X(250)}{1 - F_X(250)}, \qquad (5.10)$$

where $F_X(y)$ is the d.f. for untruncated losses based on policy 1. If we let $F_Y(y)$ be the true d.f. for observations from policy 2, then the hypothesis we want to test is

$$H_0: F_Y(y) = F_{Y*}(y).$$

Two standard methods are available. The first is the chi-square goodness-of-fit test (Section 3.6). It uses the Q statistic from Section 4.3, which was defined as

$$Q = \sum_{i=1}^{k} \frac{(O_i - E_i)^2}{E_i},$$

where O_i = observed number of losses in group i (policy 2)
$E_i = n[F_{Y*}(c_{i+1}) - F_{Y*}(c_i)]$, the expected number of losses in group i (model based on policy 1).

The test statistic, Q, has approximately a chi-square distribution with number of degrees of freedom equal to one less than the number of groups. The null hypothesis is rejected if Q exceeds the cutoff point from that chi-square distribution using the selected significance level, α. Equivalently, the p-value is the probability that a chi-square random variable takes on a value greater than or equal to the observed Q; the hypothesis is rejected if the p-value is less than α.

For the LTD data, the mixture of Pareto distributions was the fitted model for the three-month elimination period. We want to test the hypothesis that this distribution also models experience under the six-month elimination period. In Table 5.3, values of $F_n(y)$ (taken from Table 4.9) and $F_{Y*}(y)$ [from Eq. 5.10 with 6 replacing 250 and $F_X(y)$ from Eq. 5.9] are presented for selected durations. In Figure 5.1 we plotted the six-month data from Table 4.9 and $F_{Y*}(y)$ truncated at six months. It is evident from both Table 5.3 and Figure 5.1 that the model based on the three-month data is not appropriate for the six-month experience. Values

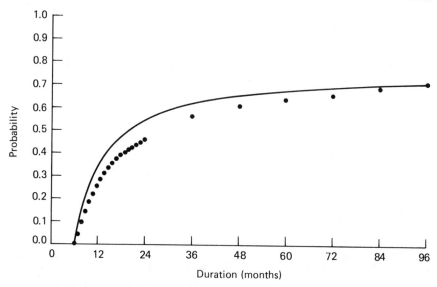

Figure 5.1. Comparison of models—long-term disability (3-month model, 6-month data).

of E_i and O_i based on $n = 1765$ are also given. The final column of Table 5.3 is used in the second testing procedure. The value of Q for this example is

$$Q = (258 - 377)^2/377 + \cdots + (514 - 511)^2/511$$

$$= 136 .$$

Table 5.3. Observed and Fitted Distributions—LTD Data

y	Six-Month Data—Observed		Three-Month Data—Truncated at Six Months		Six-Month Data
	$F_n(y)$	O_i	$F_Y(y)$	E_i	$F_Y(y)$
6	0.00000	258	0.00000	377	0.00000
9	0.14591	194	0.21339	217	0.15154
12	0.25563	238	0.33657	238	0.25213
18	0.39068	124	0.47132	126	0.37944
24	0.46102	177	0.54269	130	0.45806
36	0.56132	82	0.61613	66	0.55209
48	0.60800	53	0.65341	40	0.60763
60	0.63791	125	0.67595	60	0.64494
96	0.70888	514	0.71025	511	0.70926

With eight degrees of freedom, the p-value is less than 0.0001. This is clear evidence that experience under the six-month elimination period was different from that for the three-month period.

The second method of testing this hypothesis is a likelihood ratio test. Once again the null hypothesis gives a specific d.f. as the model for the loss distribution. The alternative hypothesis is that the correct model is some other member of the same family as the one used in H_0. The test statistic is

$$-2 \ln \lambda = 2(\ln L_1 - \ln L_0)$$

where L_0 is the likelihood function for the data evaluated at the parameters given by the null hypothesis and L_1 is obtained by finding the maximum likelihood estimates and evaluating the likelihood function at these values. As indicated in Section 3.5, with the sample size increasing to infinity, the distribution of the test statistic converges to a chi-square distribution. If H_0 is completely specified, as it is in this example, the number of degrees of freedom is equal to the number of estimated parameters. The primary difference between this and the chi-square test is that the alternative hypothesis in the likelihood ratio test includes only members of a particular family of distributions. The chi-square test has an alternative which contains all models.

For the LTD example, the null hypothesis is that the correct model is the truncated mixture of Pareto distributions. The logarithm of the likelihood function is obtained from Eq. 4.9 for the case of grouped, truncated observations. The value of $\ln L_0$ for the mixture of Pareto distributions is -4892.2. The next step is to estimate the four parameters of the mixture of Paretos (we retain the mixing proportion of 0.1). The maximum likelihood estimates are $\hat{\alpha}_1 = 0.098543$, $\hat{\lambda}_1 = 7.2517$, $\hat{\alpha}_2 = 0.73951$, and $\hat{\lambda}_2 = 3.7913$. The d.f. is given in the last column of Table 5.3. The loglikelihood value, $\ln L_1$, is -4833.0 and the test statistic is $2[-4833.0 - (-4892.2)] = 118.4$. The probability that a chi-square variable with four degrees of freedom exceeds this value is less than 0.0001. Once again, the three-month model is rejected.

Restricting the alternative hypothesis to mixtures of Paretos can lead to a problem. It may be that no mixture of Paretos adequately models the observations. In this case the null hypothesis may be accepted when it should be rejected. To prevent this, we should check that the distribution used in the computation of $\ln L_1$ provides a good model for the data. For the LTD data, it is clear from Table 5.3 that the model selected from H_1 does provide a good fit.

Exercises

1. For a disappearing deductible with breaks at d and d^* find the severity and the pure premium.

2. Consider the empirical and fitted models developed in Exercise 5 of Section 5.3. What is the LER for a franchise deductible of 100? What is it for a disappearing deductible with breaks at 100 and 1000? Compute these LERs for both the empirical and fitted models.

3. Consider, in general, a policy with a franchise deductible of d.
   (a) If inflation multiplies all losses by $1 + r$, what is the new pure premium?
   (b) Using the model from Exercise 2 and a franchise deductible of 100, by what percent will the pure premium increase if losses are inflated by 15%?

4. Suppose the sample in Exercise 5 of Section 5.3 was from policies sold in one state and that a second sample, with 20 observations, was collected from a second state. The values from this sample are

$$
\begin{array}{ccccccc}
7 & 14 & 58 & 70 & 82 & 131 & 153 \\
163 & 185 & 231 & 242 & 399 & 401 & 592 \\
614 & 698 & 1059 & 1124 & 1322 & 1656 &
\end{array}
$$

   (a) Test the hypothesis that the above sample is from the model fitted in Exercise 5. Use the chi-square procedure with class boundaries at 250, 500, 750, and 1000.
   (b) Use the likelihood ratio test to determine whether the two samples may be considered to be from the same exponential distribution.
   (c) Assume that you have accepted the hypothesis that the two samples are from the same exponential model. What is the ml estimate of that model?

5. Consider an LTD policy which provides one dollar per year beginning at the sixth month of disability and continuing until death, recovery, or the tenth payment. Compute the present value of this benefit as of the time of the first payment and conditioned upon this payment being made. Use the mixture of Pareto distributions developed in Section 4.4. The present value is $\sum_{t=0}^{9} v^t \Pr$ (payment is made at time t).

6. You have observed 2500 losses and have decided that the empirical d.f.
    provides a satisfactory model for losses up to $2000. For losses beyond
    $2000 a shifted Pareto model is to be used. The following steps will
    produce such a model:

    1. Subtract 2000 from each observation above 2000.
    2. Compute the first and second sample moments.
    3. Use the method of moments to estimate the Pareto parameters (see
        the appendix).
    4. Construct the model d.f. for $x > 2000$ as

    $$F_X(x) = F(x - 2000)[1 - F_n(2000)] + F_n(2000),$$

    where $F(\cdot)$ is the Pareto d.f. found in step 3.

    The relevant data are: $F_n(2000) = 0.7876$, first moment $= 9526$, and
    second moment $= 1,898,876,000$.

    (a) Estimate α and λ.

    (b) Verify that the formula given in step 4 provides a shifted Pareto
         distribution that is adjusted to blend in with the empirical d.f.

    (c) Given the following values from the empirical d.f., graph the
         model d.f. from 0 to 4000. Does the transition from $F_n(x)$ to
         $F_X(x)$ appear to be smooth?

x	$F_n(x)$
250	0.4168
500	0.5504
750	0.6252
1000	0.6712
1250	0.7140
1500	0.7400
1750	0.7652
2000	0.7876

5.5. LIMITS, COMPARISONS OF DISTRIBUTIONS

In addition to the deductible, there is another common coverage
modification, one that affects severity but not frequency. It is the *limitation of liability*, or more simply, *policy limit*. The insurance contract limits
the amount that will be paid to a specified number of dollars. In the first

part of this section we obtain pure premiums for such policies and the factors to be applied when increasing the limit.

The second part of this section is a continuation of the discussion of the comparison of distributions. A procedure for multiple comparisons, an extension of the likelihood ratio test developed in Section 5.4, is introduced.

This is illustrated with examples taken from the automobile bodily injury experience studied in Section 4.5. Although several models were seen to provide a good fit, we use the Burr distribution with parameters estimated by maximum likelihood to construct the illustrations.

A. Limits

Let u be the policy limit as given by the insurance contract. The amount, Y, paid by the insurance when the actual loss is X is given by

$$Y = X, \qquad X \le u$$
$$= u, \qquad X > u.$$

The severity is

$$E[Y] = \int_0^u x f_X(x)\, dx + u[1 - F_X(u)] = E[X; u] . \qquad (5.11)$$

The pure premium is then found by multiplying the severity, $E[X; u]$, by p, the frequency. Another view is that the losses eliminated are $E[X] - E[X; u]$, and so the LER for a limit of u is

$$\text{LER} = (E[X] - E[X; u])/E[X]$$
$$= 1 - E[X; u]/E[X] .$$

This, then, is another application of the limited expected value function. Its usefulness as the basic tool for obtaining pure premiums should be apparent by now. It affirms our insistence, as stressed in Chapter 4, upon finding models for which the limited expected value function closely agrees with the empirical function.

As an example, consider the Burr distributions fitted to the automobile data in Section 4.5. In Table 5.4 several values of $E[X; u]$ are presented for the distributions. The first column uses the model fitted to the combined sample. The second uses the model fitted to data obtained only from policies with a limit of u.

Table 5.4. Limited Expected Values—Automobile Bodily Injury

	$E[X; u]$	
u	Combined Data	Individual Data
5,000	1,727	1,400
10,000	2,373	1,973
25,000	3,275	2,837
50,000	3,931	3,493
100,000	4,528	5,082

Suppose a company's basic policy carries a limit of $10,000. Premiums for policies with higher limits are usually obtained by multiplying the basic limit premium by a constant referred to as the *increased limits factor* (ILF). In terms of pure premiums, if the basic limit is u and the increased limit is u', the ILF is

$$E[X; u']/E[X; u] .$$

There is one remaining problem. It is not clear which models should be used for the limited expected values. If increasing the limit does not affect the experience, then the appropriate model is found by combining the data. Such a combination has the advantage of using the largest possible volume of data. On the other hand, if experience differs, then each limited expected value should be based only upon data from that limit. Under these two approaches, the ILFs for a limit of $25,000 (using Table 5.4) are 1.38 and 1.44 respectively. In the second part of this section a statistical test which helps resolve this question is presented.

If the combined data are used, one of the advantages of using fitted models is realized. With empirical functions, it is not possible to use observations from policies with limits below u to obtain information about the severity on policies with a limit of u. The fitted model provides extrapolation beyond the individual policy limit. Additional discussion is provided in Lange (1969) and Miccolis (1977).

The presence of a limit has a moderating effect when losses are increased due to inflation. Events which formerly produced losses below the limit may, after inflation, produce losses above it. It appears that the pure premium will not increase as much as the inflation rate.

If X is the loss prior to inflation and $Z = (1 + r)X$ is the loss after inflation, the new severity is, using Eqs. 5.1 and 5.2,

$$\int_0^u z\,f_Z(z)\,dz + u[1 - F_Z(u)]$$

$$= \int_0^u z\,\frac{f_X[z/(1+r)]\,dz}{1+r} + u\left[1 - F_X\left(\frac{u}{1+r}\right)\right]$$

$$= (1+r)\int_0^{u/(1+r)} x\,f_X(x)\,dx + u\left[1 - F_X\left(\frac{u}{1+r}\right)\right] \qquad (5.12)$$

$$= (1+r)\left\{\int_0^{u/(1+r)} x\,f_X(x)\,dx + \frac{u}{1+r}\left[1 - F_X\left(\frac{u}{1+r}\right)\right]\right\}$$

$$= (1+r)\,E\left[X;\frac{u}{1+r}\right]$$

Suppose, along with inflation at rate r, the limit was raised to $u' = u(1+r)$. The new severity would then be (substituting u' for u in Eq. 5.12)

$$E\,[Z;u'] = (1+r)\,E\left[X;\frac{u'}{1+r}\right]$$

$$= (1+r)\,E[x;u].$$

Therefore, raising the limit to "keep up" with inflation produces a new pure premium (note that the frequency is not affected by any of these changes, so proportional changes in severity produce the same changes in the pure premium which is equal to the old pure premium increased by the inflation rate. Since the unadjusted pure premium based on the severity given in Eq. 5.12 is smaller, the effect of inflation is reduced when the limit is not adjusted.

For the combined automobile data and a limit of \$25,000 we have $E[X; 25,000] = 3275$. With 10% inflation we also need $E[X; 22,727] = 3182$. If the limit is unchanged the new severity is 3500, an increase of 6.87%. If the limit is increased to 27,500, the new severity is 3602.5, an increase of exactly 10%. This is also referred to as leveraging but the effect is in the opposite direction of the leveraging experienced in Section 5.3 when applying inflation to a deductible.

We close this part by noting that it is possible for a policy to have both a limit and a deductible. While it is unusual for automobile bodily injury policies to contain both restrictions, it is common for collision coverage (the upper limit being the value of the automobile). Disability insurance often has a deductible (elimination period) and a limit (age 60 or 65 for long-term disability). If the deductible is d and the limit is u, the pure premium is p times

$$\int_d^u (x - d)f_X(x)\, dx + (u - d)[1 - F_X(u)]$$

$$= \int_0^u xf_X(x)\, dx - \int_0^d xf_X(x)\, dx - d[F_X(u) - F_X(d)]$$

$$+ (u - d)[1 - F_X(u)]$$

$$= \int_0^u xf_X(x)\, dx + u[1 - F_X(u)] - \int_0^d xf_X(x)\, dx$$

$$- d[1 - F_X(d)]$$

$$= E[X; u] - E[X; d]$$

(5.13)

with the frequency being $p[1 - F_X(d)]$. This was referred to in Section 1.3 as a layer of insurance. The relative value is obtained by dividing by $pE[X]$, the pure premium for the policy with no restrictions. In Exercise 1 you are asked to evaluate the effect of inflation on this pure premium. In this setting the pure premium may increase by more or less than the rate of inflation.

B. Comparisons

In the previous section, methods of comparing two distributions were presented. Here we want to extend the problem to the case of multiple comparisons. The null hypothesis is that each of the k samples was obtained from the same probability distribution. The alternative is that at least one of the samples is from a distribution which differs from the others. The likelihood ratio procedure discussed in Section 3.5 is appropriate for conducting this test.

Under the alternative hypothesis, each sample is treated separately. Individual maximum likelihood estimates are obtained and the negative loglikelihoods are computed. The value of $-\ln L_1$ is obtained by adding the individual negative loglikelihoods. Under the null hypothesis a common model is used. A procedure for maximum likelihood estimation from a combined sample was presented in Section 4.5 and the loglikelihood which results is $-\ln L_0$. As in Section 5.4, the test statistic,

$$- 2 \ln \lambda = 2(\ln L_1 - \ln L_0),$$

has an asymptotic chi-square distribution with $(k - 1)m$ degrees of freedom, where k is the number of populations being compared and m is the number of parameters in the model.

For the automobile bodily injury data with the Burr model, we have $-\ln L_0 = 61{,}277$ (see Section 4.5) and $-\ln L_1 = 7132.5 + 2617.9 + 4851.4 + 7085.7 + 39{,}455 = 61{,}142.5$ (see Table 4.14). The value of $-2 \ln \lambda$ is $2(-61{,}142.5 + 61{,}277) = 269$. With $(5 - 1)3 = 12$ degrees of freedom, this is clearly a significant result and the null hypothesis is rejected. Had we used the lognormal model, the results would have been similar: $-2 \ln \lambda = 171.8$ with 8 degrees of freedom. One drawback of this method is that attention must be restricted to a particular parametric model. For the results to be meaningful, a model that provides a reasonable fit must be selected.

Another method of constructing a comparison focuses on the limited expected values. If u^* is the lowest limit from the k samples, we could compare the k values of $E_n[X; u^*]$. Each of these is a sample mean from a distribution censored at u^*. As such, an analysis of variance procedure is a reasonable method (although the sample is not from a normal distribution) of testing whether or not the k censored populations have the same mean. If they do, the data can be combined for the purpose of setting basic limit pure premiums. It might then be reasonable to combine the data at all levels. This approach is likely to be unreliable for grouped data. Analysis of variance requires calculation of the sample variances for each sample. The best we can do with grouped data is to replace each observation with its class mean.

Returning to the automobile example, we find that the rejection of the null hypothesis has considerable consequences for the development of pure premiums. It appears that experience is sufficiently different under differing limits to warrant use of experience under only the limit in question when developing pure premiums.

Exercises

1. Consider a policy with deductible d and limit u. If inflation increases losses by a factor of r, what is the new pure premium?

2. For the empirical and fitted models in Exercise 5 of Section 5.3:
   (a) Find $E[X; 1000]$ and $E[X; 2000]$.
   (b) Obtain the ILFs for increasing the limit from 1000 to 2000.
   (c) What is the relative value of the layer from 100 to 1000?
   (d) What is the effect on the pure premium of 15% inflation if the policy has no deductible and a limit of 1000?
   (e) Do part (d) with the addition of a deductible of 100.

3. Consider a third state to add to the two states presented in Exercise 5 of Section 5.3 and Exercise 4 of Section 5.4. The observations, from a sample of size 15, are

$$
\begin{array}{ccccccc}
1 & 2 & 3 & 12 & 23 & 25 & 36 \quad 43 \\
45 & 162 & 177 & 251 & 577 & 972 & 4585
\end{array}
$$

(a) Use the likelihood ratio test to determine if all three samples are from the same exponential distribution.

(b) Suppose a common exponential model is used for all three states. Further assume that the frequency for these observations is 0.1 for each state. Use the common model to obtain the new frequency, severity, and pure premium for a deductible of 250. Compare these figures to the empirical frequency, severity, and pure premiums obtained from each of the three individual samples. Do these comparisons support the conclusion from part (a)?

(c) Repeat part (b) replacing the deductible by a limit of 1000.

4. Use the data in Table 4.13 on policies with a $5000 limit to find the ml estimates for a Pareto distribution. Do this by the iterative method described in Section 4.3. Use the resulting information matrix to provide a 90% confidence interval for the probability a loss exceeds $5000 (this is the problem illustrated in Section 5.2). A reasonable pair of starting values is $\alpha = 0.725$ and $\lambda = 360$. You may want to reduce your calculations by eliminating the values at 3000 and 4000.

5.6. LIMITS, LAYERS, ALLOCATED LOSS ADJUSTMENT EXPENSES

In this section we take a final look at the effects of policy limits and develop further the concept of a *layer of coverage*. Layers are generally associated with reinsurance agreements, where the primary insurer assigns part of the coverage to the reinsurer. This enables several companies to share the risk and makes it possible for insurance to be offered on high-risk coverages such as professional liability.

In addition, we continue the discussion of allocated loss adjustment expenses initiated in Section 4.6. Our objective is to determine pure premiums which cover both the actual losses and the ALAE. Both topics will be illustrated with the hospital professional liability loss model developed in Section 4.6.

A. Limits and Layers

Suppose an applicant desires liability coverage with a $5 million limit. A primary insurer (company 1) offers to cover all claims up to 500,000. Insurance company 2 (a reinsurer) then takes the layer from 500,000 to 1,000,000. This means that if x is the loss, company 2 pays

$$0 \quad \text{if} \quad x \leq 500,000,$$
$$x - 500,000 \quad \text{if} \quad 500,000 < x \leq 1,000,000$$

and

$$500,000 \quad \text{if} \quad x > 1,000,000.$$

The contract is completed by insurer 3 taking the layer from 1,000,000 to 5,000,000. We want to determine the pure premium for the total coverage and how it is to be divided among the three insurers. From Section 5.5 we have that the pure premium for coverage up to a limit of 5,000,000 is equal to $E[X; 5,000,000]p$ where p is the expected number of claims. The pure premium for the layer from d to u is given (from Eq. 5.13) by p times

$$E[X; u] - E[X; d].$$

We must keep in mind that the split between frequency and severity is not obtained just by separating the value of p. The frequency for the layer from d to u is $(1 - F_X(d))p$, the expected number of claims which result in a payment made by the insurer covering this layer. The severity is then obtained by dividing the pure premium by the frequency:

$$\frac{E[X; u] - E[X; d]}{1 - F_X(d)}.$$

For the hospital professional liability data in Section 4.6, the best model for the losses was provided by a Burr distribution with parameters $\alpha = 2.2878$, $\lambda = 1502.2$, and $\tau = 0.71744$. In Table 5.5 values of the limited expected value function are presented for this Burr distribution.

So, for the above example, the pure premium is $21,904p$ for the primary insurer, $(23,301 - 21,904)p = 1397p$ for insurer 2, and $(25,025 - 23,301)p = 1724p$ for insurer 3. The frequency for insurer 3 is $(1 - 0.99834)p = 0.00166p$ and the severity is $1724p/0.00166p = 1,038,554$. It is clear, if it was not before, that insurer 3 is taking on a large risk. Payments for losses are made infrequently, but when they are made, they can be very large.

Table 5.5.   Limited Expected Value Function—Hospital Professional Liability

x	$E[X; x]$	$F_X(x)$
100,000	16,343	0.95522
250,000	19,931	0.98677
500,000	21,904	0.99519
750,000	22,783	0.99741
1,000,000	23,301	0.99834
2,000,000	24,249	0.99945
5,000,000	25,025	0.99987
∞	25,993	1.00000

Three remarks are in order at the close of this discussion. First, the term layer usually is used only in a reinsurance context. It covers losses beyond those covered by the primary insurance. It would not refer to the extra coverage provided by an increased limit as illustrated in the previous section. Second, the formulas presented in the previous section for obtaining the leveraging effects of inflation in the presence of a deductible and a limit also apply to a layer of coverage. There is no difference, other than the context in which they are applied. Third, the calculations in this section assume that experience will follow the model. This may not be the case as the data used were only from policies with a $1 million limit. We cannot be certain that the same experience will represent those who purchase a $5 million limit. Analyses like those discussed in Sections 5.4 and 5.5 would be appropriate.

B.   Allocated Loss Adjustment Expenses

We now turn to the impact of the allocated loss adjustment expenses (ALAE) on the pure premium. In Section 4.6 we modeled the ALAE by a lognormal distribution with the first parameter (the mean of the corresponding normal distribution) depending on the size of the loss. The additional premium and its allocation among the various insurers depends on the nature of the contract. In general, let the layers be broken at $0 = u_0 < u_1 < u_2 < \cdots < u_k$. The primary insurer covers all losses up to u_1, while the final reinsurer takes the layer from u_{k-1} to u_k. If y is the total ALAE, there are two (among many) methods of distributing it among the insurers. First, the primary insurer pays all of y. Second, y could be allocated in proportion to the amount paid on the loss by each carrier. Thus, if the loss, x, is between u_{j-1} and u_j, then insurer i (the one covering the layer from u_{i-1} to u_i) pays,

$$(u_i - u_{i-1})y/x \quad \text{if} \quad i < j,$$

$$(x - u_{i-1})y/x \quad \text{if} \quad i = j,$$

and

$$0 \quad \text{if} \quad i > j.$$

If the loss exceeds u_k, the ith insurer will pay $(u_i - u_{i-1})y/u_k$.

We need one more specification to complete the model. We have no information about the ALAE for losses which reach or exceed the uppermost limit, u_k, of coverage. Are they related to the actual loss, x, or to u_k? We select, with no data to provide support, the second option. We are assuming that once the loss reaches the upper limit no additional effort or expenditure is made with respect to the settlement process.

From the joint distribution developed in Section 4.6 we have the following expression for the expected ALAE:

$$E[Y] = \int_0^\infty \int_0^{u_k} yg(y|x)f_X(x)\,dx\,dy + \left[\int_0^\infty yg(y|u_k)\,dy\right][1 - F_X(u_k)]$$

$$= \int_0^{u_k} f_X(x) \int_0^\infty yg(y|x)\,dy\,dx + E[Y|X = u_k][1 - F_X(u_k)] \qquad (5.14)$$

$$= \int_0^{u_k} f_X(x)E[Y|X = x]\,dx + E[Y|X = u_k][1 - F_X(u_k)].$$

From model III in that section we have

$$E[Y|X = x] = \exp\left(a_3 + \frac{\sigma^2}{2}\right)x^{b_3}.$$

We then have

$$E[Y] = \exp\left(a_3 + \frac{\sigma^2}{2}\right)\left\{\int_0^{u_k} x^{b_3}f_X(x)\,dx + u_k^{b_3}[1 - F_X(u_k)]\right\}$$

$$= \exp\left(a_3 + \frac{\sigma^2}{2}\right)E[X^{b_3}; u_k],$$

a generalization of the limited expected value. If X has a Burr distribution, the limited expected value function for X^b is

$$E[X^b; u] = \int_0^u x^b \alpha \lambda^\alpha \tau x^{\tau-1}(\lambda + x^\tau)^{-\alpha-1}\,dx + u^b \lambda^\alpha (\lambda + u^\tau)^{-\alpha}.$$

Using the transformation $y = x^\tau/(\lambda + x^\tau)$ in the integral and then substituting γb for τ in both terms produces

$$E[X^b; u] = \alpha\lambda^{1/\gamma} \int_0^q y^{1/\gamma}(1-y)^{\alpha-1-1/\gamma} \, dy + (c^b)^{\gamma}\lambda^{\alpha}(\lambda + (c^b)^{\gamma})^{-\alpha}.$$

$$= E[Z; u^b],$$

where

$$q = (c^b)^{\gamma}/[\lambda + (c^b)^{\gamma}],$$

and where Z has a Burr distribution with parameters α, λ, and γ (see the appendix). In particular, for the model developed in Section 4.6 with $u_3 = 5,000,000$ we have

$$E[Y] = \exp(2.4135 + 2.3235/2)E[Z; 5,000,000^{0.52472}]$$

$$= 35.704(137.08)$$

$$= 4894,$$

where Z has a Burr distribution with parameters $\alpha = 2.2878$, $\lambda = 1502.2$, and $\gamma = 0.72744/0.52472 = 1.3863$.

Now consider the second method of allocating the ALAE among the insurers. For the ith insurer (taking the layer from u_{i-1} to u_i), if the loss is x, the share, y_i, of the total ALAE, y, is

$$
\begin{aligned}
y_i &= 0, & x &\le u_{i-1}, \\
&= (x - u_{i-1})y/x, & u_{i-1} &< x \le u_i, \\
&= (u_i - u_{i-1})y/x, & u_i &< x \le u_k, \\
&= (u_i - u_{i-1})y/u_k, & x &> u_k.
\end{aligned}
$$

Therefore, with $r_i = u_i - u_{i-1}$,

$$E[Y_i] = \int_0^{\infty} \int_{u_{i-1}}^{u_i} \frac{(x - u_{i-1})y}{x} g(y|x)f_X(x) \, dx \, dy$$

$$+ \int_0^{\infty} \int_{u_i}^{u_k} \frac{r_i y}{x} g(y|x)f_X(x) \, dx \, dy$$

$$+ \left[\int_0^{\infty} \frac{r_i y}{u_k} g(y|u_k) \, dy \right][1 - F_X(u_k)]$$

$$= \int_{u_{i-1}}^{u_i} E\left[\frac{x - u_{i-1}}{x} Y | X = x \right] f_X(x) \, dx$$

$$+ r_i \int_{u_i}^{u_k} E\left[\frac{Y}{x} | X = x \right] f_X(x) \, dx$$

$$+ \frac{r_i}{u_k} E[Y|X = u_k][1 - F_X(u_k)].$$

Again using model III from Section 4.6, we have

$$E\left[\frac{x - u_{i-1}}{x} Y | X = x\right] = \frac{x - u_{i-1}}{x} \exp\left(a_3 + \frac{\sigma^2}{2}\right) x^{b_3},$$

$$E\left[\frac{Y}{x} | X = x\right] = \frac{1}{x} \exp\left(a_3 + \frac{\sigma^2}{2}\right) x^{b_3} = \exp\left(a_3 + \frac{\sigma^2}{2}\right) x^{b_3 - 1},$$

and

$$E[Y | X = u_k] = \exp\left(a_3 + \frac{\sigma^2}{2}\right) u_k^{b_3}.$$

Using these in the previous equation gives

$$E[Y_i] = \exp\left(a_3 + \frac{\sigma^2}{2}\right) \left\{ \int_{u_{i-1}}^{u_i} (x^{b_3} - u_{i-1} x^{b_3 - 1}) f_X(x)\, dx \right.$$

$$\left. + r_i \int_{u_i}^{u_k} x^{b_3 - 1} f_X(x)\, dx + r_i u_k^{b_3 - 1} [1 - F_X(u_k)] \right\}.$$

Recall that, in general,

$$\int_a^b h(x) f_X(x)\, dx = \int_0^b h(x) f_X(x)\, dx - \int_0^a h(x) f_X(x)\, dx$$

$$= E[h(X); b] - h(b)[1 - F_X(b)]$$

$$- E[h(X); a] + h(a)[1 - F_X(a)].$$

Thus,

$$\exp\left(-\mu - \frac{\sigma^2}{2}\right) E[Y_i] = E[X^{b_3}; u_i] - E[X^{b_3}; u_{i-1}] - u_i^{b_3}[1 - F_X(u_i)]$$

$$+ u_{i-1}^{b_3}[1 - F_X(u_{i-1})] - u_{i-1} E[X^{b_3 - 1}; u_i] + u_{i-1} E[X^{b_3 - 1}; u_{i-1}]$$

$$+ u_{i-1} u_i^{b_3 - 1}[1 - F_X(u_{i-1})] - u_{i-1}^{b_3}[1 - F_X(u_{i-1})] + r_i E[X^{b_3 - 1}; u_k]$$

$$- r_i E[X^{b_3 - 1}; u_i] - r_i u_k^{b_3 - 1}[1 - F_X(u_k)] + r_i u_i^{b_3 - 1}[1 - F_X(u_i)]$$

$$+ r_i u_k^{b_3 - 1}[1 - F_X(u_k)].$$

After considerable canceling and rearranging, we are left with

$$\exp\left(-\mu - \frac{\sigma^2}{2}\right) E[Y_i] = E[X^{b_3}; u_i] - E[X^{b_3}; u_{i-1}] + u_{i-1} E[X^{b_3 - 1}; u_{i-1}]$$

$$- u_i E[X^{b_3 - 1}; u_i] + r_i E[X^{b_3 - 1}; u_k].$$

In our example, insurer 2 (who has the layer from 500,000 to 1,000,000) will have an expected ALAE equal to

$$35.704\{E[Z_1; 1,000,000^{0.52472}] - E[Z_1; 500,000^{0.52472}]$$
$$+ 500,000E[Z_2; 500,000^{-0.47528}] - 1,000,000E[Z_2; 1,000,000^{-0.47528}]$$
$$+ 500,000E[Z_2; 5,000,000^{-0.47528}]\},$$

where Z_1 has a Burr distribution with parameters 2.2878, 1502.2, and 1.3863, and Z_2 has a Burr distribution with parameters 2.2878, 1502.2, and $0.72744/(-0.47528) = -1.5306$. When the third Burr parameter (τ) is negative, the Burr d.f. is no longer a legitimate distribution function; as x goes from 0 to infinity, $F_X(x)$ decreases from 1 to 0. However, all we are interested in here is the evaluation of the limited expected value function. It can be defined for any function $F(x)$, whether or not it is a d.f. as

$$\int_0^d xf(x)\, dx + d[1 - F(d)],$$

provided $F(x)$ has a derivative, $f(x)$, and the integral exists. This will be the case if the third Burr parameter is less than -1 (or, of course, if it is positive). Evaluation of the limited expected values, and of the corresponding quantities for the other two insurers (note that for the primary insurer, $u_0 = 0$ and the corresponding limited expected values are zero) produces

Insurer	Layer	Frequency	Expected Loss	Expected ALAE	Pure Premium
1	0–500,000	p	21,904	4,798	26,702p
2	500,000–1,000,000	0.00481p	1,397	62	1,459p
3	1,000,000–5,000,000	0.00166p	1,724	34	1,758p
			25,025	4,894	29,919p

One part of the loss process has been ignored up to this point. Recall that in Table 4.17 there were 1856 claims which were settled for zero loss. Nevertheless, these claims had ALAEs averaging 1030. This portion of the ALAE must also be included in the pure premium. The frequency of this extra cost is estimated as $(1856/1132)p = 1.6396p$ where 1132 was the number of nonzero losses. The total pure premium is then $29,919p + (1030)(1.6396p) = 31,608p$. If the primary insurer is absorbing all of the ALAE, the entire amount of this increase will be assigned to its pure premium. If ALAE is allocated it may be reasonable to allocate this portion of it on the basis of the remainder of the pure premium. For insurer 2 this share is $(1459/29,919)(1030)(1.6396p) = 82p$ to bring the final pure premium up to $1541p$. For insurers 1 and 3 it is $28,209p$ and $1857p$ respectively.

We have no information about the distribution of the ALAE for claims settled for no payment. It would not be appropriate to use the regression model at $x = 0$ since these ALAEs are from a broad spectrum of cases, some of which would have produced large losses had the decision been different. The anticipation of a favorable settlement may encourage even greater expenditures. On the other hand, many cases are routinely opened at the first hint of a possible loss (e.g., an investigation by the hospital of a surgical procedure) even though a claim is not likely to be filed. These situations produce little, if any, ALAE. The number of factors influencing this distribution are just too many to allow us to speculate on a model. More information must be made available if we are to complete this part of the loss distribution.

We close this chapter by repeating the qualifications mentioned throughout the last two chapters. While all the data used were from actual experience, we do not claim that any of the numerical results are appropriate for use by an insurer. Many of the results were obtained by making assumptions that would have to be verified, while others are based on industry-wide figures which would have to be modified to reflect the potential experience of a specific company. Finally, of course, all of the data were collected from past experience. They would have to be trended if the objective is to model future losses. This topic is beyond the scope of this book.

Exercises

1. Consider a lognormal model with $\mu = 9$ and $\sigma = 2$. Suppose the frequency is 2.5. The insured retains all losses up to 200,000 and then purchases excess insurance from Company A which covers losses from 200,000 to 5,000,000. In turn, Company A purchases reinsurance from company B to cover the layer from 2,000,000 to 5,000,000.

   (a) What is the expected amount of losses to be paid by the insured?
   (b) What are the frequency, severity, and pure premium for the coverage retained by insurer A? Repeat for reinsurer B.
   (c) Repeat parts (a) and (b) with inflation increasing all losses by 15%.

2. Consider the following model for losses plus ALAE. The loss, X, has an exponential distribution with the parameter equal to 0.002 (recall

that this is a Weibull distribution with $c = 0.002$ and $\tau = 1$). If $X = x$, the ALAE, Y, also has an exponential distribution. The parameter is $0.1/\sqrt{x}$.

(a) What are $E[X]$, $E[Y|X = x]$, $E[Y]$, and $E[S]$, where $S = X + Y$. *Hint*: To obtain $E[Y]$ use Eq. 5.14 with the upper limit on x set at infinity. Also, $\Gamma(1.5) = \sqrt{\pi}/2$.

(b) Suppose three insurers are covering the losses and the ALAE with each paying the ALAE in proportion to their share of the loss. The limits are $u_1 = 1000$, $u_2 = 2000$, and $u_3 = \infty$. Find the pure premium for each insurer. Express your answer in terms of incomplete gamma (see appendix) values.

References

Bohman, H. and Esscher, F. (1963). Studies in Risk Theory with Numerical Illustrations Concerning Distribution Functions and Stop Loss Premiums, Part I. *Skandinavisk Aktuarietidskrif*, **46**, 173–225.

Bohman, H. and Esscher, F. (1964). Studies in Risk Theory with Numerical Illustrations Concerning Distribution Functions and Stop Loss Premiums, Part II. *Skandinavisk Aktuarietidskrif*, **47**, 1–40.

Boos, Dennis D. (1981). Minimum Distance Estimators for Location and Goodness of Fit. *Journal of the American Statistical Association*, **76**, 663–670.

Brown, Kenneth M. and Dennis, J. E. (1972). Derivative Free Analogues of the Levenberg–Marquardt and Gauss Algorithms for Nonlinear Least Squares Approximations. *Numerische Mathematik*, **18**, 289–297.

Burr, Irving W. (1942). Cumulative Frequency Functions. *Annals of Mathematical Statistics*, **13**, 215–232.

Chambers, J. M. (1977). *Computational Methods for Data Analysis*. Wiley, New York.

Cramér, Harald (1946). *Mathematical Methods of Statistics*. Princeton University Press, Princeton.

Hall, W. J. and Wellner, Jon A. (1981). Mean Residual Life. In M. Csörgö, D. A. Dawson, J. N. K. Rao, and A. K. Md. E. Saleh, Eds., *Statistics and Related Topics*. North-Holland Publishing Company, Amsterdam, pp. 169–184.

Herzog, T. N. (1984). An Introduction to Stochastic Simulation. In *Society of Actuaries Part Three Study Note*, Society of Actuaries, Chicago.

Hewitt, Charles C. and Lefkowitz, Benjamin (1979). Methods of Fitting Distributions to Insurance Loss Data. *Proceedings of the Casualty Actuarial Society*, **66**, 139–160.

Hogg, Robert V. and Craig, Allen T. (1978). *Introduction to Mathematical Statistics*, 4th ed. Macmillan, New York.

Hogg, Robert V. and Tanis, Elliot A. (1983). *Probability and Statistical Inference*, 2nd ed. Macmillan, New York.

Huber, Peter J. (1970). Studentizing Robust Estimates. In M. L. Puri, Ed., *Nonparametric Techniques in Statistical Inferences*. Cambridge University Press, London, pp. 453–463.

Kellison, Stephen G. (1975). *Fundamentals of Numerical Analysis*. Richard D. Irwin, Homewood, Ill.

215

Kennedy, W. J. and Gentle, J. E. (1980). *Statistical Computing*. Marcel Dekker, New York.

Lange, Jeffrey T. (1969). The Interpretation of Liability Increased Limits Statistics. *Proceedings of the Casualty Actuarial Society*, **56**, 163–173.

Marquardt, Donald W. (1963). An Algorithm for Least-Squares Estimation of Nonlinear Parameters. *Journal of the Society for Industrial and Applied Mathematics*, **11**, 431–441.

Miccolis, Robert S. (1977). On the Theory of Increased Limits and Excess of Loss Pricing. *Proceedings of the Casualty Actuarial Society*, **64**, 27–59.

Moore, D. S. (1978). Chi-Square Tests. In R. V. Hogg, Ed., *Studies in Statistics*, Vol. 19. Mathematical Association of America, Washington, D.C., pp. 453–463.

Patrik, Gary (1980). Estimating Casualty Insurance Loss Amount Distributions. *Proceedings of the Casualty Actuarial Society*, **68**, 57–109.

Ralston, Mary L. and Jennrich, Robert I. (1978). DUD, A Derivative-Free Algorithm for Nonlinear Least Squares. *Technometrics*, **20**, 7–14.

Rao, C. R. (1965). *Linear Statistical Inference and Its Applications*. Wiley, New York.

Seal, Hilary L. (1977a). Approximations to Risk Theory's $F(x, t)$ by Means of the Gamma Distribution. *ASTIN Bulletin*, **9**, 213–218.

Seal, Hilary L. (1977b). Numerical Inversion of Characteristic Functions. *Scandinavian Actuarial Journal*, **1977**, 48–53.

Sprott, D. A. (1980). Maximum Likelihood and Small Samples: Estimation in the Presence of Nuisance Parameters. *Biometrika*, **67**, 515–523.

Venter, Gary G. (1983). Transformed Beta and Gamma Distributions and Aggregate Losses. *Proceedings of the Casualty Actuarial Society* (to appear).

Von Lanzenauer, Christoph H. and Wright, Don (1977). Multistage Curve Fitting. *ASTIN Bulletin*, **9**, 191–202.

Wald, Abraham (1943). Tests of Statistical Hypotheses Concerning Several Parameters When the Number of Observations Is Large. *Transactions of the American Mathematical Society*, **54**, 426–482.

Weber, Donald C. (1971). Accident Rate Potential: An Application of Multiple Regression Analysis of a Poisson Process. *Journal of the American Statistical Association*, **66**, 285–288.

Wilks, S. S. (1938). The Large-Sample Distribution of the Likelihood Ratio for Testing Composite Hypotheses. *Annals of Mathematical Statistics*, **9**, 60–62.

Wilks, S. S. (1962). *Mathematical Statistics*. Wiley, New York.

APPENDIX

Characteristics, Values, and Estimators for Selected Distributions

The following sections of this appendix contain detailed descriptions and formulas for each of the eight distributions used for obtaining models in Chapters 4 and 5. The following notation is used throughout the appendix.

Distribution function: $F(x)$

Probability density function: $f(x)$

Limited expected value function: $E[X; x] = \int_0^x yf(y)\, dy + x[1 - F(x)]$

Gamma function: $\Gamma(\alpha) = \int_0^\infty x^{\alpha-1}e^{-x}\, dx = (\alpha - 1)\Gamma(\alpha - 1)$

Digamma function: $\psi(\alpha) = d \ln \Gamma(\alpha)/d\alpha = \Gamma'(\alpha)/\Gamma(\alpha)$

Incomplete gamma function: $\Gamma(\alpha; x) = \int_0^x y^{\alpha-1}e^{-y}\, dy/\Gamma(\alpha)$

Incomplete beta function:

$$\beta(a, b; x) = \frac{\Gamma(a + b)}{\Gamma(a)\Gamma(b)} \int_0^x y^{a-1}(1 - y)^{b-1}\, dy = 1 - \beta(b, a; 1 - x) = F\left[\frac{bx}{a(1 - x)}\right]$$

where F is the d.f. for the F distribution with $2a$ and $2b$ degrees of freedom.

217

Normal distribution function: $\Phi(x) = \int_{-\infty}^{x} \exp\left(-\frac{y^2}{2}\right) dy / \sqrt{2\pi}$

Normal density function: $\phi(x) = \exp\left(-\frac{x^2}{2}\right) / \sqrt{2\pi}$

The integrals for the moments and the limited expected value function can be obtained by appropriate substitutions. Two examples are presented below.

1. *Burr Distribution*

$$E[X; x] = \int_{0}^{x} y\alpha\tau\lambda^{\alpha} \frac{y^{\tau-1}}{(\lambda + y^{\tau})^{\alpha+1}} dy + x\left(\frac{\lambda}{\lambda + x^{\tau}}\right)^{\alpha} ;$$

$$z = y\lambda^{-1/\tau}, \qquad y = z\lambda^{1/\tau}, \qquad dy = \lambda^{1/\tau} dz$$

$$= \lambda^{1/\tau}\alpha\tau \int_{0}^{x\lambda^{-1/\tau}} z^{\tau}(1 + z^{\tau})^{-\alpha-1} dz + x\left(\frac{\lambda}{\lambda + x^{\tau}}\right)^{\alpha} ;$$

$$y = (1 + z^{\tau})^{-1}, \qquad z = (y^{-1} - 1)^{1/\tau},$$

$$dz = -\frac{1}{\tau}(y^{-1} - 1)^{1/\tau-1}y^{-2} dy$$

$$= -\lambda^{1/\tau}\alpha \int_{1}^{(1+x^{\tau}/\lambda)^{-1}} (y^{-1} - 1)^{1/\tau}y^{\alpha-1} dy + x\left(\frac{\lambda}{\lambda + x^{\tau}}\right)^{\alpha}$$

$$= \lambda^{1/\tau}\alpha \int_{\lambda/(\lambda+x^{\tau})}^{1} (1 - y)^{1/\tau}y^{\alpha-1/\tau-1} dy + x\left(\frac{\lambda}{\lambda + x^{\tau}}\right)^{\alpha}$$

$$= \lambda^{1/\tau}\alpha \frac{\Gamma(1 + 1/\tau)\Gamma(\alpha - 1/\tau)}{\Gamma(\alpha + 1)}\left[1 - \beta\left(\alpha - \frac{1}{\tau}, 1 + \frac{1}{\tau}; \frac{\lambda}{\lambda + x^{\tau}}\right)\right]$$

$$+ x\left(\frac{\lambda}{\lambda + x^{\tau}}\right)^{\alpha}$$

2. *Weibull Distribution*

$$E[X^{n}] = \int_{0}^{\infty} x^{n}c\tau x^{\tau-1}e^{-cx^{\tau}} dx ; \qquad y = cx^{\tau}, \qquad x = (y/c)^{1/\tau},$$

$$dx = \tau^{-1}y^{1/\tau-1}c^{-1/\tau} dy$$

$$= \int_{0}^{\infty} c^{-n/\tau}y^{n/\tau}e^{-y} dy = c^{-n/\tau}\Gamma\left(1 + \frac{n}{\tau}\right)$$

Approximations for the incomplete gamma and beta functions can be obtained by using a finite number of terms from the following expansions.

$$\Gamma(\alpha; x) = \frac{x^{\alpha} e^{-x}}{\Gamma(\alpha)} \sum_{n=0}^{\infty} \frac{x^n}{\alpha(\alpha + 1) \dots (\alpha + n)}$$

$$\beta(a, b; x) = \frac{\Gamma(a + b)x^a(1 - x)^b}{a\Gamma(a)\Gamma(b)} \left[1 + \sum_{n=0}^{\infty} \frac{\Gamma(a + 1)\Gamma(a + b + n + 1)}{\Gamma(a + b)\Gamma(a + n + 2)} x^{n+1} \right]$$

The four gamma functions in the sum reduce to

$$\frac{(a + b)(a + b + 1) \dots (a + b + n)}{(a + 1)(a + 2) \dots (a + n + 1)} .$$

The gamma function itself may be approximated by

$$\Gamma(\alpha) = (\alpha - 1)(\alpha - 2) \dots (\alpha - k)\Gamma(\alpha - k)$$

where k is selected so that $1 < \alpha - k < 2$. Finally, for $0 < x < 1$,

$$\Gamma(1 + x) \approx 1 - 0.577191652x + 0.988205891x^2 - 0.897056937x^3$$

$$+ 0.918206857x^4 - 0.756704078x^5 + 0.482199394x^6$$

$$- 0.193527818x^7 + 0.035868243x^8 .$$

The sample p.d.f.s graphed (later in this appendix) for each distribution are selected to show the variety of shapes possible. For those which have means, the parameters are selected to keep the mean constant. The first example for each distribution has parameters which are similar to the model fitted in Section 4.5 to the automobile bodily injury data with a 25,000 limit. All of the examples selected portray heavy-tailed members of the respective families.

The formulas for estimation by percentile matching are obtained by setting

$$F(x_i) = F_n(x_i)$$

where $F_n(x)$ is the empirical d.f. and then solving for the parameters. To simplify the formulas we set $p_i = F_n(x_i)$.

The formulas for estimation by the method of moments are obtained by setting

$$E[X^i] = \sum_{j=1}^{n} \frac{x_j^i}{n} .$$

To simplify the formulas we set

$$m_i = \sum_{j=1}^{n} \frac{x_j^i}{n}.$$

I. BURR DISTRIBUTION

Support: $x > 0$

Parameters: $\alpha > 0,\ \lambda > 0,\ \tau > 0$

D.f.: $F(x) = 1 - \left(\dfrac{\lambda}{\lambda + x^\tau}\right)^\alpha$

P.d.f.: $f(x) = \alpha \tau \lambda^\alpha x^{\tau-1}(\lambda + x^\tau)^{-\alpha-1}$

Moments: $E[X^n] = \lambda^{n/\tau} \Gamma\left(\alpha - \dfrac{n}{\tau}\right)\Gamma\left(1 + \dfrac{n}{\tau}\right)/\Gamma(\alpha),\quad \alpha\tau > n$

Mode: $0, \tau \le 1;\quad \left[\dfrac{\lambda(\tau - 1)}{\alpha\tau + 1}\right]^{1/\tau}, \tau > 1$

Limited expected value function:

$$E[X; x] = \frac{\alpha \lambda^{1/\tau}\Gamma(\alpha - 1/\tau)\Gamma(1 + 1/\tau)}{\Gamma(\alpha + 1)} \beta\left(1 + \frac{1}{\tau},\ \alpha - \frac{1}{\tau};\ \frac{x^\tau}{\lambda + x^\tau}\right) + x\left(\frac{\lambda}{\lambda + x^\tau}\right)^\alpha$$

Derivatives of d.f.:

$$\frac{\partial F(x)}{\partial \alpha} = -\left(\frac{\lambda}{\lambda + x^\tau}\right)^\alpha \ln\left(\frac{\lambda}{\lambda + x^\tau}\right)$$

$$\frac{\partial F(x)}{\partial \lambda} = -\frac{\alpha x^\tau}{\lambda^2}\left(\frac{\lambda}{\lambda + x^\tau}\right)^{\alpha+1}$$

$$\frac{\partial F(x)}{\partial \tau} = \frac{\alpha x^\tau}{\lambda}(\ln x)\left(\frac{\lambda}{\lambda + x^\tau}\right)^{\alpha+1}$$

Percentile matching: Set $q_i = 1 - p_i$, $i = 1, 2, 3$ and $\eta = -1/\alpha$. Also,

$$y_1 = \frac{\ln x_3 - \ln x_2}{\ln x_2 - \ln x_1}, \qquad y_2 = \frac{\ln x_1 - \ln x_3}{\ln x_2 - \ln x_1}.$$

Solve for η:

$(q_1^\eta - 1)^{y_1}(q_2^\eta - 1)^{y_2}(q_3^\eta - 1) = 0$ by Newton's method. The derivative is

$y_1(q_1^\eta - 1)^{y_1-1}q_1^\eta(\ln q_1)(q_2^\eta - 1)^{y_2}(q_3^\eta - 1)$

$+ (q_1^\eta - 1)^{y_1}y_2(q_2^\eta - 1)^{y_2-1}q_2^\eta(\ln q_2)(q_3^\eta - 1) + (q_1^\eta - 1)^{y_1}(q_2^\eta - 1)^{y_2}q_3^\eta \ln q_3.$

Then

$$\lambda = (q_1^\eta - 1)^y (q_2^\eta - 1)^{-y-1}$$

where

$$y = \frac{\ln x_2}{\ln x_1 - \ln x_2}.$$

Finally,

$$\tau = \frac{\ln (\lambda (q_1^\eta - 1))}{\ln x_1} \quad \text{and} \quad \alpha = -\frac{1}{\eta}.$$

Sample distributions:

Parameters						
α	λ	τ	Mean	Standard Deviation	Mode	Graph
2.25	250	0.7	3397	—	0	——
4.5	822	0.7	3396	8440	0	· · · ·
2.25	1,822,269	1.7	3421	3121	1547	-----

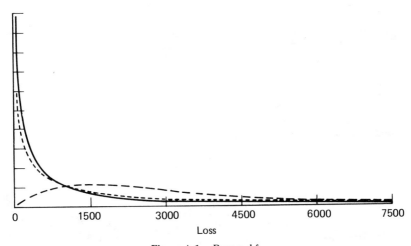

Figure A.1. Burr p.d.f.

II. PARETO DISTRIBUTION

Support: $x > 0$

Parameters: $\alpha > 0, \lambda > 0$

D.f.: $F(x) = 1 - \left(\dfrac{\lambda}{\lambda + x}\right)^{\alpha}$

P.d.f.: $f(x) = \alpha\lambda^{\alpha}(\lambda + x)^{-\alpha-1}$

Moments: $E[X^n] = \dfrac{\lambda^n n!}{\prod\limits_{i=1}^{n}(\alpha - i)}, \quad \alpha > n$

Mode: 0

Limited expected value function:

$$E[X; x] = \frac{\lambda}{\alpha - 1}\left[1 - \alpha\left(\frac{\lambda}{\lambda + x}\right)^{\alpha - 1} + (\alpha - 1)\left(\frac{\lambda}{\lambda + x}\right)^{\alpha}\right] + x\left(\frac{\lambda}{\lambda + x}\right)^{\alpha}$$

Derivatives of d.f.:

$$\frac{\partial F(x)}{\partial \alpha} = -\left(\frac{\lambda}{\lambda + x}\right)^{\alpha}\ln\left(\frac{\lambda}{\lambda + x}\right)$$

$$\frac{\partial F(x)}{\partial \lambda} = -\frac{\alpha x}{\lambda^2}\left(\frac{\lambda}{\lambda + x}\right)^{\alpha + 1}$$

Percentile matching: Set $g_i = (1 - p_i)^{-1/\alpha}, \quad i = 1, 2.$ Solve $g(\alpha) = (g_2 - 1)/(g_1 - 1) - x_2/x_1 = 0$ by Newton's method, using

$$g'(\alpha) = \frac{(g_1 - 1)g_2 \ln(1 - p_2) - (g_2 - 1)g_1 \ln(1 - p_1)}{\alpha^2(g_1 - 1)^2}.$$

Then

$$\lambda = \frac{x_1}{g_1 - 1}.$$

Method of moments:

$$\alpha = \frac{2(m_2 - m_1^2)}{(m_2 - 2m_1^2)}$$

$$\lambda = \frac{m_1 m_2}{(m_2 - 2m_1^2)}$$

Sample distributions:

Parameters					
α	λ	Mean	Standard Deviation	Mode	Graph
0.8	500	—	—	0	——
1.5	1500	3000	—	0	· · · ·
3.0	6000	3000	5196	0	- - - - -

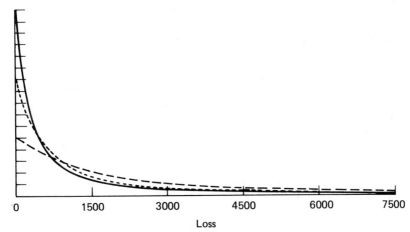

Loss

Figure A.2. Pareto p.d.f.

III. GENERALIZED PARETO DISTRIBUTION

Support: $x > 0$

Parameters: $\alpha > 0,\ \lambda > 0,\ k > 0$

D.f.: $F(x) = \beta\left(k, \alpha; \dfrac{x}{\lambda + x}\right)$

P.d.f.: $f(x) = \dfrac{\Gamma(\alpha + k)\lambda^{\alpha}x^{k-1}}{\Gamma(\alpha)\Gamma(k)(\lambda + x)^{k+\alpha}}$

Moments: $E[X^n] = \lambda^n \dfrac{\prod\limits_{i=0}^{n-1}(k+i)}{\prod\limits_{i=1}^{n}(\alpha - i)},\quad \alpha > n$

Mode: $0, k \leq 1$; $\dfrac{(k-1)\lambda}{\alpha+1}, k > 1$

Limited expected value function:

$$E[X; x] = \frac{\lambda k}{\alpha - 1} \beta\left(k+1, \alpha-1; \frac{x}{\lambda+x}\right) + x\left[1 - \beta\left(k, \alpha; \frac{x}{\lambda+x}\right)\right]$$

Derivatives of d.f.:

$$\frac{\partial F(x)}{\partial \alpha} = [\psi(\alpha+k) - \psi(\alpha)]F(x) + \frac{\Gamma(\alpha+k)}{\Gamma(\alpha)\Gamma(k)} \int_{\lambda/(\lambda+x)}^{1} (1-y)^{k-1} y^{\alpha-1} \ln y \, dy$$

$$\frac{\partial F(x)}{\partial \lambda} = -\frac{\Gamma(\alpha+k)}{\Gamma(\alpha)\Gamma(k)} \left(\frac{x}{\lambda+x}\right)^{k} \left(\frac{\lambda}{\lambda+x}\right)^{\alpha-1} \frac{1}{(\lambda+x)}$$

$$\frac{\partial F(x)}{\partial k} = [\psi(\alpha+k) - \psi(k)]F(x) + \frac{\Gamma(\alpha+k)}{\Gamma(\alpha)\Gamma(k)} \int_{0}^{x/(\lambda+x)} y^{k-1}(1-y)^{\alpha-1} \ln y \, dy$$

Sample distributions:

Parameters

α	λ	k	Mean	Standard Deviation	Mode	Graph
1.2	2,500	0.5	6,250	—	0	——
2.2	15,000	0.5	6,250	25,769	0	....
1.2	625	2.0	6,250	—	284	-----

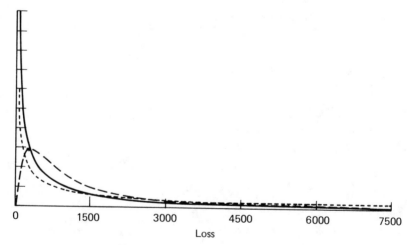

Figure A.3.   Generalized Pareto p.d.f.

IV. TRANSFORMED GAMMA DISTRIBUTION

Support: $x > 0$

Parameters: $\alpha > 0,\ \lambda > 0,\ \tau > 0$

D.f.: $F(x) = \Gamma(\alpha;(\lambda x)^\tau)$

P.d.f.: $f(x) = \lambda^{\tau\alpha}\tau x^{\tau\alpha-1}e^{-(\lambda x)^\tau}/\Gamma(\alpha)$

Moments: $E[X^n] = \dfrac{\Gamma(\alpha + n/\tau)}{\lambda^n \Gamma(\alpha)}$

Mode: $0,\ \tau\alpha \le 1;\quad \left(\dfrac{\tau\alpha - 1}{\lambda^\tau \tau}\right)^{1/\tau},\ \tau\alpha > 1$

Limited expected value function:

$$E[X;x] = \frac{\Gamma(\alpha + 1/\tau)}{\lambda\Gamma(\alpha)}\Gamma\left(\alpha + \frac{1}{\tau};(\lambda x)^\tau\right) + x[1 - \Gamma(\alpha;(\lambda x)^\tau)]$$

Derivatives of d.f.:

$$\frac{\partial F(x)}{\partial \alpha} = -\psi(\alpha)F(x) + \frac{1}{\Gamma(\alpha)}\int_0^{(\lambda x)^\tau} y^{\alpha-1}e^{-y}\ln y\, dy$$

$$\frac{\partial F(x)}{\partial \lambda} = \frac{\tau x}{\Gamma(\alpha)}(\lambda x)^{\tau\alpha-1}e^{-(\lambda x)^\tau}$$

$$\frac{\partial F(x)}{\partial \tau} = \frac{(\lambda x)^{\tau\alpha}}{\Gamma(\alpha)}e^{-(\lambda x)^\tau}\ln(\lambda x)$$

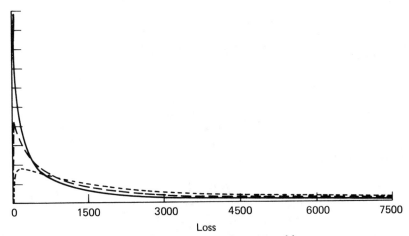

Figure A.4. Transformed gamma p.d.f.

Sample distributions:

	Parameters			Standard		
α	λ	τ	Mean	Deviation	Mode	Graph
2.75	0.025	0.3	3443	9327	0	——
2.75	0.0029956	0.5	3443	4220	188	. . . .
4.5	0.09012	0.3	3443	6713	19	- - - - -

V. GAMMA DISTRIBUTION

Support: $x > 0$

Parameters: $\alpha > 0, \ \lambda > 0$

D.f.: $F(x) = \Gamma(\alpha; \lambda x)$

P.d.f.: $f(x) = \lambda^\alpha x^{\alpha-1} e^{-\lambda x} / \Gamma(\alpha)$

Moments: $E[X^n] = \dfrac{\prod\limits_{i=0}^{n-1} (\alpha + i)}{\lambda^n}$

Mode: $0, \ \alpha \leq 1; \quad \dfrac{\alpha - 1}{\lambda}, \ \alpha > 1$

Limited expected value function:

$$E[X; x] = \frac{\alpha}{\lambda} \Gamma(\alpha + 1; \lambda x) + x[1 - \Gamma(\alpha; \lambda x)]$$

Derivatives of d.f.:

$$\frac{\partial F(x)}{\partial \alpha} = -\psi(\alpha) F(x) + \frac{1}{\Gamma(\alpha)} \int_0^{\lambda x} y^{\alpha-1} e^{-y} \ln y \, dy$$

$$\frac{\partial F(x)}{\partial \lambda} = \frac{x}{\Gamma(\alpha)} (\lambda x)^{\alpha-1} e^{-\lambda x}$$

Methods of moments:

def'n of m_i
top of p. 220

$$\alpha = \frac{m_1^2}{m_2 - m_1^2}$$

$$\lambda = \frac{m_1}{m_2 - m_1^2}$$

Sample distributions:

Parameters

α	λ	Mean	Standard Deviation	Mode	Graph
0.3	0.0001	3000	5477	0	——
1.5	0.0005	3000	2450	1000	. . . .
7.5	0.0025	3000	1095	2600	- - - - -

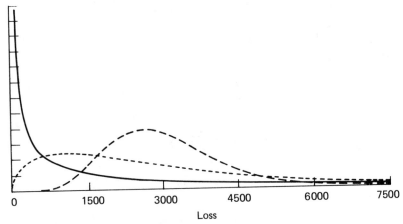

Loss

Figure A.5. Gamma p.d.f.

VI. LOGGAMMA DISTRIBUTION

Support: $x > 1$

Parameters: $\alpha > 0,\ \lambda > 0$

D.f.: $F(x) = \Gamma(\alpha; \lambda \ln x)$

P.d.f.: $f(x) = \dfrac{\lambda^{\alpha}(\ln x)^{\alpha - 1}}{x^{\lambda + 1}\Gamma(\alpha)}$

Moments: $E[X^n] = \left(1 - \dfrac{n}{\lambda}\right)^{-\alpha},\ \lambda > n$

Mode: $1,\ \alpha \le 1;\quad \exp\left(\dfrac{\alpha - 1}{\lambda + 1}\right),\ \alpha > 1$

Limited expected value function:

$$E[X; x] = \left(\frac{\lambda}{\lambda - 1}\right)^\alpha \Gamma(\alpha; (\lambda - 1) \ln x) + x[1 - \Gamma(\alpha; \lambda \ln x)], \quad \lambda > 1$$

$$= \frac{(\lambda \ln x)^\alpha \exp((1 - \lambda) \ln x)}{\Gamma(\alpha)} \sum_{i=0}^\infty \frac{[(\lambda - 1) \ln x]^i}{\alpha(\alpha + 1) \ldots (\alpha + i)}$$

$$+ x[1 - \Gamma(\alpha; \lambda \ln x)], \quad \lambda > 0$$

Derivatives of d.f.:

$$\frac{\partial F(x)}{\partial \alpha} = -\psi(\alpha)F(x) + \frac{1}{\Gamma(\alpha)} \int_0^{\lambda \ln x} y^{\alpha-1} e^{-y} \ln y \, dy$$

$$\frac{\partial F(x)}{\partial \lambda} = \frac{\lambda^{\alpha-1} x^{-\lambda}}{\Gamma(\alpha)} (\ln x)^\alpha$$

Methods of moments: Set

$$m_i' = \sum_{j=1}^n \frac{(\ln x_j)^i}{n}, \quad i = 1, 2$$

$$\alpha = \frac{m_1'^2}{(m_2' - m_1'^2)}$$

$$\lambda = \frac{m_1'}{(m_2' - m_1'^2)}$$

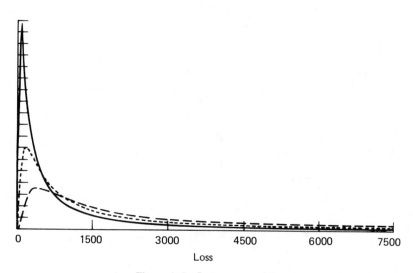

Figure A.6.   Loggamma p.d.f.

Sample distributions:

Parameters

α	λ	Mean	Standard Deviation	Mode	Graph
13	2	8,192	—	55	———
20	2.7569	8,192	410,903	157	· · · ·
30	3.8543	8,192	57,832	393	- - - - -

VII.   LOGNORMAL DISTRIBUTION

Support: $x > 0$

Parameters: $-\infty < \mu < \infty, \sigma > 0$

D.f.: $F(x) = \Phi\left(\dfrac{\ln x - \mu}{\sigma}\right)$

P.d.f.: $f(x) = \dfrac{\exp\left[-\dfrac{1}{2}\left(\dfrac{\ln x - \mu}{\sigma}\right)^2\right]}{x\sigma\sqrt{2\pi}}$

Moments: $E[X^n] = \exp\left(n\mu + \dfrac{1}{2}n^2\sigma^2\right)$

Mode: $e^{\mu - \sigma^2}$

Limited expected value function:

$$E[X; x] = \exp\left(\mu + \frac{\sigma^2}{2}\right)\Phi\left(\frac{\ln x - \mu - \sigma^2}{\sigma}\right) + x\left[1 - \Phi\left(\frac{\ln x - \mu}{\sigma}\right)\right]$$

Derivatives of d.f.:

$$\frac{\partial F(x)}{\partial \mu} = -\frac{1}{\sigma}\phi\left(\frac{\ln x - \mu}{\sigma}\right)$$

$$\frac{\partial F(x)}{\partial \sigma} = -\frac{\ln x - \mu}{\sigma^2}\phi\left(\frac{\ln x - \mu}{\sigma}\right)$$

Percentile matching: Set

$$g_i = \Phi^{-1}(p_i), \quad i = 1, 2$$

$$\sigma = \frac{\ln x_1 - \ln x_2}{g_1 - g_2}$$

$$\mu = \ln x_1 - \sigma g_1$$

Method of moments: Set

$$m'_i = \sum_{j=1}^{n} \frac{(\ln x_j)^i}{n}$$

$$\mu = m'_1$$

$$\sigma = (m'_2 - m'^2_1)^{1/2}$$

Sample distributions:

Parameters

μ	σ	Mean	Standard Deviation	Mode	Graph
6.5	2.0	4,915	35,981	90	——
7.0	1.7321	4,915	21,471	194	....
7.5	1.4142	4,915	12,423	440	-----

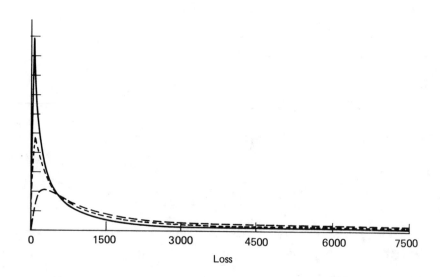

Figure A.7.   Lognormal p.d.f.

VIII. WEIBULL DISTRIBUTION

Support: $x > 0$

Parameters: $c > 0, \tau > 0$

D.f.: $F(x) = 1 - e^{-cx^{\tau}}$

P.d.f.: $f(x) = c\tau x^{\tau-1} e^{-cx^{\tau}}$

Moments: $E[X^n] = \dfrac{\Gamma(1 + n/\tau)}{c^{n/\tau}}$

Mode: $0, \tau \le 1;$ $\left(\dfrac{\tau - 1}{c\tau}\right)^{1/\tau}, \tau > 1$

Limited expected value function:

$$E[X; x] = \frac{\Gamma(1 + 1/\tau)}{c^{1/\tau}} \Gamma\left(1 + \frac{1}{\tau}; cx^{\tau}\right) + xe^{-cx^{\tau}}$$

Derivatives of d.f.:

$$\frac{\partial F(x)}{\partial c} = x^{\tau} e^{-cx^{\tau}}$$

$$\frac{\partial F(x)}{\partial \tau} = cx^{\tau} e^{-cx^{\tau}} \ln x$$

Percentile matching: Set

$$g_i = -\ln(1 - p_i), \quad i = 1, 2$$

$$\tau = \frac{\ln g_1 - \ln g_2}{\ln x_1 - \ln x_2}$$

$$c = \frac{g_1}{x_1^{\tau}}$$

Method of moments: Solve

$$\ln \Gamma\left(1 + \frac{2}{\tau}\right) - 2 \ln \Gamma\left(1 + \frac{1}{\tau}\right) - \ln m_2 + \ln m_1 = 0.$$

The derivative is $-\dfrac{2}{\tau^2} \psi\left(1 + \dfrac{2}{\tau}\right) + \dfrac{2}{\tau^2} \psi\left(1 + \dfrac{1}{\tau}\right).$

Then $c = \left[\dfrac{\Gamma(1 + 1/\tau)}{m_1}\right]^{\tau}.$

Sample distributions:

Parameters

c	τ	Mean	Standard Deviation	Mode	Graph
0.024	0.5	3472	7764	0	——
0.000288	1.0	3472	3472	0	· · · ·
0.0001?254	1.1	3472	3160	407	- - - - -

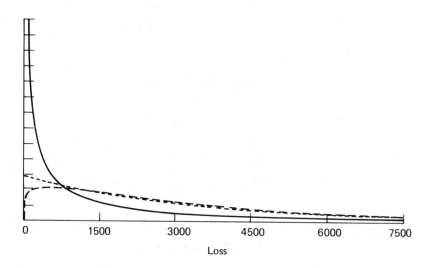

Figure A.8. Weibull p.d.f.

Index